AT HOME WITH THE DIPLOMATS

EXPERTISE

**CULTURES AND
TECHNOLOGIES
OF KNOWLEDGE**

EDITED BY DOMINIC BOYER

A list of titles in this series is available at www.cornellpress.cornell.edu.

At Home with the Diplomats

Inside a European Foreign Ministry

Iver B. Neumann

Cornell University Press
Ithaca and London

First published 2012 by Cornell University Press
First printing, Cornell Paperbacks, 2012
Printed in the United States of America

Library of Congress Cataloging-in-Publication Data

Neumann, Iver B.
    At home with the diplomats : inside a European foreign ministry / Iver
B. Neumann.
        p. cm. — (Expertise)
    Includes bibliographical references and index.
    ISBN 978-0-8014-4993-2 (cloth : alk. paper)
    ISBN 978-0-8014-7765-2 (pbk. : alk. paper)
    1. Diplomatic and consular service, European.   2. Diplomatic and
consular service, Norwegian.   3. Diplomats—Europe.   4. Diplomats—
Norway.   5. Europe—Foreign relations.   6. Norway—Foreign
relations.   7. Neumann, Iver B.   I. Title.   II. Series: Expertise
(Ithaca, N.Y.)
    JZ1570.A59N48 2012
    327.4—dc23   2011022560

Cornell University Press strives to use environmentally responsible
suppliers and materials to the fullest extent possible in the publishing of
its books. Such materials include vegetable-based, low-VOC inks and
acid-free papers that are recycled, totally chlorine-free, or partly composed
of nonwood fibers. For further information, visit our website at www.
cornellpress.cornell.edu.

Cloth printing   10   9   8   7   6   5   4   3   2   1
Paperback printing   10   9   8   7   6   5   4   3   2   1

To Cecilie, the most fleeting of foreign ministry occupants

The social science that we want to concern ourselves with is a *science of actuality*. We want to understand *in its particularity* the encompassing actuality of the life in which we are placed—on one hand, the coherence and cultural *significance* of individual occurrences in their contemporary configuration, and on the other hand, the reasons for those occurrences being historically so and not otherwise.

Max Weber

CONTENTS

PREFACE

My first experience with the diplomatic world came in 1980, when, at the ripe age of nineteen, I had just finished as a draftee at the Army Language School and set off to serve my last six months of service as a guard and interpreter at the Royal Norwegian Embassy in Moscow. I then took up work at a think tank where social and professional contact with diplomats was frequent. In 1995 I arrived at the European University Institute with a postdoc project in political science on the European Union's main internal diplomatic institution, COREPER (the Committees of Permanent Representatives of the EU's member states). I discovered that the lack of studies of diplomacy could not be overcome by drawing on the methods at my disposal as a political scientist. My reaction was to retrain as an anthropologist, and to work in the Norwegian Ministry of Foreign Affairs for three and a half years, first as a planner (1997–99), and then as a senior adviser on European politics (2001–3), on the explicit understanding that I was to write on diplomacy. I then went on to write the archival-based centenary history of the ministry for its 2005 centenary (the result is available as Neumann and Leira 2005). This work builds on field data and archival data collected throughout these experiences.

I thank Morten Andersen, Matti Bunzl, Benjamin de Carvalho, Costas Constantinou, James Der Derian, Bud Duvall, Nora Eggen, Thomas Hylland Eriksen, Anette Fagertun, Ulla Gudmundson, Ole Dahl Gulliksen, Hege Haaland, Martin Hall, Helga Hernes, Patrick T. Jackson, Fuat Kayman, Mark Laffey, Halvard Leira, Daniel Nexon, Cecilie Basberg Neumann, Knut Nustad, Vincent Pouliot, Bahar Rumelili, Niels Nagelshus Schia, James C. Scott, Ole Jacob Sending, Paul Sharp, May-Len Skilbrei, Inger Skjelsbæk, Jorun Solheim, Inger Lise Teig, Henrik Thune, Ann Towns, Torunn Tryggestad, and Geoffrey Wiseman for conversations and written comments. Ulf Hannerz, Knut Nustad, and Cris Shore read the entire manuscript and were very encouraging. Douglas Holmes steered me in Dominic Boyer's direction. Thanks Dominic, and please forward my thanks to your anonymous referees. And thanks to Roger Haydon for the most thorough editing I have ever experienced.

What is now chapter 3 draws on two previous publications; "On Generating State Voice," *State Formation: Anthropological Explorations,* ed. Knut Nustad and Christin Krohn-Hansen (London: Pluto, 2005), 195–211, used here with the permission of Pluto Press; and "'A Speech That the Entire Ministry May Stand for,' or: Why Diplomats Never Produce Anything New," *International Political Sociology* 1 (2) (2007): 183–200, used here with the permission of Wiley-Blackwell. Half-length versions of chapters 4 and 5 have been published previously. Material from "To Be a Diplomat," *International Studies Perspectives* 6 (1) (2005): 72–93, is used with the permission of Wiley-Blackwell; and material from "The Body of the Diplomat," *European Journal of International Relations* 14 (4) (2008): 671–94, is used with the permission of SAGE journals.

At Home with the Diplomats

INTRODUCTION

Who Are They and Where Do They Come From?

Handbooks are a fascinating source for social inquiry. They tell us how things should be. If enough people use them, what began as a recipe may become a social reality. In 1917, Sir Ernest Satow, a naturalized British citizen born in Sweden to an English mother and a German father, who had enjoyed a distinguished diplomatic career in East Asia, published a *Guide to Diplomatic Practice.* Satow defined diplomacy as "the conduct of official relations between the governments of independent states." All six subsequent editions, the latest of which appeared in 2009, retain that definition. "Satow" remains a key authority in the world's foreign ministries, many of whose practices have evolved along the lines described in the book (Otte 2001). To those unfamiliar with the inner workings of diplomacy, modern diplomacy may look like what Satow wanted it to be. Prescription has become description.

This book is to Satow what the meal is to the recipe. It is a historically informed ethnography of diplomacy, in which I ask what diplomats do and how they came to do it. Diplomacy is an integrating mechanism for what is now emerging as a global polity. It is, I believe, just as significant as trade and war. We need to understand what diplomats and diplomacy do and what they believe they are doing.

The Need for Ethnography

Handbooks give us a sense of how things should be, but they do not necessarily tell us how things are. Those who have a lived experience of diplomacy know the difference between the prescriptions of the handbook and the way state diplomats represent what they are doing to the outside world, on the one hand, and actual diplomatic practices, on the other. There are inevitable frictions between prescription and description, for guides to practice and practices themselves are different things. First, state diplomacy is not continuously fixated on state-to-state relations, but works through all sorts of channels. From his own life as a practicing diplomat, Satow knew full well that diplomacy was only ideally a state-to-state affair. Satow (1843–1929) was, after all, a contemporary of the likes of Mata Hari (1876–1917), the courtesan who peddled vital information between France, Germany, and other warring parties during the First World War. Second, diplomats may end up working in all kinds of social locales, not only in foreign capitals. They may work as consuls in major cities that are not capitals, in state delegations to international organizations (IOs), in IOs themselves, or on secondment from an international organization. In fact, for the greater part of their careers they are not even posted to another country but work "at home," by which they mean in the ministry of foreign affairs (MFA) of the state of their employ—which for the last couple of hundred years has been the state of which they are citizens. There are still remnants of a time when this was not so, however, and here we have a third friction between prescription and description; a number of microstates routinely hire foreign nationals to be their diplomats. Before the age of nationalism, this was a widespread practice. To mention but one example, the Dutchman Hugo Grotius, a founder of international law, served as Sweden's ambassador to the French court from 1634 to 1644. A direct parallel may be drawn to the world of the soldier. During the Napoleonic Wars, the Prussian soldier Carl von Clausewitz spent a year in Russian employ without being considered a mercenary the way he would have been if he had taken up foreign employ some years later (cf. Thomson 1994).[1] Fourth, and this is where diplomacy as a set of practices begins to detach itself from states, other actors such as transnational companies (TNCs), counties, nongovernmental organizations (NGOs) are increasingly hiring their own diplomats (cf. Ross 2007). Indeed, IOs and NGOs are increasingly training people in diplomatic skills in-house, and I will return to the transformative potential of these developments in the conclusion (see also Sharp 2009: 17–36; Neumann 2008b). Since my own ethnographic work took place in a state setting, however, the main focus of this book is state diplomacy.

There is a key instrumental reason why we should pay heed to what diplomats actually do, and how they think about what they are doing. Another diplomatic practitioner turned scholar, Adam Watson (1984), spelled out a corollary of Satow's definition, namely that we may understand the work of a state's diplomats taken together as no less than a state's "national interest." It is the hands-on work of diplomats—their reports from abroad, their desk analyses, their drawing of all this information into recommendations for state policies and priorities—that make up the substance of what has for some 150 years been known as "foreign" policy making. Still, it took the end of the Cold War for a literature on diplomacy to form. This is a positive development not only for our understanding of international relations (IR), but also of the state itself. It is that diplomacy is what states do. It is also that states are what diplomacy does. The state takes shape as a result, among other things, of interaction with other states. For this reason, diplomacy is a key institution of global politics. It is also critical for state formation and state building.

Nonetheless—and this became very clear as purported pundits around the world commented on the American diplomatic correspondence that WikiLeaks made available in the autumn of 2010—very little seems to be known about the standard operational procedures and everyday routines of diplomacy, even by many of those who make their living as political insiders. This book contains examples of how a state institution like the foreign ministry is integrated by dint of specific practices predicated on the idea that state institutions have to present themselves as unitary actors toward the outside world in general, and toward other states in particular.

---

1. Today, most foreign ministries employ locals in their missions abroad, but these will be servants, chauffeurs, and information workers, never diplomats.

The Need for History

By treating the state as the obvious precondition for diplomacy, Satow's definition obscures the fact that diplomacy is much older than the modern European state. Defining a phenomenon may erase that phenomenon's history, and this is precisely what Satow's definition of diplomacy does. We have historical examples of diplomacy from before the rise of the modern European state (such as the more than three-thousand-year-old Amarna system centered on Pharaonic Egypt) and we know of diplomatic systems that are non-European (such as the Iroquois system). This book demonstrates that today's organization of diplomacy, centered as it is on foreign ministries with staffs usually numbered in the thousands, is a very recent and historically specific phenomenon. The modern state is only some five hundred years old, and foreign ministries go back little more than two centuries. In fact, their merging with field diplomacy began only about a hundred years ago, and in the Netherlands, the foreign ministry, the diplomatic service, and the consular service merged into an integrated foreign service only in the 1980s. Moreover, the increase in the number of diplomats is even more recent, beginning in the wake of the First World War and exploding as recently as in the 1960s.[2]

To the degree that diplomacy as prescribed by Satow may be said to have existed in the twentieth century, its very newness should be a reminder that it could easily have taken other forms. Any phenomenon is shaped not only by its present form but also by our awareness of its pasts and our expectations about its futures. It follows that debates about diplomacy's future stand to gain from an awareness of diplomacy's pasts. The book therefore opens with a discussion of how diplomatic systems, understood as institutionalized interaction between polities with some degree of formal autonomy that lasts over time, have emerged historically. All known cases include the construction of shared myths of kinship which have made communication possible in the first place, as well as what we

---

2. I estimate the total number of full-time diplomats around the world in 1850 to have been perhaps a thousand, twelve hundred at most. Most of them knew of one another. Today, the number of Norwegian diplomats alone is around seven hundred, and we find twice as many employees on the payroll of the Norwegian Ministry of Foreign Affairs. Norway has a population of 4.9 million.

may call shared sociabilities—mutually recognized times, places, and formats for meetings (Sahlins 1981)—which have eased communication. Then there have evolved common practices—socially recognized forms of good or bad behavior—that have been specific to each system. This historical discussion is not merely an exercise in documentation and comparison. Foreign ministries customarily commission in-depth studies of previous conferences when they sense that a new one is in the offing—so, for example, toward the end of the First World War the British Foreign Office asked C. K. Webster (1919; cf. also Fair 1992) to write a history of the Congress of Vienna of 1814–15. It did so because such stocktaking is key to the conversation about where diplomacy is going.

All this should be of central interest to our understanding of globalization. Awareness of diplomacy's past has a wider salience for the study of global politics than what pertains specifically to diplomacy. Globalization is nothing if it is not an increase in the density of social relations. Historically, diplomacy is one of the three principal phenomena at the core of this process. There was trade, which was constituted by relations among merchants. There was war, which was constituted by relations among soldiers. And there was diplomacy, which was constituted by relations among diplomats. Diplomacy may not deploy material resources on a par with war—the United States spends more on its military brass bands than on its State Department—but that is no reason to neglect it.

While entire libraries are dedicated to the merchant and the soldier, the diplomat does not even have a full shelf. Harold Nicolson (1963), an interwar British diplomat, published a slender and elegant book on the overall history and conduct of European diplomacy, and his book has its valuable modern imitators (Watson [1982] 1984, Anderson 1993, Berridge 1995, Hamilton and Langhorne 1995). Ragnar Numelin (1950), a Finnish anthropologist who trained at the London School of Economics in the interwar period, wrote a thesis on the early evolution of diplomacy that was eventually published. Garrett Mattingly (1955), an American historian, wrote a deservedly well-known book on Renaissance diplomacy; and James Der Derian (1987), a British-trained American IR scholar, wrote a genealogy of diplomacy in which he argues that diplomacy is about handling alienation between polities. Sharp (2009) makes a sophisticated attempt at furthering Satow's and Watson's agenda, which was to (re)instate an interest in diplomacy at the heart of international relations. We have a whole host of memoirs by diplomats, and a few interesting testimonies by people writing in midcareer about what it is like to be a diplomat (Dickie 2004, Ross 2007, Murray 2007). This book complements the sparse extant literature by bringing anthropology and international relations to bear on the quotidian work of diplomats. Diplomats are organized in specific ways and have been so over time, and in transnational networks at that. They are an elite awaiting its ethnography (cf. Cohen 1981, Shore and Nugent 2002).

Diplomacy Is Quotidian Policy-Making

Why, if diplomacy and diplomats are as important as I believe, have they not been studied more widely? One key reason is that Satow's and Watson's privileging of the diplomat is a minority view in the literature on foreign policy making. This literature, the main part of which goes by the name of diplomatic history, has an implied hero, but that hero is not the diplomat. It is the "statesman," that is, the monarchs and the presidents and the politicians who are said to make the decisions. The implication becomes perhaps most evident in Henry Kissinger's *Diplomacy* (2004). In his characteristically brilliant style, Kissinger celebrates not the diplomat, as his title would seem to indicate, but the statesman (Kissinger is instructively vague about whether the statesman has to be a head of state or, say, his security adviser). To Kissinger, as to the diplomatic historian, the diplomat is simply there to furnish the statesman with information and to carry out the "statesman's" orders. In those rare moments when diplomatic historians want to be self-critical, they talk about their trade as the study of what one clerk wrote to another. Here we are in a rather different world from Satow's and Watson's. I suggest, however, that Kissinger's work (so much better than most diplomatic history because it is theoretically informed, see esp. Kissinger 1957) does not allow us to dismiss Satow's and Watson's perspective. It only limits its area of validity, by questioning the reach of their claims. It is true that the statesman is the last link in the decision-making chain and, by implication, the first link in the implementing chain. Regardless of whether the diplomat is seen as a hero in her own right or as a subcontractor to the hero-statesman, however, the point stands that everyday policy formation in this area is in the hands of diplomats.

Had that not been the case, Kissinger would have had little reason for his steady critique over more than half a century of how diplomats are organized and how they work.

As a form of knowledge production, diplomacy has yet to be studied. The heavy pressure on field diplomats to produce knowledge leads to a great deal of improvisation, ad-libbing and corner-cutting (cf. Callon 1998). The result is knowledge about highly specific and ephemeral social constellations. Hedley Bull, an Australian student of international relations, describes how knowledge produced by the field diplomats is

> information about the views and policies of a country's political leadership, now and in the near future. It is knowledge of personalities rather than of the forces and conditions which shape a country's policy over the long term. It is knowledge of the current situation and how it is likely to develop rather than of the pattern of past regularities. It derives from day-to-day personal dealings with the leading political strata in the country to which a diplomatist is accredited, sometimes to the detriment of his understanding of society at large in that country. (Bull 1977: 181)

When diplomats are working at home, however, they are primarily engaged in a different and much more bureaucratic mode of knowledge production. When diplomats are in charge of producing a text, they seek out the opinion of each and every part of the foreign ministry that may conceivably have, or may be expected to gain, an interest in the matter at hand. As a result, the writing up of a diplomatic text is not primarily a question of communicating a certain point of view to the outside world, or producing a tight analysis. It is rather an exercise in consensus building. One effect of this mode of knowledge production is that texts emanating from a foreign ministry are all, at least ideally, in the same voice. Another effect is that, when left to their own devices, diplomats will tend to reproduce extant knowledge rather than produce something new.

The ephemeral and idiosyncratic mode of knowledge production that dominates the life of the field diplomat is very different from the form of knowledge production that is standard currency "at home" in the ministry. As a result, the diplomat who is coming home from a posting abroad may come to experience the transition as what one of my interlocutors referred to as "bureaucracy shock." Diplomacy is about negotiating between different positions held by different polities. To be a diplomat is to take part in such negotiations. It is also to take part in a lifelong balancing act between one's own shifting positions and modes of knowledge production. The kind of expertise that the diplomat needs in order to pull this off is not unlike the expertise that the ethnographer needs in order to analyze it (cf. Holmes and Marcus 2004). Marcus (1998: 119) maintains that the ethnographer

> tries to get at a form of local knowledge that is about the kind of difference that is not accessible by working out internal cultural logics. It is about difference that arises from the anxieties of knowing that one is somehow tied into what is happening elsewhere but, as noted, without those connections being clear or precisely articulated through available internal cultural models. In effect, subjects are participating in discourses that are thoroughly localized but that are not their own.

I believe that what Marcus writes about ethnographers holds for diplomats as well. I also believe that this representation of diplomats flies in the face of widespread stereotypes about them.

The Stereotypes

The field of diplomacy does not only differ from the prescriptions to be found in Satow. It also differs quite radically from the widespread stereotypes that shape newspaper reports, popular culture, and, I think, the opinions of social scientists who have had no personal experience with diplomats and diplomacy.[3] To take one of the root metaphors of diplomacy as an example: after twenty years among diplomats, I have yet to attend a cocktail party. Cocktails have to be mixed one by one, and that requirement requires waiting. Waiting breaks up the easy flow of conversation that diplomats deem conducive to their business and that food and drink are supposed to sustain. So whereas the cocktail is nowhere to be seen, invariably

---

3. I note this in the spirit of Gupta and Ferguson (1997: 5) when they insist that "the attention to 'reading' cultural products and public representations here does not displace but complements the characteristically anthropological emphasis on daily routines and lived experiences."

lunches and receptions and dinners feature when diplomats meet. Sharing food and drink is a reminder of our biological unity as a species, and can be observed cross-culturally when negotiations are in progress, so this is hardly surprising. The particular form that eating and drinking tends to take in diplomatic circles today does, however, owe much to a specific cultural practice, namely the European dinner party.

Because of their ubiquity, food and drink are also good markers of hierarchy. When Norway left the personal union with Sweden in 1905 and needed to set up its own Ministry of Foreign Affairs, Thor von Ditten left Stockholm to lend a hand. He had been the highest-ranking civil servant in the Swedish ministry, and he knew the procedures intimately. Laying down new routines turned out to be easy. What was hard was to convince the Norwegian Parliament that Norway's representatives abroad had to be properly paid. Von Ditten persuaded them by evoking international and national hierarchies in a way that tells us much about diplomacy in the years before the First World War. There were two categories of small states, Ditten argued:

On the one hand, we have the diplomats from Denmark, Belgium, Holland and sometimes Portugal, who participate in social life, are well known and come across as worthy representatives of their countries all around. On the other hand we have Serbia, Rumania, Greece and sometimes Switzerland, whose representatives do not participate in social life and so are not well known and in no way measure up to the first category. Of course, that is where we will continue to find Sweden, and that is where Norway should also be. However, Norway cannot draw on private fortunes and aristocratic names who would make it possible for its representatives to make their mark, which means that everything hangs on paying them a salary that will enable them to lead a social life that will place them in the first category. Of course one may pay our minister to London an annual salary of 36.000 kroner, but the consequence is that he cannot afford his own transportation, so cannot participate in social life, nor frequent the best clubs, nor rent a comfortable apartment, etc. As a result, he will end up like the Greek, whom no one knows and whose address is basically unknown.[4]

---

4. Norwegian National Archives, Ministry of Foreign Affairs (hereafter NNA MFA), G3A 9/22, box 677, Pro Memoria (hereafter PM) written by von Ditten 19 July 1905.

Where one ate, and with whom, was critically important. Diplomacy to von Ditten was a field where aristocrats representing historically colonialist European states made rules and set the tone over a good meal. The wining and dining man about town remains one of the imagined personae of the diplomat. Von Ditten also pinpointed another: the diplomat was expected to have been born in an exalted social station.[5] Sir Henry Wotton, an English diplomat and minor poet, quipped in 1604 that "an ambassador is an honest man, sent to lie abroad for the good of his country."[6] There is now a touch of James Bond to the public image of the diplomat, and it is true that the diplomat's supposed power may in no small measure rest on that of the state he represents. But something must be added to Wotton's quip, for we also expect the diplomat if not to be above the use of physical force, then at least to view its use as a last resort, even an admission of defeat. Perhaps popular culture's closest equivalent to James Bond the spy is *Star Trek* captain Jean-Luc Picard the diplomat (Neumann 2001). Picard is not only the captain of a starship. He is also a gallant opponent, a famed negotiator, and a polymath with a degree in archaeology.

Picard (and Bond for that matter) belongs to the upper bourgeoisie. In Satow's and von Ditten's day, the bourgeoisie had begun to flood the ranks of diplomats. Sixteenth-century Dutch merchants who tried to make contact with the Chinese emperor were summarily dismissed once the emperor learned that they were not aristocrats (Zhang, forthcoming). European bourgeois scribes actually began to enter service of kings in the seventeenth century. If they did well, however, their anomalous class background was simply resolved, as the king proceeded to ennoble them. Furthermore, these bourgeois scribes were active only at home. In those days, the term diplomat was reserved for the representative of the state who traveled or lived abroad, using his own resources. The collaborators attached to him—his attachés, as it were—did not receive any salary, either. Diplomats remained aristocrats, for good hierarchical and material

---

5. As suggested by Der Derian (1987), the panache of the diplomat probably has even more stellar origins. Diplomats are, among other things, messengers (Gr. *angeloi*) who specialize in dealing with the unknown, as do priests. And like priests, when popular culture honors them by hanging them out to dry, it is invariably their implied transgressions and sanctimonious way of being in the world that are being parodied.

6. "Legatus est vir bonus peregre missus ad mentiendum rei publicae causa" (quoted in Mattingly 1955: 274).

reasons. Soldiery and diplomacy are historically core tasks for the state, and they were the parts of the state apparatus to which the European aristocracy clung as the bourgeoisie rose to become the new state-bearing class. Throughout the nineteenth century, the typical diplomat was a male aristocrat. Even in Norway, a country whose small aristocracy was stripped of legal privileges in 1821, aristocrats were key when the new state's Ministry of Foreign Affairs was established in 1905. Still, bourgeois diplomats were in a huge majority. Like Picard and Bond, however, they were upper bourgeois who to a large degree had emulated aristocratic ideals. There is still a lingering expectation that diplomats will hail from the upper echelons of their societies, and will have the easy social ways of the naturally superior. This stereotype survives even though in the aftermath of the Second World War, bourgeois diplomats were joined by people from more humble stations and then, from the 1970s onward, by women. Now, people from minority ethnic backgrounds are also joining the service. Mutatis mutandis, a similar diversification is happening in other ministries all over the world. The result is tension within a diplomatic corps whose esprit de corps has been legendary.

A Day at the Office

There are plenty of integrative factors, however. Since we are considering a profession here, it is hardly surprising that the central integrating factor is work. Wining and dining are also important in this respect. Lunch is the major opportunity for maintaining and expanding one's organizational network, particularly when the diplomat is stationed at home. Important business calls for good eating about town. The beef tartar that I had for lunch one day in September 2001, in the dignified Library Bar of Oslo's Bristol Hotel, was certainly tasty, and the full-bodied red wine matched it well. The conversation, which turned on how to write the centenary history of the Norwegian Ministry of Foreign Affairs, had an easy flow to it. As I returned to the ministry, where I was working as a senior adviser, I was quite pleased with my attempt at the diplomatic art of blowing my trumpet without seeming to do so. Looking at my watch, I noted that it was 1:40. Maybe the job would be mine. The luncheon had lasted for well over the usual hour, and that was a good sign. Food, drink, setting, timing: diplomats leave none of this to chance. At diplomatic dinner parties, the done thing is to take your leave around 10.30 p.m., so that all concerned may put in a full day in the office the next day. If the host insists that you stay, it is because something is to be discussed, or because something has already gone right.

On that particular day, however, the good feeling did not last. When I entered the Department for European Affairs and Bilateral Relations with North America, my slight inebriation dissipated. Something was wrong; there was none of the usual hustle and bustle. I walked down the corridor to find a group assembled around the department's TV. The boss himself was on the phone to the foreign minister, to make certain that the minister knew that a plane had just crashed into the Twin Towers in New York City. Two of my senior colleagues were discussing which of their European counterparts to call. A second plane emerged on the screen, flying straight into the South Tower. The boss broke the long silence and asked us to go back to our offices and finish whatever we were doing. New work would definitely materialize.

It did. Over the next few days, the entire ministry was abuzz. Official condolences were sent. Information was gathered. The different departments were in contact with their opposite numbers in other MFAs. Discussions about how to handle the press, always the key item in the morning meetings between the minister, the secretary general, and the heads of departments, took on even greater urgency. There were talks with the prime minister's office, and with the Ministry of Defence, which had the best contacts in the Pentagon and was therefore a key player as the MFA tried to foresee American responses. There were consultations within the NATO framework. There was debate about how wise it was of "the Americans" (meaning American diplomats and politicians) to define the situation as one of war. And then there were responses to all the calls for help from Norwegian individuals and nongovernmental organizations who were affected by the attacks.

9/11 was an extraordinary event, and so was the activity that it spawned in two hundred MFAs around the world. It was extraordinary not in the sense that the activity was different from what the MFAs usually did, however, only in the sense that there was more of it. Every day, MFAs are involved in a huge number of transnational processes. Many are long and meandering, others simply materialize and have to be responded to. Carl von Clausewitz maintained that war was 90 percent waiting. Diplomacy is also about waiting, in the sense that diplomats are always collecting and analyzing information with a view to what *may* be the next big thing. This information has a very short time horizon, which means that it constantly has to be renewed. Another similarity between the diplomat and the soldier is that both are infatuated by rank.

A Life at the Office

The diplomatic career is a nomadic trek between postings at home and abroad. In the Norwegian diplomatic service, after two years at home, which includes both on-the-job and academy training, the young secretary has two postings abroad. This eight-year period may be seen as one long rite of passage, complete with integration into the fold, detachment, and then a homecoming as a fully fledged diplomat, and it is characterized by routinized casework at the bottom of various hierarchies and an often intense social schedule. The homecoming diplomat is typically in his mid- to late thirties. The make-or-break forties usually include one, sometimes two, tours abroad. By the age of fifty, members of the lead pack have served as ambassadors in a small station, typically with a first secretary career diplomat, a consular employee, and an office person (in Norway's case, examples include embassies in Rabat and Havana).[7] Of roughly equal importance is service as counselor (number two) in a medium-sized station or as a head of section at home. The lead pack is the key knowledge-producing group in the organization; they set up and supervise the work of the juniors, and deliver the results to the seniors (who then proceed to parse them). If you have not made any of the positions mentioned by fifty, your career will usually peak with a stint as ambassador in a small station (which is wholly acceptable) or you will find yourself in some office at home with nowhere to go (which is not). At a rough estimate, about one in five or six makes the lead pack. Cohorts help one another and also serve as yardsticks for their members to see how they are doing.

---

7. Since diplomats are accredited to sovereigns who live in capitals, they usually speak of Rabat and Havana rather than Morocco and Cuba.

Since there are more high-ranking jobs abroad (103 stations) than at home, homecomings are usually tense moments, with competition for positions as head of section and deputy head of department being particularly fierce. At this stage, a temporary dearth of slots or some contingent situation may knock one off track. To take an example from Sweden: in the only Cold War spy scandal involving a diplomat in Norway,[8] in the early 1980s counterintelligence taped some of the suspect's dinner conversations. One of these involved a very promising Swedish midcareer diplomat. As sometimes happens at professional dinners, the participants compared their bosses, with the Swedish diplomat saying some unfavorable things about his foreign minister. Norwegian intelligence sent records of the conversation to the Swedish MFA. After that, the diplomat later told me, his career ground to a halt for years and had never really recovered.

Beyond the age of fifty, those in the lead pack compete for the most coveted embassies (London, Washington, Moscow, Paris, Berlin) and delegations (NATO, the UN) as well as for jobs at home as head of department and particularly political director and secretary general. Party affiliation plays some role here, and occasionally a nondiplomat is appointed to an ambassadorial job. (European states are, however, a far cry from the so-called spoils system practiced in the United States, where each new administration sends a whole swathe of political appointees to serve as ambassadors abroad.) At this level, quotidian life is dominated by representation. Lunches and dinners are given and attended on a massive scale. When, in 1976, the secretary general of the Norwegian ministry talked about his regular working day to the greenhorns attending the in-house academy, he gave as an example of how these events evolve the obligatory luncheon for departing ambassadors.[9] He would give a set speech, which he summarized as follows: "We will miss the ambassador. The ambassador has made no end of friends in Norway. The ambassador has been very hospitable. The ambassador has done valuable work that has further advanced relations between our two countries. Then I decorate the

---

8. There were three others centered on other Foreign Ministry personnel.

9. An important part of the secretary general's duties is attending to the *corps diplomatique,* the body of diplomats accredited to a sovereign (in other words, the foreign diplomats in a capital taken as a whole).

ambassador with the Grand Cross of St. Olav."[10] If stationed abroad, one has to retire on one's sixty-eighth birthday. If one is working at home, the mandatory retirement date is the seventieth birthday.

The Book

In order to account for the nimbus surrounding the diplomat, and also to defend the claim that diplomacy is a historical cross-cultural phenomenon on a par with trade and war, I start with a discussion of the key diplomatic systems known in history. It may come as a surprise that all known diplomatic systems seem to have rested on shared myths of kinship. At the core of a diplomatic system, one finds "metaphors which serve to bulwark common values, but come themselves from a quite different quarter" (Strathern 2004: 25). To mention some key examples, this is true of the Amarna system; for ancient Greece and ensuing systems converging on Rome and Byzantium; for interaction among aborigines in precontact Australia; for the diplomacy among Italian city-states and among emerging European territorial states from the late fourteenth century onward; as well as for what has been called the forest diplomacy of the Six Nations of the Iroquois. European practices became the dominant template for today's global diplomacy, and so I concentrate on that experience and discuss the lingering importance of the Christian myths that underpinned European diplomacy historically. And since I did my fieldwork in the Norwegian MFA, I concentrate on the diplomatic experience of one specific European state, namely the Danish composite state of which Norway was a part until Denmark ended up on the wrong side of the Napoleonic Wars and lost Norway to Sweden.

With the broader historical and social context established, I then turn to a discussion of what it is like to be a diplomat. Present-day diplomats are in their element when they are in the thick of negotiation. This is when they get to mediate between states, which, *pace* Satow, is what diplomats define as their major task. Since this particular activity makes up very little

---

10. NNA MFA 2.25/7, speech by Sverre Gjellum, "En utenriksråds arbeidsoppgaver" (The tasks of a secretary general), 18 February 1976.

of a diplomat's life work, however, diplomats are left to square the practice of actually doing a lot of bureaucratic work with a discourse that instructs them to spend as much time as possible in negotiation. Furthermore, negotiation is always done on behalf of a seemingly disembodied collective, namely the state, and as a result the ideal of being a negotiator is also a threat to the integrity of the diplomat's self.

The changes in MFA recruiting patterns have made for a more diverse body of diplomats. Class and gender have changed what used to be first a male aristocratic and then a male upper bourgeois pursuit. I outline the ensuing tensions by tracking first the emergence of the female diplomat and then the emergence of different class and gender scripts for how to be a diplomat. I then compare the narrative identities in play and conclude that the upper bourgeois male is still dominant in the MFA.

Diplomats may believe that negotiation is at the core of their work, but most of their time is spent producing texts. These texts speak to widely different concerns and are read and listened to by very different audiences. Still, they are all suspiciously similar. IR realists would say that this is because they all give voice to the national interest. Neo-institutionalists would say it is because they are all produced by the same organization. I challenge these armchair views by tracking the production of actual texts. I find that, in the name of the social integration of the MFA itself, everyone is supposed to have his or her say. The result is that any one text tends to look like the next one. It is not that some specific person or unit wants things to stay the same. Rather, the mode of knowledge production is such that a text produced by the MFA will of necessity repeat what has been said before. The hands-on political work of the diplomat is to create consensus and find ways of making processes come together in a way that will cause as little friction as possible. Revolutionaries of all stripes—Communist, Conservative Crusader, Ecologist—have never liked diplomats. Hitler thought that "diplomats do not represent their countries, but an international Society clique" (quoted in Irving 1978: 166). The focus of diplomacy is maintenance, not change. By the same token, however, any order will need its diplomats, and any one kind of diplomacy will have its own, characteristic kind of knowledge production. For the last two centuries, diplomacy's knowledge production has taken the form that is presented in this book.

In the conclusion, I speculate about how globalization may be changing the face of diplomacy. We may be seeing a move away from a reactive kind of knowledge production which sprang from certainty about the supremacy of the state to a forward-leaning kind where the point is actively to change the way people represent global issues, wherever those people may be found. Diplomacy certainly does not stand still. An emerging global polity seems to be generating its own kind of diplomatic knowledge.

1

ABROAD

The Emergence of Permanent Diplomacy

> We can trace the gradual broadening of the feeling of fellowship during the
> advance of civilization. The feeling of fellowship in the horde expands to the
> feeling of bonds established by a neighbourhood of habitat, and further on
> to the feeling of fellowship among members of nations. This seems to be the
> limit of the ethical concept of fellowship of man which we have reached at
> the present time . . . the ethical point of view which makes it justifiable at the
> present time to increase the well-being of one nation at the cost of another,
> the tendency to value our own form of civilization as higher—not as dearer
> to our hearts—than that of the whole rest of mankind, are the same as those
> which prompt the actions of primitive man, who considers every stranger an
> enemy, and who is not satisfied until the enemy is killed.
>
> FRANZ BOAS, 1911

The public image of the diplomat as the wining and dining man about town is grounded in fact.[1] It is not unusual for a senior field diplomat to travel for a month or two out of the year and, while at home, to eat another hundred working dinners, some of which he will have to host. The food may be fancy, the drinks plentiful, the staff helpful, but the hours are long, and family life suffers. I never came across a diplomat who complained about this. "It's all part of the job." "This is how it is." "This is what we

---

1. Particularly in the 19th century, however, he was also depended on by his family. Regarding social history, Jones 1983 makes the key point that the nineteenth-century embassy was a family business. My own previous work on the Norwegian case suggests that the family aspect was important well into the interwar period (Neumann and Leira 2005).

do." The diplomat puts up with it because she is out to gather information, and she is on the look out for ways to broaden the interfaces of information between her home country and her host country. One easy way to pursue both goals is to socialize with those locals who have already developed what the founder of American anthropology referred to as "feelings of fellowship" for her sending country (Boas [1911] 1983: 224), for example, people who have studied in her home country. The Norwegian Oxford committee, of which I am a member, can always count on Her Britannic Majesty's ambassador to put up our annual guest from our old university and even to host a dinner for us. One year, as part of the proceedings, the ambassador joined Professor Adam Roberts and the rest of us for a weekend at the seaside, some two hours' drive out of Oslo, just across the Swedish border. As we chatted amiably, the ambassador told the professor that, when she had phoned her Swedish colleague (by which she meant Her Majesty's ambassador to Stockholm) to inform him about the trip, she had mentioned that the professor would be coming along, and the ambassador to Sweden had sent his greetings. Once the networking was out of the way, I asked why the ambassador had phoned her Swedish colleague, and she told me that it was a standard courtesy for a country's ambassadors to give warning when they trespassed onto another's territory. I asked since when this had happened, and she looked at me and said: "Well, always."

In this grain of sand we see two major aspects of the diplomat's world. Information gathering is so important to diplomats that they regularly put their private lives on hold when a chance to pursue it comes along. To this topic I will return once I have discussed the second aspect of diplomatic discourse on display here, namely the diplomat's studied disregard of her own profession's history.

What makes you a professional, an insider, is among other things that you take your situation for granted. Diplomats rarely question the conditions that structure their life, and they are not particularly interested in the history of their trade. The British ambassador was typical of her profession in that she had naturalized diplomacy. In the public eye as well, diplomacy seems timeless. Even eminent historians have treated diplomacy as a given. For example, Herbert Butterfield (1966: 182–83) wrote that:

> if there are rules of diplomacy and laws of foreign policy, these must be
> valid whether the business is conducted by men or women, whites or blacks,

monarchies or democracies, cabinets or parliaments. . . . It may be true that some of the routines of diplomacy—some of the techniques and detailed practices—may depend on conditions (on the state of communications, for example, or the character of the *régimes* involved); but this can hardly be the case with rules of policy and the way in which consequences proceed out of causes in international relations. . . . If the principle of the balance of power was useful or valid in the eighteenth century, it was likely to be useful or valid in the twentieth century.

To say that diplomacy has "always" been thus is not an innocent move, for it shrinks our understanding of a historically and socially rich phenomenon to today's constellation, and it elides the power struggles that went into producing that particular constellation. This chapter, which looks at the discourse of diplomacy, and the following one, which looks at foreign ministries, are intended as antidotes.

Present-day diplomatic discourse has a history. There are specific historical reasons that, as I discussed in the introduction, "the Greek" came across as an outsider to the diplomatic corps of early twentieth-century London and that, with the number of states in the world having quadrupled since then, this fact may strike the contemporary reader as odd. There are specific reasons why the head of the diplomatic corps in London is the diplomat who has been accredited to the Court of St. James the longest, whereas the head of the diplomatic corps in Berlin is always the Pope's representative, the nuncio. The diplomat who professes no interest in history simply accepts a particular understanding by default. This chapter begins with a discussion of the traditional European understanding of diplomacy's history. I then discuss four basic problems with this understanding, all of which will be immediately familiar from general historiographical debates: a privileging of its Greek origin, an elision of ancient Greek and European diplomacy, an erasure of what happened in the millennium in between, and a blindness to what happened outside Europe and to how polities interacting with European ones experienced those interactions. In discussing diplomats' implicit understanding of the history of their profession and presenting the ongoing discussions within the field of diplomatic studies, I also mean to situate the book within those discussions. In conclusion, I return to the question of information gathering, which is, I believe, the key knowledge-producing practice anchored by permanent diplomacy.

Diplomatic Histories

If Satow is the authoritative diplomatic handbook of the twentieth century, then Sir Harold Nicolson's *Diplomacy* (1939), which has seen three editions and also received elaboration in his *Evolution of Diplomatic Method* (1954), still seems to be the most widely read history of diplomacy in diplomatic circles. As behooves a text written by an English aristocrat-diplomat, Nicolson's book is elegant, erudite, and tactful. It is also a work that emerges from the British colonial experience. Nicolson is typical of his time and his class in seeing the beginning of most things in Greece (ancient Greece, that is, not the Greece whose representative to London was so marginalized within the diplomatic corps). Etymologically, he is certainly right, in that the word diplomacy hails from the Greek verb *diploein,* which means to fold. The written document (the diploma) that certified a herald as such, had to be folded and kept in a wooden contraption that shielded it against the weather. The verb turned into a noun that signified first the document, then the carrier (Constantinou 1996). Nicolson's history of diplomacy then moved to the city states of the Italian Renaissance, which he identified as the birthplace of so-called permanent diplomacy, that is, exchanges based not on embassies in the old sense of groups of people journeying from one seat of power to another on a specific mission but on embassies in the sense of permanent physical structures that housed a resident representative. For Nicolson, Italian Renaissance diplomacy then transmuted into modern European diplomacy.

Nicolson's history fits the grand narrative of Western civilization very well: Greece is the cradle, there is a rebirth of the Greek ethos in Italy, and then we arrive at the present. The insightful histories of diplomacy that have appeared more recently contain material that undermines Nicolson's grand narrative, but they nonetheless stick to his general outline (see Watson 1984, Anderson 1993, Berridge 1995, Hamilton and Langhorne 1995). Take, for example, a present-day practice, the country note, which is a regularly updated *précis* of how things stand and are going for a particular state, perhaps ten pages long. As pointed out by Hamilton and Langhorne (1995: 53), it is the direct descendant of an Italian Renaissance practice, the *relazione:*

> The Venetian *relazione* gave a full picture of the geography, politics and society of the territory from which the ambassador had returned, as well as

the nature and relative success of Venetian policy in relation to it. The initial purpose when *relazioni* were instituted in 1268 was to give the senior statesmen of Venice an extended verbal report of a mission, but after the 1530s when *relazioni* began to be written and retained in the chancellery, they were available for the instruction of future ambassadors to the same places and, as it turned out, became a mine of useful evidence for their future political and social, as well as diplomatic, historians. For those who want to chart the development of diplomacy itself, the *relazioni* are not as helpful as ordinary dispatches, however.[2]

Hamilton and Langhorne go on to deliver a detailed and highly convincing discussion of how the present-day dispatch—"a formal and therefore stylized letter from a head of mission abroad to the Foreign Secretary, and vice versa; and also from one head of mission to another" (Berridge and James 2001: 62)—is the direct descendant of the Renaissance Italian specimen. Indeed, such traditional histories of diplomacy are right to point out that several present-day practices—anchoring ones such as permanent diplomacy as well as specific ones such as the writing and distribution of country notes—are the direct descendants of Italian Renaissance practices. They are also right in pointing to the importance of ancient Greece, for Greek diplomatic discourse was rich in distinctions, and so of particular interest as a social form. As the Renaissance unfolded, it became a direct source of inspiration for emergent European diplomacy.

Problem One: The Privileged Account

These traditional histories of diplomacy are not, however, the only form of knowledge about the preconditions for today's diplomacy. General debates about the possibility of grand narratives and the place that should be allotted to the Western experience are highly pertinent to the field of diplomacy. One early attempt to undermine the traditional account was Ragnar Numelin's (1950) book on the beginnings of diplomacy, in which

---

2. Compare Queller's (1980: 173) reported definition of a *relazione* as a report on "the power and disposition of all great lords and princes of the world as well as of the condition of the great lands and of the people who dwell in them." To Bismarck, always a skeptic when it came to everything diplomatic, dispatches were "paper freely daubed with ink."

he looked into prehistoric practices such as those of precontact Australia in order to demonstrate that diplomacy is an aspect of political life wherever different polities come into contact. Since archaeological studies increasingly underline the importance of relations among different groups in order to account for the emergence of large-scale polities (Renfrew and Cherry 1986, Stein 1999, Smith 2003), I believe we may claim that diplomacy is ubiquitous once political life is lived on a scale larger than the band.

Numelin's point has been further substantiated by work documenting a diplomatic system centered on Egypt and involving polities such as Mesopotamia, Assyria, and Hatti, some thirty-five hundred years ago (for a recent discussion of what has come to be known as Amarna diplomacy, see Cohen and Westbrook 2000).[3] Building on these and other works allowed Jönsson and Hall (2005) to present a rather different history of diplomacy, one where European conventions appear as only one set among many.

Such a decentering of Europe undermines Nicolson's historiographical project. It also undermines Satow's and Nicolson's definition of diplomacy as the conduct of official relations among the governments of independent states, for it demonstrates that practices which we may call "diplomatic" were in evidence long before the emergence of the state in Continental Europe, let alone of government.

---

3. The Amarna system is named after the village Tell el-Amarna on the Nile. Here, in 1349 BCE, the Egyptian Pharaoh Akhenaten built his new capital. In 1887, excavations yielded around 350 letters, some 50 of which were correspondence with foreign polities, mostly from the other great powers of the day: Assyria, Babylonia, Hatti (the Hittite kingdom), and Mittani (the kingdom of the Hurrians; Cohen and Westbrook 2000). Read with other archival and archaeological evidence from the Middle and Late Bronze Ages (ca. 2000–1100 BCE), we have enough to capture a glimpse of what Amarna diplomacy looked like, to identify its forerunners, and to estimate its two-century heyday (Liverani 1990, Munn-Rankin 1956). The great kings made up a brotherhood (in Akkadian, the system's *lingua franca, ahhûtu,* also brotherliness or group of persons of equal status; Cohen and Westbrook 2000: 268 n. 7, Cohen 1996). According to Liverani (2000: 18), "international relations were shaped on a model of interpersonal relations currently obtaining at the level of face-to-face communities: family or village or neighborhood. . . . The family metaphor is immediately evident in the pervasive use of the term 'my brother' (*ahî*) to address the partner (the 'my father' (*abî*) metaphor being reserved for a more aged partner). Yet the most suitable model for external relations could not be the nuclear family or the self-sufficient household but rather the small community. . . . From the most trivial but socially meaningful usage, to 'ask (news of) the health' . . . to the most demanding negotiations for interdynastic marriages, the interpersonal level is the only one in use."

Problem Two: The Elision

The problems with the traditional account of diplomacy do not stop with the privileging of Europe and the modern state. As James Der Derian's (1987) work on the genealogy of Western diplomacy stresses, the traditional account of its emergence is deeply flawed in that it elides substantial differences between forerunners and descendants. As a social form, Greek diplomacy was simply different from what came later.

Greek diplomacy was founded on myths stressing kinship and religion (Jones 1999). Diplomatic practices converged around the Amphictyonic leagues and the Olympic Games, both of them religious institutions (Adcock and Mosely 1996 [1975]). As to the importance of kinship, note that the man after whom the leagues were named, Amphictyon, was also said to be the common ancestor of all the Greeks. When Greeks came into contact with other groups and relations with these groups proved to take on some degree of permanence, their members were "discovered" to be kin (Jones 1999). In an anthropological perspective, this is hardly surprising, for as Strathern (2004: 37) notes,

> When writers use the language of kinship, say, to draw attention to affinities and similarities, is the connection one of analogy and metaphor (that is, how language is being used) or is the connection a genetic one (that is, a demonstrable kinship between phenomena)? Where does the creative energy lie? In the study of language itself, the contrast collapses when resemblances between languages are taken to indicate . . . connections between them.

Inasmuch as religion and kinship cannot be said to be anchoring practices of contemporary diplomacy (though see below), ancient Greek and European diplomacy must be said to be different creatures, and in my view too different to be elided in the way Nicolson and his followers do. In fact, by Satow's and Nicolson's own lights, Greek diplomacy is no diplomacy at all, not only because there are no states involved but also because its modus operandi differs radically from the way they define diplomacy. Recall that, to Satow ([1917] 1979: 3), "diplomacy is the application of intelligence and tact to the conduct of official relations." As the classicist J. R. Grant (1965: 262–63) points out, tact had no place in Greek diplomacy: "Greek diplomats talked like any other Greeks. [Threats were commonplace.] A Greek speaker wishing to utter a threat did not trouble to disguise it by nicely graded conversational phrases, and the recipient did not go into an emotional tailspin but weighed the matter on its merits" (Grant 1965: 262–63).

If the first problem with the traditional account of how diplomacy emerged is the elision of its ubiquitous roots and the privileging of ancient Greek origins, then the second problem is the sleight of hand that simply postulates that Greek diplomacy was similar to modern European diplomacy.

Problem Three: Erasure

A third problem with the traditional account is the way it cuts out of its grand narrative everything that does not fit. At the very least, in a standard "Western civilization" account, one would expect the Roman Empire and Christianity to make a bridging appearance between Greece and the Renaissance. They cannot have been erased for a lack of diplomacy, for diplomatic practices are heavily in evidence in both cases. Among the early Romans, there was an expectation that once their city-state ran up against other polities, it also ran up against autochthonous gods that needed to be appeased and ideally brought to some kind of stalemate with Roman gods.[4] Specialists known as *fetiales* therefore performed one ritual in Rome as a prelude to any contact, another ritual upon crossing the city-state's *limes* or boundary, and a third in foreign territory. Only then could the mundane part of the business at hand commence (Adcock and Mosely 1995).

In the case of medieval Christendom, too, diplomatic discourse was imbricated with religious discourse. In his genealogy of Western diplomacy, Der Derian highlights the role of Augustinian thinking in Western Christian diplomacy. St. Augustine specified the historical existence of what he called cities (i.e., polities), stretching from the fall of the angels until Doomsday, and saw the historical task of the city as the purification of its resident souls. The cities were ideally united, just as humanity was ideally united in Christ. When united, there would be peace and justice all around. Augustine observed, however, that empirically, cities strayed

---

4. Note the parallel to Amarna diplomacy: the earliest peace treaty of which we know is that of Kadesh, from the twelfth century BCE, between the Egyptian pharaoh Ramses II and the Hittite king Hattussili III. It explicitly states that there shall be peace not only between the two kings but also between the gods involved on either side (Grimal 1992: 256–57).

from their course. Diplomatic relations were required only when what was to Augustine the natural state of things, namely peace, was in jeopardy. Consequently, diplomacy was a necessary but tainted business, since the need for it arose only when humans strayed from God. As Der Derian (1987) points out, to the degree that diplomatic messengers deserved the Greek name for messenger—*angeloi*—they are probably best considered as black angels. Medieval diplomacy had specific practices regarding the messenger's letter of authority (procuration), his letter of credence ("short letters naming the ambassador and asking that credence be given to him"; Dickinson 1955: xviii, cf. Cuttino 1985: 8), and instructions. They also had rules of procedure for negotiations, many of them taken over from the great church meetings. The diplomatic practices I have touched on so far were explicitly religious, as were most medieval Christian practices. For example, the practice of verification in use involved kissing a cross (Vernadsky 1948: 95), with the implicit sanction being heavenly punishment for breaking promises. A wonderful example of how this norm could fare in practice is furnished by the official Soviet history of diplomacy:

> In 1152 the Galician prince Vladimir Volodarevich [Volodymyrko of Halich] did not fulfill the agreement that had been sealed with a kiss of "the cross of St. Stephen." When the ambassador of the Kievan prince Izyaslav held this against him, his answer was that "It is a small cross!" When the ambassador pointed out that he who reneged on a holy promise should not live, Vladimir simply told him to pray that it should be so, and then be off. (Zorin 1959: 138; cf. Hamilton and Langhorne 1995: 50)

The fact that the practice was honored in the breach demonstrates its existence (and serves as a reminder that the existence of practices need not necessarily determine specific action). Note that the norm is unchallengeable on its own merits; Vladimir is reduced to quibbling over ritual execution. One problematic effect of downplaying what came between ancient Greek and Italian Renaissance diplomacy, then, is that it also downplays the importance of religion and kinship for diplomatic discourse generally and for the emergence of contemporary diplomacy in particular. Consider the practice of the immunity of envoys, which is the centerpiece of the key legal code on diplomacy and diplomats, the Vienna Convention on

Diplomatic Relations of 1961 (Frey and Frey 1999). Variants of this practice may be found in all known diplomatic systems, but genealogically the modern variant hails directly from medieval Christendom. Having established the functionality of reciprocity (if I grant immunity to your envoy, then you will grant immunity to mine), all stress the importance of religious sanction. It was God's will that His children should live in peace with one another, and Christendom stood to gain from the existence of envoys between worldly power holders. These are the specific ideas to which Bertrand du Rosier referred in the first-ever textbook for diplomats from 1436, when he wrote that "an ambassador is sacred because he acts for the general welfare" (quoted in Mattingly 1955: 42; see also Hamilton and Langhorne 1995: 40–43). This idea found its way into legal Christian discourse, where the ambassador—one's own as well as that of an enemy—was described as a representative of Christendom in its entirety. Many lawyers held that, for this reason, murdering an envoy was not just a worldly crime but also sacrilege, and that the murderer thereby earned the status of enemy of mankind. The centerpiece of the Vienna Convention on Diplomatic Relations thus began as a specifically Christian practice. More generally, modern diplomacy still carries the marks of its Christian origins. To take but one example, since the eighteenth century, when states gradually discontinued ranking resident ambassadors according to the status of the kings they represented and instead began to rank them according to the date of their accreditation, the dean of any particular capital's diplomatic corps has been its longest-serving diplomat. In Catholic states, however—and in this regard Germany is a Catholic state—the dean of the corps is always the papal nuncio (Rana 2007).

Another problematic effect of simply deleting a millennium or so of history is that it forecloses inquiries into specific continuities, or for that matter into the origins of any European diplomatic practice that predates Italian Renaissance diplomacy. Consider the very practice that makes of the Italian Renaissance a historical break in the traditional account, namely permanent diplomacy. In 1455, the duke of Milan sent Nicodema de Pontremoli to Genoa in order to set up a permanent representation. Within a few decades, permanent representation was in evidence in other city-states as well. Nothing has only one origin, however, and James Der Derian notes that as early as 453, Pope Leo the Great and the archbishop of

Ravenna had exchanged representatives (Der Derian 1987: 92).[5] On closer inspection, however, it turns out that this exchange was part of institutionalized permanent representation between the Eastern and Western churches. In the first volume of the *New Catholic Encyclopedia* (1907) we find an article on the Apocrisiarius, a character that extant scholarship has either written off as irrelevant (Mattingly 1955: 56) or simply noted (Jönsson and Hall 2005: 112). Due to its great genealogical interest, the passage deserves reproduction in its entirety:

(Greek *apocrisis,* an answer; cf. Latin *responsalis,* from *responsum*). This term indicates in general the ecclesiastical envoys of Christian antiquity, whether permanent or sent temporarily on missions to high ecclesiastical authorities or royal courts. In the East the patriarchs had their *apocrisiarii* at the imperial court, and the metropolitans theirs at the courts of the patriarchs. The popes also frequently deputed clerics of the Roman Church as envoys, either for the adjustment of important questions affecting the Church of Rome, or to settle points of discipline in local dioceses, or to safeguard the interests of the Church in religious controversies. In the letters of St. Gregory the Great (590–604) very frequent mention is made of such envoys (*responsales*). In view of the great importance attaching to the relations between the popes and the imperial court of Constantinople, especially after the fall of the Western Empire (476), and during the great dogmatic controversies in the Greek Church, these papal representatives at Constantinople took on gradually the character of permanent legates and were accounted the most important and responsible among the papal envoys. The first of these *apocrisiarii* seems to have been Julianus, Bishop of Cos, accredited by St. Leo the Great to the court of Emperor Marcian (450–57) for a considerable period of time during the Monophysite heresies. From then until 743, when all relations between Rome and Constantinople were severed during the iconoclastic troubles, there were always, apart from a few brief intervals,

---

5. Der Derian also notes the large ecumenical councils as a forerunner of congress diplomacy as in 1648, 1815, and 1878. "Probably the most significant congress was the Peace of Cateau-Cambrésis in 1559. Open to several interpretations, it represents a last-ditch effort to preserve a disintegrating Christendom—or, alternatively, an enlightened approach for ushering in a new system of European states. Old proto-diplomatic procedures, such as the exchange of hostages (one was William of Orange) to ensure the treaty, coexist with a very modern balancing act in which the powers alienated internal estrangement to the *boundaries* of Christendom by a verbal agreement *not* to consider hostilities west of the Azores and south of the Tropic of Cancer in breach of the peace" (Der Derian 1987: 129–30).

apocrisiarii in Constantinople. On account of the importance of the office, only capable and trustworthy members of the Roman Clergy were selected for such missions. Thus Gregory I, while Deacon of the Roman Church, served in Byzantium for several years as *apocrisiarius*.[6]

Note that Gregory the Great was one of the original four Church fathers. Here we have an example of how the *apocrisiarii* were recruited from the very top. Furthermore, when the iconoclasts were defeated about a century after the year 743, there ensued a regular flow of envoys back and forth. This flow increased, rather than decreased, after the schism in 1054. We have here a fully fledged case of institutionalized diplomacy, which included permanent representation. Note, furthermore, the close contacts between Byzantium and the Italian city-states.[7]

The point about Byzantium's importance for European diplomacy and the way it has been occluded by the traditional history of diplomacy may be further underlined by revisiting the specific practice of the Italian Renaissance's *relazione* and its contemporary descendant, the country note. In his study of cultural influences between Byzantium and what he calls Western cultures, Geanakoplos (1976: 73; cf. Mattingly 1955) writes that

> Venice, whose relations with Byzantium were always closer than those of other Western powers, seems to have profited most from the Byzantine example. Indeed, a comparison of Venetian and Byzantine diplomatic practices in the late medieval and Renaissance periods—for instance, the transmission by ambassadors of periodic reports to the home government (*relazioni*) or the organization of an intelligence service—would probably reveal no small degree of direct or indirect Byzantine influence.

In sum, the traditional account traces both the anchoring practice of permanent representation and specific practices such as the country note back to the Italian Renaissance. On closer inspection, however, it turns out that the Renaissance was *not* such an important turning point in the emergence

---

6. http://www.newadvent.org/cathen/01600a.htm. Note that the pope also had permanent representatives at various courts.

7. After all, Byzantine hegemony in the area had only been broken by the Lombards in 751, and Sicily only finally fell to the Arabs in 902. In fairness to Nicolson (1988: 24), it should be noted that he does indeed stress that the Byzantines "taught diplomacy to Venice." For a magisterial overview of their relations that is less than optimally helpful on diplomatic forms, see Nicol 1988.

of European diplomacy. Indeed, considering that diplomacy overall was imbricated with religious life, I believe that it is a mistake to accept Nicolson's view that what happened in the Italian city-states was a clear historical break. On the contrary, I stress the continuity between the diplomacy of the Renaissance and what came before.

Problem Four: Eurocentrism

This leads us to a fourth and final shortcoming of the traditional account. Byzantine practices were significant for European diplomacy, and Byzantine models were also important for Ottoman society and politics (bear in mind that, as the Ottomans changed from a nomadic to a sedentary existence, they had to learn the ways of townspeople and thereby were transformed). It would be a significant omission to ignore how the emergence of diplomacy is also tied into diplomatic practices other than the European model.[8] To the diplomats of the Italian Renaissance themselves, there was certainly no sharp divide between dealing with the Byzantines and dealing with their Ottoman successors. For example, in 1205, 250 years before the traditional account notes the emergence of permanent diplomacy, the city-state of Venice had placed a representative called a *bailo* permanently in Constantinople, where he took care of typical diplomatic and consular functions (see Steensgaard 1967). The city fell to the Ottomans in 1453, and after a brief absence the *bailo* returned in the following year.[9]

---

8. European, not Western. Former settler colonies often had a cold coming of it. "In the summer of 1811 George Erving visited France before assuming a position as special minister to Denmark. In Paris, dirty and dressed in boots, 'he called on the Danish minister [and] announcing himself as the bearer of letters was taken for a courier and treated at first as that'. He later called on the French foreign minister, but 'in his uniform trimmed with galloon he was thought to be a footman in livery'" (Nickles 2008: 297).

9. Note that the Ottoman *ahdname* extended to the Venetian *bailo* by the Porte explicitly made it a continuation of the previous Byzantine-Venetian setup. *Ahdname* (from Arabic *ahd*, treaty, and Persian *name*, writ), translated into English as capitulations (from Latin *capitulum*, chapter heading and hence a legal provision), were granted to merchants for a year at a time, and gave them the right to trade without having to pay taxes. "Such concessions," Lewis (1988: 84) explains, "perceived by European trading states as treaties, by the Muslim rulers as edicts, were granted by Muslim sovereigns in North Africa, Egypt, Turkey, Iran and elsewhere. The capitulations, in Ottoman *ahdname*, "covenant-letter," were granted by the sultans as an act of condescension. The rights and privileges accorded to the foreign merchant communities in the Empire were a logical extension of the autonomy of the *dhimmi* communities and of the medieval Muslim

If European and Ottoman practices share a common origin in Byzantine diplomacy, this raises the question of how the two are related. That question leads to an even broader one, which is how Europe's diplomatic practices have been marked by the practices of its interlocutors, whether Chinese, Indian, or Iroquois. An ethnography of contemporary diplomatic practices is not the place to pursue this huge topic, but I mention it in order to demonstrate that the traditional account of diplomacy's history, embraced by Western diplomats, is under fire from scholars (cf. Neumann 2012). Not surprisingly, it is also under fire from non-Western diplomats, who tend to stress how they stand not only in a Western diplomatic tradition but also in the tradition embodied by the country that they represent.[10] The diplomats with whom I worked at the Norwegian Ministry of Foreign Affairs, and whose practices I analyze at length in this book, were acting from an unacknowledged position of power, which lent their acts a taken-for-grantedness relative to non-European diplomats.

The Diplomatic Mode of Knowledge Production

To return to the Swedish incident which opened this chapter, with one proviso the British ambassador was right when she said that her predecessors had "always" informed their colleagues accredited to other courts when they traveled into the realms of those courts. If "always" means the period since the seventeenth and eighteenth centuries, when permanent diplomacy made such practices possible, then she was right. To this day, diplomats accredited to a particular capital will always inform the host state about their leaving and returning to that state. The traditional account does not privilege the transformative potential of permanent diplomacy without reason. All three categories of present-day diplomatic practices—information gathering, negotiation, and communication of how the polity one represents works and how it represents the world (cf. Wight 1977)—are anchored by permanent diplomacy. Note, however, that the older

---

practice of *amān*." *Amān*, roughly safety or security, meant that you were under somebody's protection; *dhimmi* communities were Jewish and Christian ones, cf. Ye'or 1985.

10. For a Chinese example, see Zhang, forthcoming; for Russia, see Zorin 1959; for Vietnam, see Nien 2004: 31 et passim.

practice of the perambulatory embassy was never entirely supplanted by permanent diplomacy, and that the perambulatory embassy seems to have increased in importance over the last 150 years or so. To note some examples: the special envoy is a perambulatory embassy of one, who has a limited period in which to do her work. The state visit is a ritualized embassy led by the head of state, and the summit is a meeting of two or more heads of state whose deliberations are prepared and assisted by diplomats (known, for the last half-century or so, as sherpas; Constantinou 1996). We may even identify a hybrid practice anchored in both forms of diplomacy, namely the ambassador-at-large, who is based in the state that he represents but is accredited to several different host countries.

The entire point of permanent diplomacy is to lodge diplomacy more firmly within the territory of another state; permanence of stay implies extraterritoriality. The perambulatory embassy, on the other hand, is a passenger in both time and space: it is a trek "there" and "back," for as long as it takes. Changes in technology that increase the speed of communication and render the importance of space relative by making possible the rapid movement of persons have facilitated practices rooted in perambulatory diplomacy. The telegraph, the telephone, the fax, and the Internet join the steamship, the railway, and the airplane in challenging the significance of permanent diplomacy. Embassies and delegations are typically involved in negotiations, but the most important sequences of negotiation take place elsewhere. The increased density of global politics increases communication all around, reducing the status of embassies from the face of a polity to organizer of special events such as concerts, fairs, and lectures. No doubt information gathering is also challenged: witness the greater speed at which journalists may convey news, the greater depth in which other purveyors may provide analysis, and the importance of the "fact-finding mission," a diplomatic practice rooted in the perambulatory embassy. Nonetheless, I argue, like Hedley Bull, that the working diplomat's information gathering produces a certain kind of knowledge that still cannot be matched by any other social actor. To repeat a quote, the personnel of permanent diplomatic missions abroad are

> uniquely skilled in gathering a particular kind of information that is essential to the conduct of international relations. This is information about the views and policies of a country's political leadership, now and in the near

future. It is knowledge of personalities rather than of the forces and conditions which shape a country's policy over the long term. It is knowledge of the current situation and how it is likely to develop rather than of the pattern of past regularities. It derives from day-to-day personal dealings with the leading political strata in the country to which a diplomatist is accredited, sometimes to the detriment of his understanding of society at large in that country. (Bull 1977: 181)

Note that gathering information, processing it into stories, and feeding it to one's foreign ministry is also a precondition for negotiation and communication to succeed. Information gathering is a key category of practices anchored by permanent diplomacy. What Bull describes is nothing less than the diplomatic mode of knowledge production. The present-day field diplomat is first and foremost an information gatherer who writes dispatches back to her foreign ministry. Small wonder that, since the emergence of permanent diplomacy, the dispatch has remained as a practice largely unchanged. Given its fundamental importance for permanent diplomacy, the dispatch is logically written as if it emanates from the embassy or delegation, and not the actual person writing it. The dispatch is the voice not only of the field diplomat but of the entire embassy to which she belongs, and in the final analysis the voice of permanent diplomacy itself.

2

AT HOME

The Emergence of the Foreign Ministry

Every organisation also involves a discipline of being—an obligation to be of
a given character and to dwell in a given world.

ERVING GOFFMANN, 1961

I had not seen Giles since we both studied international relations back
in the late 1980s. He had gone on to join the British diplomatic service, and
now he had just finished a tour as ambassador to one of the Soviet successor states. I asked him what it was like to be back in Whitehall. Well, he
said, "there is not an obvious connection between what you do and what
happens."

One often overlooked forerunner of today's diplomat is the adviser
working not abroad, but first at the king's court, then in the state's administration. When posted abroad, the diplomat is a representative of his
country; with the country absent, he is present. When posted abroad, diplomats will regularly say things like "it is the opinion of the United States"
or "Norway thinks." My friend Vidar, then the Norwegian ambassador to
Cuba, once described to me the celebrations marking "my national day"
on that island (referring to what the rest of us think of as Norway's national day). When Giles and Vidar wrote home to their respective foreign
ministries, their reports would be read and would often have immediate
and tangible consequences for policy. Not so after their return, when, as

Giles somewhat ruefully observed, one may no longer make much of a difference. "You have a much freer position when you are abroad (*ute*)," Klara told me as we brainstormed about how to obtain the information we needed for a ministry note. "When you come home you make umpteen mistakes, you send faxes here and you forget to obtain a signature there. You get a bureaucracy shock *(Du får byråkratisjokk)*." Here we are far from the focused and wide-reaching information gathering which is at the heart of the diplomatic mode of knowledge production. Diplomats at home are unwilling bureaucrats. As far as they are concerned, it is just as well that the public image of the diplomat does not really involve the diplomat's working life back in the home capital.

The state started life as a small cadre of people whose functions were not particularly distinct. Advisers rode with the king, and he sent them on sundry missions, to his own subjects as well as to other kings. The permanent diplomat emerged only as a consequence of permanent diplomacy. He was the king's personal representative abroad, and today's ambassador remains the personal representative of the head of state. At home, however, early modern European kings continued to draw on court officials to advise on and implement the business at hand, whether that business pertained to relations with subjects or relations with other kings. In addition to the diplomatic service, which was always very small, a growing number of advisers at home were involved in relations with other states. In the early twentieth century, the diplomatic service—the representatives of a state abroad understood as a collective—was merged with the consular service and with the foreign ministry. Foreign ministries themselves date from the end of the eighteenth century. The foreign ministry was, as this chapter will detail, the result of a glacially slow differentiation within the state administration, whereby personnel who specialized in dealing with other courts were gathered within one institution.

The merging of these three entities was a crucial turn in the genealogy of today's foreign service. It was an advance in state building, in the sense that it brought about an institution more differentiated than those preceding it. It was the last in a long succession of steps away from a state run by aristocrats, as the aristocrat-dominated diplomatic service became a small part of a larger bourgeois-dominated whole. For the diplomatic profession, it was a return to the days before the emergence of permanent diplomacy, in the sense that time abroad became shorter, broken up by stays at home.[1] By the twentieth century, however, diplomacy had become professionalized, so that the diplomat's periods at home were spent working at the foreign ministry. As Satow has it, not only were those stationed abroad diplomats, but "all the public servants employed in diplomatic affairs, whether serving at home in the department of foreign affairs, or abroad" (Satow [1917] 1922: 4, repeated verbatim in the 5th ed., 1979: 7). Postings abroad typically last for three years or less and rarely exceed five. Where nineteenth-century diplomats were permanent expatriates, present-day diplomats are paid nomads.[2] When diplomatic service and foreign ministry merged, the diplomat took on a double heritage, which makes for a disjointed existence involving two different forms of knowledge production. When working abroad, today's diplomat is the successor to those who were permanently stationed abroad. At home, she is the successor of the adviser who stayed at court and never went on missions abroad.

I root this abstract story in concrete historical material by discussing the preconditions for the emergence of a Norwegian foreign service. Since that service is the immediate subject of the book, the chapter also serves as an introduction to my field of study. From the late Middle Ages and through the Napoleonic Wars, Norway was part of the Danish conglomerate state. Norway became a state under Swedish suzerainty only in 1814, when the great powers decided to take the territory of Norway from Denmark, which had been on the losing side of the war, and award it to Sweden, as compensation for Sweden's loss of Finland to Russia five years earlier. The Norwegian state which came into being 1814 was constitutional (Seip [1974] 1997). Parliament met in the Norwegian capital of

---

1. Early permanent diplomats were often appointed for limited periods of time, as little as two years (Jones 1983: 4), but the phenomenon of the extended stay was quick to emerge.

2. Like other nomads, diplomats abroad have interesting patterns of interaction with the sedentaries. Most missions (but not, for example, the North Korean embassy in Oslo) will have nationals of the receiver country serve as so-called "local hires." When I worked at the Norwegian embassy in Moscow in 1980, the upheavals that might be expected to follow the fairly fast-paced rotations in Norwegian personnel were significantly smoothed by the fact that Irina and Lyudmila had worked as the embassy's receptionists for years, and Nikolai had been driving ambassadors around since the days of Khrushchev. The woman who came in to give us daily Russian classes was also a mainstay, as was the washerwoman Mirova, widely rumored to be the local KGB officer. Since the ambassador's residence was in the same building, there were also local kitchen and servant personnel.

Christiania (present-day Oslo), but the king was located in the Swedish capital of Stockholm and paid only an occasional visit to Christiania. A common Ministry of Foreign Affairs was located in Stockholm, and the two states also shared the same diplomatic service.

As a consequence of these historical developments, discussing the emergence of the Norwegian Foreign Ministry in 1905 is a two-step exercise. Step one is to detail how the Danish conglomerate state evolved a separate foreign ministry in 1772. Step two, which is much shorter, introduces the Swedish-Norwegian Ministry of Foreign Affairs in its capacity as the main point of departure for the foundation of the Norwegian MFA in 1905. This adds up to a distinct history, although it must also be said that the emergence of the Danish MFA was fairly typical of a larger European pattern. Norway is, furthermore, typical of the great majority of the world's 203 states in having gained its sovereignty and formed a foreign ministry only in the twentieth century. For these reasons, the genealogy of the Norwegian MFA should also throw light on the general emergence of foreign ministries and the effects on the conduct of diplomacy.

Before Bureaucracy

State building is a protection racket, wherein a small cadre of people forces peasants and townspeople to pay for military protection. There is usually competition between different noblemen and their retinues to become king, systematizing tribute-taking in the process. Little is demanded in terms of administration. As Durkheim ([1913] 1992: 82, 85) puts it, "the State comes into existence by a process of concentration that detaches a certain group of individuals from the collective mass . . . it is above all the agent of external relations, the agent for the acquisition of territory and the organ of diplomacy." Olesen (2000: 4) discusses how the king went about tribute-taking before a local administration was in place:

> The king had to raise his income as he criss-crossed the realm, just as judicial procedures were carried out at the local "tings" [assemblies] to ensure a modicum of control over the legal process. In remote areas, such a rule implied virtual autonomy, with power entrusted to local nobility, with whom communications were scarce.

Communication, apart from royal visits, had from the late twelfth century been carried out by members of the king's retinue (*hird*) who, inspired by how affairs were ordered in Germany, were consolidating their standing as the king's closest advisers and were increasingly becoming his representatives in the districts. There was no distinction between domestic and foreign administration, since both were carried out on an ad hoc basis and involved only a small number of advisers, whose function was institutionalized in the 1280s (Helle 1972: 316–22). A similar situation may be observed where England is concerned (Cuttino 1971: 127–43).[3] Developments in knowledge production mirror developments in institutional patterns; the second half of the thirteenth century is also the period when the tradition of writing handbooks for kings reaches Norway (Bagge 1987; for an earlier Byzantine example, cf. Constantine Porphyrogenitus 1967). The advisers were recruited from the aristocracy, which had its own institution distinct from the king's court, the Council of the Realm. Among their tasks was to serve as envoys. Arve Johansen (1983: 90, cf. 102) concluded a detailed study of the adviser as envoy as follows: "Their work was not specialized enough during the thirteenth century for us to discuss the existence of a separate division for foreign affairs."[4] This was true for all

---

3. Like Nordic historians, Cuttino is remarkably lax in his use of concepts. He announces his study as being one of the *custos processuum*, an archivist, but then goes on to "draw a rough analogy," the result of which is that this official emerges as "a sort of permanent under-secretary of state for foreign affairs" (Cuttino 1971: 1, 127). Neglecting to note that those acting as envoys to other courts are also those who take care of other business, he remarks that "the first outstanding fact about the foreign service" was "the continuity of its personnel," only to stress in numerous other places that medieval administration was messy (Cuttino 1971: 140 et passim). Elsewhere, however, Cuttino (1985: 2) makes the important point that the conceptual history of "diplomacy" in English seems to date only from the late eighteenth century. A conceptual history of diplomacy is certainly called for.

4. With regard to the retinue (*hird*), Johansen substantiates the point by showing how the chancellor was the only one who had envoy duties as part of his general instructions upon entering office, and that he traveled more than the second in command, who again traveled more than numbers three and four. The argument about frequency of travel is convincing, but Johansen is wrong to see proof of embryonic administrative specialization. In a situation with limited institutionalization, as here, hierarchical status must continuously be confirmed: the most important people must handle the most important tasks. One would expect that the hierarchy to which Johansen refers can be found for all important tasks, and indeed that seems to have been the case. It follows that we cannot assume any division between domestic and foreign at this point in time. Johansen is thus guilty of an anachronism, writing of a certain period in terms that emerged later but were unknown to the period itself. The historical literature repeats the mistake, which may be traced back to Johansen's supervisor, cf. Bjørgo 1975, also Bjørgo, Rian, and Kaartvedt 1995, Riste 2005.

polities at the time. Oikonomides (1992: 83) writes of one of the best-honed administrative apparatuses in Europe at the time, Byzantium, that it

> did not have a diplomatic service, any more than it had had one in the past; ambassadors were selected on the basis of the emperor's confidence in them personally; but they mostly came from a well defined social group, the great families, and one has the impression that they were selected more on the basis of their origins than on the position that they held in court or on the administration; a special place was reserved among them for members of the clergy.

Following bubonic plague and agricultural decline in the fourteenth century, state-building in Northern Europe was furthered by a feudalization of agriculture, with smallholders relinquishing control over their land in return for protection from feudal lords. The resulting increased strength of the aristocracy was balanced by a strengthening of the king's chancellery, which now found a territorial basis in Copenhagen and played a role in administering the king's three realms—Denmark, Sweden, and Norway (Gustafsson 2000, Olesen 2000: 30). As seen from the court, there was a distinction between what happened vis-à-vis the three realms and what happened in relation to other courts, since the king was elected as ruler of the three realms (Gustafsson 2000). But the relevant distinction is not between domestic and foreign (territorial and administrative), but between the court of the king and other courts (personal relations between sovereigns). This is clear in the way that the court used envoys as the regular means of communications well into the fifteenth century, with other courts as well as within the domain that the king himself ruled; and in the fact that the establishment of unified control in the chancellery was not followed by any differentiation of work as between domestic and foreign. Relations became distinctly "foreign" only when there emerged a postulated unity among king (sovereign), subjects, and territory. That would not happen until a later period.

From the fifteenth century the chancellery was manned by scribes. These positions did not tempt the nobility and were filled by the king's German-speaking subjects. (Note the difference from diplomacy, where the aristocracy dominated.) The work of the chancellery was organized on a territorial principle, so that different scribes were responsible for different parts of the realms and territories beyond. The scribes made drafts of letters in the chancellery, and the chancellor took these drafts to the king. The nobility and the Council of the Realm resisted the continuous expansion of the chancellery, as it was a powerful tool for the king. After prolonged contest, a compromise in 1536 established that the top personnel in the chancellery would be recruited from the aristocratic Council of the Realm. The net result strengthened the king's court at the expense of the aristocrats, for the king could draw on a steadily increasing administrative capacity. After the Reformation in 1536, the king's position was strong enough to divide the chancellery into two parts, the Danish and the German. It is tempting to read this as an example of administrative differentiation between domestic and foreign. I believe that such a reading, de rigueur among Nordic historians, is mistaken, and that the basic principle is simply which language of correspondence should be used: Danish and Latin vs. German. In the days before nationalism, this was not a question involving patriotism but rather a practical one of communication. Consider the following authoritative statement regarding the differentiation of functions between the Danish and the German chancelleries:

> The Danish chancellery took care of all traditionally domestic issues, and, also by tradition, relations with the eastern neighbors, Sweden, the Order of Teutonic Knights, and Russia. . . . The German chancellery, the ministry of foreign affairs, represents an invention or a modification. Traces of a foreign service can be found in the late Middle Ages, but the real starting point can be found in 1523, when [King] Fredrik I brought the chancellery from his dukedom of Gottorp. . . . This was nonetheless assimilated and divided into two parts, one domestic that took care of the royal lands within the dukedoms and one foreign that took care of the foreign relations of the monarchy. The latter is thus an innovation of some magnitude, necessitated by the rapidly increasing contacts with the outside world, particularly the troubled Protestant Germany, and from ca. 1560 the rapidly expanding trading and maritime states, the Netherlands and England. (Petersen 2000: 60–61; cf. Jespersen 2000: 102)

The term "ministry of foreign affairs" for the German chancellery seems premature. The German chancellery received dispatches from Denmark's diplomats and consuls stationed abroad, but as late as in 1740, 29 out of 51 employees were to be found within the state, but outside the capital.[5] The chancellery also continued to handle what we would categorize as domestic issues.

I suggest two reasons why historians have mistakenly postulated a divide in state administration before the coming of modernity. First, our contemporary world is institutionalized into a domestic and a foreign sphere; historians have not considered that the division of the political world into territorially based sovereign states is a precondition for such a divide to emerge. The second reason concerns how the relevant archives, key for historians' research, have been anachronistically rearranged. Current archives make it appear that the divide between domestic and foreign did exist back then, when in fact it was not a principle of archival organization at the time.

Sovereignty as a Precondition for Bureaucratic Specialization

In the 1990s there emerged a literature showing how the development of the modern state and the European state system reified a division between the inside and the outside of the state (Walker 1993, Bartelson 1995). The importance of this literature for an ethnography of diplomacy is that during modernity, the principal agents of diplomacy were sovereign states, and these states categorized their policy as domestic and foreign. Ever more distinct territorial divisions among states were strengthened by a host of social, political, economic, military, and cultural differences. The result was a categorization of the world into two different spheres that seemed to offer starkly diverging sets of preconditions for social life. Within the state, a juridical apparatus consisting of police, courts, and prisons ostensibly guaranteed a sphere of peace, where one could seek to attain social and political progress or, in the American idiom, life, liberty, and the pursuit of happiness.[6] Outside the state, or more precisely between states, in what came

---

5. In 1740, there were eight diplomats and consuls, to be found in Paris, The Hague, Amsterdam, Warsaw/Dresden, St. Petersburg/Moscow, Madrid, London, and Stockholm, cf. Kjølsen 1991: 157.

6. An example of the all-European character of this process on the level of naming is how "the state" came to become a self-description of more polities. This process, which in Northern Europe meant that "the state" partially replaced "the realm," is imbricated with the power struggle between the king and the aristocracy in ways that would be key to a social analysis of the emergence of foreign policy but are too complex to be analyzed here. See Neumann 2007, Leira 2011.

to be known as international relations, there was nothing but anarchy (in the technical sense of there being no ruler, what anthropologists, following Evans-Pritchard [1940: 181], often refer to as an acephalous or headless state of affairs). The literature in question makes two main points. First, it demonstrates how the thoroughgoing categorization of the world into inside and outside was established in a specific period of time, roughly from the wars of religion to the Enlightenment.[7] Second, the literature on sovereignty demonstrates how all people who presuppose this dichotomy, and make it the basis of their actions in the social world, by that very presupposition are reproducing the division between inside and outside. Actions that assume the primacy of the division between inside and outside confirm the division. Since knowledge production within academic disciplines such as political theory, international relations, history, and the burgeoning anthropology of the state are based on such a division, the ontic division of foreign and domestic policy on which these disciplines are based perpetuates the existence of that distinction. These academic disciplines uphold a discourse in which the world is divided between the inside and outside of a state. Historians who argue in favor of a domestic/foreign divide before the coming of modernity have naturalized this division and projected it back to a time before sovereignty emerged.

Archival Order and Anachronistic Knowledge Production

An additional and more specific reason why historians talk about a divide between the domestic and the foreign before any such divide actually existed is the outcome of the anachronistic practices followed by modernity's archivists, who have reorganized premodern archives according to this divide. Because the way people categorize their world is itself of key interest to anyone trying to understand the past, it is a golden rule of archival science never to change the ordering principles of archives. Trusting this principle, one enters an archive expecting to find it close to the state it was in when it was actually in use. When the contents

---

7. Among the many who have tried to explode the dichotomy, we find Durkheim ([1913] 1992: 74), who advocated imagining "humanity in its entirety organized as a society."

are rearranged, experts in archival science hold that a false impression is made. If such a rearrangement mirrors the doxa of the generation that actually undertakes the rearranging, then the effect is to read historical archives and organizing principles as predecessors of our own (cf. Fabian 1983). A statement in the standard guide to the Danish state archives illustrates the problem:

> With the establishment of absolutism [in 1661] the king's personal control over foreign policy was acknowledged, and with the establishment of the Privy Council [*Gehejmekonseillet*] in 1670 the foreign service was given a solid institutional basis, as the conduct of foreign policy was left to it while the chancelleries became post offices. During the rule of Griffenfeldt (1670–76) most foreign issues were handled in the Danish chancellery, but after his downfall in 1676 the Danish chancellery stopped dealing with foreign affairs. From 1676 to 1770, political issues pertaining to foreign states were exclusively handled by the German chancellery, where one from the 1670s onwards can see a specific office for foreign affairs. This office is nonetheless not explicitly mentioned until 1736. Correspondence with foreign states pertaining to the issues of private citizens were mostly handled through the domestic office of the German chancellery. (Gelting and Korsgaard 1983: 301)

The authors of the archival guide insist that one can find a specialized office for foreign affairs from the 1670s onward. Two pages further on, one nonetheless reads that "The current archival division between the domestic and foreign offices of the German chancellery does not at all times match the actual order of business, since drafts and attachments pertaining to 'foreign private affairs' mostly are archived with the foreign office's archive, although the matters were handled in the domestic office" (Gelting and Korsgaard 1983: 304). This raises the question what kind of bureaucratic office goes unmentioned in any archival source for sixty-six years. Worse is to come. A few paragraphs further on is a brief mention of the "Foreign Office of the Danish Chancellery 1571–1676," which in its entirety reads as follows: "This heading is not representative of any particular office in the Danish chancellery; it is simply an indication that the foreign matters were registered separately" (Gelting and Korsgaard 1983: 304).

What we have here is an anachronistic set-up of the archives. The ordering of the material mimics an institutional order that did not exist at the time. The effect of such an ordering is that the clear division between domestic and foreign politics that grew up only in the late eighteenth century is projected backward onto earlier periods. This knowledge-reconfiguring, nationalist move is not peculiar to Denmark. In the British case, when the State Papers were compiled at the Public Record Office during the nineteenth century, the correspondence of kings with foreign nationals was edited so that things which did not strike *the compilers* as relevant to what *they* held to be foreign policy (such as Henry VIII's correspondence with Martin Luther) were left out (Doran and Richardson 2005: 1–3). Nor is the Danish method of classifying the domestic and foreign as a territorial division rather than a politico-social one peculiar to Denmark. It was the European norm. According to the historian of the Foreign and Commonwealth Office and his co-author,

> The habit of combining both domestic and foreign policy administration in the same departments was common throughout the greater states until the early eighteenth century. It particularly took the form of giving to domestic departments the management of policy of foreign states which lay on the edges of the provinces under their control. In France, for example, in the first half of the sixteenth century, the provinces and their neighbours were divided in this fashion among the four financial secretaries. (Hamilton and Langhorne 1995: 73)[8]

The Institutionalization of the Foreign

As a principle for how to categorize the world, sovereignty is a precondition and a recipe for bureaucratic specialization. It tells a story about

---

8. Writers on the history of diplomacy often do not take this vital point into account, with quaint results. For example, Hamilton & Langhorne (1995: 60) on the emergence of foreign ministry: "The Italian city-states in their record keeping and more or less continuous control of their foreign relations, had evolved embryo foreign ministries in their chancelleries; across the rest of Europe, this evolution was much slower. The principal problem arose out of the uncertainties surrounding the position of royal secretaries. Sometimes they were really foreign secretaries—and many other things besides—sometimes they were merely clerks and cipher writers. Their responsibilities were often bizarrely [i.e., differently] arranged, particularly, as in France for much of the sixteenth century, if there were several of them. Philip II of Spain sought to control his secretaries by duplicating them and often operated independently, as he also, though decreasingly, spied on his ambassadors while they were abroad. . . . Secretaries, ambassadors and ministers did not

how the domestic and the foreign add up to two different worlds. The story calls for two different kinds of administration, one appropriate to the domestic, and one to the foreign. In terms of concrete institutionalization, it took states a long time to answer this call. Whereas sovereignty as a legal and political principle was firmly in evidence in the seventeenth century, the institutionalization of the foreign as a separate sphere of administration may be dated to the end of the eighteenth century.[9]

In the first half of the seventeenth century, the administration was still small enough that the king was supposed personally to oversee all business at hand. "A note from Jørgen Seefeldt illustrates how the chancellery could work. He wrote that on 6 August 1627, he had read a number of extracts aloud to the king, and that his comments in the margin were dictated and commanded by the king" (Jespersen 2000: 104). A variant of this practice lives on. A document written in the lower echelons of the bureaucracy may still be passed up the chain of command to higher-ranking officials and, if the case so requires, also politicians for comment, until it finally reaches the level where a decision may be taken. In 1623, however, there was no administrative chain. All documents were supposed to reach the king. The degree of differentiation remained very low.

This was about to change. Short stints at the chancellery had now become a springboard for future administrative posts, so these positions were predominantly held by young sons of the nobility (previously the incumbents were predominantly Germans). In the years around 1600, young nobles qualified for their posts by traveling on the continent on so-called *peregrinationes*. With the establishment of an academy at Sorø in 1623, the recruits received a more standardized training, on Danish soil. The king's

---

generally have a reliable sense of the distinction between state and private papers [i.e., their categories were different], and might simply remove them on leaving office or changing post." The critique of diplomatic history given in chapter one applies here as well.

9. The separation was never complete, and with the coming of internationalization in the late nineteenth century and particularly globalization in the late twentieth, it has been diminishing. For example, at the time of writing, every single Norwegian ministry, including the prime minister's office, has its own representative or representatives to the Norwegian delegation to the EU in Brussels. For a discussion of how and why states disaggregate their administrations, see Neumann and Sending 2010.

advisers were thus trained for a purpose rather than being haphazardly re-cruited.[10] In 1660, the king established an absolutist system, abolishing the aristocracy's Council of the Realm and replacing it with a Privy Council. A supreme administrative body was set up in charge of a central admin-istration divided into separate branches. With institutionalized opposition to his rule gone, the king was firmly in control of the administration. He maintained his court, but important business was increasingly conducted in the chancelleries. The new administration increasingly became the curse of the nobility and the domain of the bourgeoisie. Throughout the seventeenth century and into the eighteenth, an ever more detailed and anonymous hierarchy was established, where royal officials by the thou-sands were promoted ahead of the old nobility and placed just below the king, the counts, and the barons. Day-to-day work was carried out by a growing number of clerks, all of them bourgeois and typically hired by the heads of each office. The clerks were the ones carrying out the "mind-numbing proofing and copying, the never-ending writing of protocols, and the tedious copying of the books and accounting records. Anyone who has spent any time over eighteenth-century archival records will have felt how the clerk must have been snoring with his eyes wide open while copy-ing the piles of documents" (Feldbæk 2000: 318). The clerks had twelve-hour days and could also be put to work on religious holidays, whereas the head of office who appeared around 10:30 a.m. and left four hours later was considered the epitome of diligence (Feldbæk 2000: 330).

Left to themselves, administrations are wont to continue doing what they have always done, in the way they have always done it (more on this below). The coming of absolutism did not in and of itself change everyday

---

10. One of the key reasons for this professionalization was the threat of Catholic or other for-eign influence during the *peregrinationes*. Much could be said about the imbrication of religion with sovereignty and its importance for the institutionalization of foreign policy here, and also about the relevance of the power struggle between the king and the Danish-speaking nobility who manned the Danish chancellery and also knew of its doings through their Council of the Realm (for an overview, see Neumann 2007). The nobility's grip on the German chancellery was much looser, making it suspicious of the uses to which the king put it. When the Holy Roman Empire was dissolved by Napoleon in 1806 and the Duchy of Holstein became part of the conglomerate state, the local nobility won acceptance for the so-called *biennium*—that a precondition for a posi-tion in the duchies of Schleswig and Holstein was a two-year stay at Christian Albrecht Univer-sity in Kiel, the realm's oldest university outside the capital. Thus was a systematic difference in professional training reintroduced in the state (Feldbæk 2000: 237).

practices. "The two chancelleries wrote the same kind of letters, with standard formulations that were only changed as much as constitutionally necessary, and they continued to archive their work in the same way as before" (Lind 2000: 167). It was Peder Griffenfeld, a key adviser to the king and the chief ideologue of absolutism, who first attempted to group business with all foreign courts together and thus set in motion what would prove to become the Danish variant of a European change:

> Foreign relations had pride of place in the chancelleries. In the beginning of the period they were still divided according to linguistic criteria, so that the Danish chancellery took care of relations with Sweden and Russia, and the German chancellery the rest. At the peak of his power, Griffenfeld was able to gather all foreign correspondence in "his" Danish chancellery, but when he fell from power in 1676, all matters, including Swedish and Russian, were moved to the German chancellery. The foundation was laid for the gradual foundation of a ministry of foreign affairs within the German chancellery. Nevertheless, nothing happened. We are not able to find a division between domestic and foreign fields of work among the secretaries of the German chancellery until the 1720s, and even then only a hint of it. (Lind 2000: 170)

Although Lind uses the term "ministry of foreign affairs," he is himself the first to point out that deep into the eighteenth century, there existed no such thing. Even by 1750 it makes little sense to describe the German chancellery as a distinct ministry of foreign affairs. However, when in 1766 absolute power fell into the hands of the raving mad Christian VII, the political situation became destabilized and made room for a de facto coup d'état by the king's personal surgeon, Johann Struensee. Even though the good doctor was removed in another coup within two years, the episode led to permanent changes in the administration, largely inspired by Enlightenment thinking. In 1773 candidates with law degrees were given precedence for positions in the chancelleries, and in 1776 the precedence of national citizens was established. At this point the division between domestic and foreign became more solidly institutionalized. On Christmas Eve 1770, Struensee removed the administration of foreign affairs from the chancelleries and created a separate Ministry of Foreign Affairs. While Struensee's coup was a failure, his institutional innovation survived, and the Danish Foreign Ministry celebrates 1772 as its year of origin. The all-European character of this administrative move is clear from the dates of the institutionalization of the divide: Britain, 1782; France, 1789; Sweden, 1791; Russia, 1802; Spain, 1814.[11] The United States also fits the pattern, with the State Department hailing from 1789. Other sovereign states followed: Siam 1840, Japan 1885, Turkey 1920, until by the mid-twentieth century MFAs had become a generally acknowledged accoutrement of statehood. Note, however, that the emergence of foreign ministries did not put an end to the separation of diplomatic and consular services.

To sum up: the principle of sovereignty divided up the world into discrete territorial states and suggested an ontic difference between domestic and foreign. There was a steady increase in the size of administration, helped along in the Danish case by absolutism. Around 1800, knowledge production reflected this domestic/foreign divide. Toward the end of the eighteenth century, we also find apparently the first manual on government in the conglomerate state organized along such lines. In the years 1773–76, Andreas Schytte, a central ideologue of the state, wrote seven volumes on its government, and organized them as five volumes on internal government and two on external government. In both practice and theory, the divide between domestic and foreign policies was firmly in place toward the end of the eighteenth century.

The Emergence of a Unified Foreign Service

The Congress of Vienna streamlined diplomatic practice. Since 1815, international law has recognized only sovereign polities (states, the Holy See, and the Sovereign Military Order of Malta) as diplomatic subjects. Another innovation held that only great powers—defined as those who took part in the work of all the congress committees—could exchange ambassadors. These were Prussia, Great Britain, France, Austria, and Russia. Middle powers—those who took part in the work of some but not all committees—as well as small powers, who took part in none,

---

11. Hamilton and Langhorne (1995: 73) are thus mistaken when they argue that the Foreign Office was founded "very late by the standards of the rest of Europe."

were allowed only to send and receive ministers. The number of great and middle powers was fairly stable throughout the nineteenth century, with German and Italian unification accounting for most of the changes. Toward the end of the century, Denmark, the Netherlands, Spain, Sweden, and Turkey were generally seen to be the middle powers (cf. Hinsley 1963: 250n). Those middle powers where the bourgeoisie had come to dominate politically—the Netherlands, Sweden, Denmark—as well as small powers such as the Swiss Confederation and Belgium, needed fewer diplomatic legations and more consulates, and they allocated their own resources according to this principle. For example, Denmark had 44 diplomats in 1797 but was down to 28 by midcentury and only 20 by 1914. Foreign ministries, on the other hand, were expanding: the Swedish MFA had 19 employees in 1905 but by 1918 it had 88 (Anderson 1993: 110). This reduction of the diplomatic service may have resulted from an onslaught on the one part of the state apparatus that was still dominated by the aristocracy.[12] The aristocratic diplomat spent his time being received in foreign salons; the bourgeois scribe at home beavered away in obscurity. An investigation of Norwegian working practices carried out in 1854 found that many of the tasks facing the scribes were "so tiresome and mind-numbingly dull that one simply cannot demand that the personnel should carry them out without pause throughout the working day . . . without it being a danger to his [the scribe's] mental state of mind" (Omang 1955: 113). This may sound grave. But as the office day a hundred years earlier had been twelve hours and was now four hours, the main point of interest is that bourgeois hegemony allowed the issue to surface at all. Bureaucratic work was carried out by bourgeois, which meant that scribes—soon to be called bureaucrats—were now considered people of high social standing, with a right to fairly tolerable working conditions. In a parallel development throughout liberal Europe, diplomatic posts became more open to the bourgeoisie. Here is a key social

---

12. This has been a topic of much debate in Great Britain, where the position of the aristocracy was stronger. For a summing up, see Jones (1983), whose main focus is the relationship between the diplomatic service ("In 1815, there was only a rudimentary hierarchical organization, hardly any specialization of function . . . an undeveloped bureaucracy" [Jones 1983: 215–16)] and the Foreign Office. For an excellent overview, see Otte 2008.

factor that paved the way for the amalgamation of foreign ministries, diplomatic services, and consular services which began in Sweden in 1906 and spread to the rest of the world.[13]

Sweden is of key interest here not only because it initiated the unified foreign service, but also because the Norwegian diplomatic service and the Norwegian MFA are the direct descendants of their Swedish counterparts. Between 1891 and 1905, the year when the Norwegian Parliament declared Norway a sovereign state, the key issue in the tug-of-war between Norway and Sweden was how to organize consular business. This had been a point of contention since midcentury. Norway wanted consulates worldwide to serve the needs of its merchant navy. Sweden's interest in consulates, while positive, was more restrained, as was the Swedish attitude to the idea that Norway should evolve something which looked more like a separate foreign policy with a separate policy apparatus to match. The Norwegian Parliament was directly engaged in a further practice that pointed in the same direction. From 1874 to 1905, it awarded twenty-four stipends to young Norwegian men who were to be attached to the diplomatic service. The explicit aim was to place Norwegians in the diplomatic service.

The political campaign that resulted in Norwegian sovereignty fastened on the shape of foreign policy decision making. In 1890, the campaign's key ideologue, Sigurd Ibsen, previously employed by the foreign ministry in Stockholm and the son of the playwright Henrik Ibsen, tried to broaden the debate about the ordering of the consular institution to a debate about the ordering of foreign policy, by introducing the idea that Norway should have its own foreign ministry. He met with resistance, and reacted by more or less single-handedly building the ministry inside the existing Norwegian state administration (Neumann and Leira 2005: 31–37). Ibsen planned his foreign ministry by collecting and drawing on institutional models employed by other states, particularly Belgium, Germany, Great Britain, and the United States. Here we have an example of

---

13. Another institutional change constitutive of bourgeois hegemony was the rise of the parliamentary committee for foreign affairs. It first cropped up in revolutionary France. In 1816, the U.S. Senate formed such a committee. In 1860, Liberal MPs in the lower house of the UK Parliament initiated an informal campaign aiming for the same thing. A formal committee emerged in Britain in 1911, whence the phenomenon spread to the rest of Europe. The relevant year for Norway was 1923.

a key practice of diplomatic services since at least the eighteenth century, namely that different states exchange information relatively freely about how they order their offices. All parties concerned know that a key task is to speak to opposite numbers, and that the more compatible the institutional structures, the smoother will be the communication. This practice ensures a high degree of formal homogeneity between states. As dominant states tend to have their innovations copied, it also has a hegemonic aspect. The practice explains not only why MFAs around the world are relatively similar, but also why they are frequently somewhat out of sync with bureaucratic developments within their own states' central administrations.

When the Norwegian Ministry of Foreign Affairs was established in the summer of 1905, this happened as an upgrading of Ibsen's already existing mini-ministry. At the time of the break with Sweden, four of the sixteen ministers who headed missions to other states were Norwegians. One stayed on in the Swedish diplomatic service and became a naturalized Swede, whereas the other three came to play pivotal roles in building the Norwegian MFA and the Norwegian diplomatic service. This work included laying down practices by writing handbooks. The key person was the former Stockholm MFA official Thor von Ditten, who copied some practices directly from his former place of work, from rules for correspondence to set phrases for reporting (such as "the legation will not omit to point out," a formulation still used when embassies report back to Oslo).

The Norwegian MFA became properly institutionalized in the spring of 1906, at which time it employed sixteen civil servants and seven typists. Following some hefty domestic opposition, the social hegemony of the leading states asserted itself and the Norwegian MFA was fashioned after the Swedish and European standard of the day, with two directors general each heading a department (*avdeling*), both of which consisted of two divisions (*kontor*) under their respective heads (*byråsjef*).[14] There was also an archival detachment. The diplomatic service, which was kept separate from the MFA, consisted of six missions in Europe, one in Washington,

---

14. At present, the following titles are used for senior officials or *embedsmenn: departementsråd* (secretary general), *politisk director* (political director), *ekspedisjonssjef* (director general), *avdelings-direktør* (deputy director general), *underdirektør* (assistant director general, but deputy director general if the person ranks as number two in the department), *seksjonsleder* (head of section, previously *byråsjef,* head of office). There also exist senior *spesialrådgiver* (special advisers with ambassadorial rank).

and one in Argentina. In the early years, the minister to London was informally considered to be the service's *primus inter pares*.

In 1922, Norway followed Sweden's lead and amalgamated the Foreign Ministry with the diplomatic and consular services. The new, unified foreign service streamlined its professional personnel by insisting that each and every member accept a legal obligation to fill posts anywhere in the world on a similar level to the one that the person already held (that is, subject to *flytteplikt,* literally a duty to move). It established the position of secretary general (*utenriksråd*) as well as a specific body of civil servants and business people whose job was to interview, assess, and accept applicants to the MFA. For those accepted (*aspiranter*), an in-house training program was established. The reform brought the number of employees to around sixty, with another twenty working on short-term contracts (Fure 1996: 53–71). The pace of work in the interwar period was somewhat meandering:

> Life at the office was pretty unfettered. We could always take a stroll about town if we so pleased. Still, working hours were long. We were rarely home for supper before 4.30 p.m., and then we had to return and work into the evening. The thing was that foreign mail arrived late, and when it had been registered and handed out to the heads of office, it was already 3 p.m. and after hours. Telegrams came at about the same time, which meant that we were often called in by the office heads to take care of urgent business. (Fay 1959: 44)

Following German occupation in April 1940, the king and the government went into exile in Britain, where a shoestring MFA of seven persons was established. Most of the archives sat out the war in neutral Sweden. When the MFA was reorganized in Oslo in 1945, it had 156 employees, and it had a general, a political, and an economic department as well as a temporary department to handle questions regarding expense claims in the wake of the war. Like other MFAs of industrialized countries, the Norwegian MFA added some delegations for multilateral work to its foreign service during the first half of the Cold War. In 1942, in the spirit of a reward for acting honorably, the allied great powers discussed bestowing on Belgium the right to send ambassadors, only to decide that the privilege had to be extended to all powers. As a result, Norway sent its first ambassador (to

Washington) in 1943. Increases in the number of embassies and legations abroad came in spurts. In 1973, the number stood at 69. By 2002, it had reached three figures. Many of these stations are manned by only two diplomats, typically an ambassador and a first secretary, as well as an administrative officer (*kansellist*).[15] When I started my first period as a diplomat in 1997, the MFA's budget was NOK 12.4 billion (more than $1.5 billion) and it fielded around 500 people abroad. When I finished my second period in 2003, the budget had shot up by more than a third, to NOK 17.3 billion, whereas the number of people sent abroad was pretty stable (Neumann and Leira 2005: 380, 435). The total number of employed professional diplomats, at home and abroad, increased to around 650. Regarding the nature of their tasks, a major change concerned aid and development to developing countries. Together with other like-minded countries such as Sweden, Denmark, and the Netherlands, in 1978 Norway decided to heed the UN's call to allocate 1 percent of gross national income to such projects, and the work was organized under the MFA's umbrella (Stokke 1979: 50–53). During my years of service, development aid made up almost 90 percent of the ministry's total budget.

Summing Up

States evolved corps of advisers during the thirteenth century. Before the sixteenth and seventeenth centuries, the period when sovereignty and permanent diplomacy emerged, diplomats were simply advisers who were sent on missions abroad. The seventeenth and eighteenth centuries saw a gradual differentiation of domestic and foreign work within steadily growing state administrations, and distinct foreign ministries emerged at the end of the eighteenth century. Thereafter, advisers and scribes working at home were overwhelmingly bourgeois, whereas permanent diplomats tended to be aristocrats. Even in Norway after the gaining of sovereignty, whose aristocracy consisted of only a handful of families whose privileges were legally revoked in 1821, the leading diplomat was a count. From the beginning of the twentieth century onward, states began to amalgamate

---

15. Parliamentary report no. 11, 1989–90, *Om utviklingstrekk i det internasjonale samfunn og virkninger for norsk utenrikspolitikk*, p. 74.

their MFAs with diplomatic and consular services. By midcentury, permanent expatriate diplomats were all but gone.[16] In one sense, we are now back to the days before permanent diplomacy, when envoys were simply advisers to the king sent on specific missions abroad. Today's diplomats are paid nomads, shuttling between postings abroad and at home. They are the immediate successors both of the diplomat permanently stationed abroad and of the adviser working at home. While abroad, their mode of knowledge production depends on information gathering. Their mode of knowledge production at home is the topic of the next chapter, which is ethnography based. The transition from history to ethnography is a vexed one, however, which requires some elaboration.

Connecting History and Ethnography

The problem is a fairly new one. It did not arise in nineteenth-century debates, which focused on something other than lived history, namely historiosophy, understood as the temporal fate of humanity at large. The conservative answer was to celebrate the here and now as if it equaled the human condition as such. Diplomacy, in that case, was simply a question of maintaining the status quo. Herbert Butterfield's understanding of diplomacy, discussed in the previous chapter, is a recent example of such an attitude. Liberals and Marxists had a different answer: history was moving in stages, and whatever forces moved it, diplomacy was not among them. Nineteenth-century liberal and Marxist thinkers both write off diplomacy as a bit of a nuisance in the present and an epiphenomenon in the long run. When Marx and Engels argued in the *Communist Manifesto* that man makes his own history, but not under conditions that he himself has chosen, they were definitely not thinking about diplomats. They did, however, open a vista that they themselves did not explore, namely the relationship between how we got here and how we go further.

In one sense the birth of the social sciences happened in opposition to history and historiosophy. Instead of speculating about the fate of humanity at large, the project was to understand and explain the integration of

---

16. A partial exception to this rule is the papal nuncio, who may stay in his post for prolonged periods of time.

humanity's groups in the here and now. Consequently, some social scientists have written off history as irrelevant and concentrated on structures, as when A. R. Radcliffe-Brown (1958: 168–69) wrote that "The inhabitants of Europe are arranged into nations, and this is therefore a structural feature of the social life of Europe. . . . Ultimately, a social structure is exhibited either in interactions between groups, as when one nation goes to war with another, or in interactions between persons." For Radcliffe-Brown, war, or diplomacy for that matter, was to be treated as an unobservable structure, that performed certain observable tasks or functions which upheld that structure. The consequence of such an approach for history was the same as for nineteenth-century conservatives: diplomacy is system maintenance.

So far, we have two approaches to social life that have no place for history understood as lived life. The liberal-Marxist approach tends to treat history as determined outside of lived life. The structuralist-functionalist approach simply brackets history altogether. The early Marx and Engels open the door to studies of how human agency changes history, however, when they postulate that present conditions are both the effect of past actions and the precondition for future ones. The emergence of diplomacy discussed so far is the precondition of present actions as they are to be analyzed in the rest of this book.

Some social scientists have tried to specify Marx and Engels's postulate. The anthropology of elites is dominated by people who study history as the outcome of attempted elite manipulation and resistance thereto. Let a complaint by two avowed post-Marxists serve as examples of this approach[17]: "How is it that—if *all* meaning were potentially open to contest, *all* power potentially unfixed—history keeps generating hegemonies that, for long periods, seem also to impose a degree of order and stability on the world? How come relatively small groups of people—class fractions, ethnic minorities, or whatever—often succeed in gaining and sustaining control over large populations and in drawing them into a consensus with dominant values?" (Comaroff and Comaroff 1991: 17). The main point here is the old Marxist one, that the dominant thoughts in a society are the thoughts of the dominant.

---

17. Cf. other key works such as Cohen 1981, Coronil 1997, and Shore 2000. For an overview, see Shore and Wright (1997).

The problem with this mode of analysis is that it anchors the analysis either in a historical necessity—dominant thoughts are a function of materiality—or in intention—it is the willed domination by elites that explains human action. Either way, these are presuppositions that reduce ethnographic work to demonstrating an already postulated axiom about the human condition. History is reified, and human agency read out. But that will not do: there are specific historical reasons why present-day diplomacy has states as agents and negotiation as its basic modus operandi. These things are "potentially open to contest"—look no further than this book—but they are also not easily changed. This is not (only) due to unconscious influences, but because in order to say something about diplomacy that makes sense in an everyday setting, one has to start from the present social fact that diplomacy is tactful communication between states. The entire point of including a historical discussion in this book is to demonstrate that diplomacy has had various agents, who have interacted in various ways, tactful and otherwise. We cannot account for such a phenomenon by drawing on a post-Marxist approach.

One alternative is to investigate action where the meaning (including the Marxian "dominant values") that actors ascribe to it is in evidence, i.e. in language. What we need in order to do so is a concept of diplomacy as a bundle of utterances linked together in narrative and repeated over and over, so that new instantiations of the narrative confirm the previous ones and, at the same time, keep alternative narratives at bay. Discourse is such a concept (cf. Clifford and Marcus 1986: 299; Marcus 1998: 119, 125; Holmes and Marcus 2004).

Discourse

Foucault presented the concept of discourse as a concept for the social sciences in *The Archaeology of Knowledge* ([1970] 1972). A discourse is a system for the formation of statements (Bartelson 1995: 5).[18] Discourse analysis studies meaning where it arises, namely in the language itself. As the founder of modern linguistics, Ferdinand de Saussure ([1916] 1986:

---

18. For a definitional and conceptual clarification, see Neumann 2008a.

114), wrote: "The content of a word is determined in the final analysis not by what it contains but by what exists outside of it." Saussure's way of seeing language as a system of relations, is a central prerequisite for discourse analysis. The so-called linguistic trend in social science follows Saussure's thought that relations form or constitute a language, by seeing relations as constitutive of *everything* social. Discourse analysis has a history that emanates from about the same time and place as Saussure's theory of language. The leading French philosopher of the Third Republic, Charles Renouvier, held that things had a material inside and a social outside. If we pay too much attention to the inside, we end up with materialism; if too much to the outside, we end up with idealism. Durkheim sociologized Renouvier's program by marking out the social fact, which I take to be Renouvier's outside of the thing, as the object of social study, and to insist that social facts should be explained in terms of the social. Mutatis mutandis, there is a clear line to be drawn from Renouvier and Durkheim through Mauss and Lévi-Strauss to Foucault and discourse analysis (Jones [1996] 2001; Allen 2000: 95–103; Lukes 1975: 56–57; Fournier 1994: 55–57). What I have done so far in this book is try to map diplomacy as emergent discourse. At any one time, discourse is the precondition for action. Discourses offer a distinct set of socially recognized actions, as well as means of recognizing when they are appropriate and how they should be performed. The concept that captures actions so patterned by discourse is practice.[19]

Practices

The two key thinkers for discourse analysis, Wittgenstein and Foucault, both analyzed how humans make their own history, but not under conditions they themselves have chosen, by focusing on language in use—on discursive practices.[20] The analysis of diplomatic discourse understood as the

---

19. An alternative to discourse analysis is offered by Sahlins (1987: 152), who suggests that "Symbolic action is a duplex compound made up of an inescapable past and an irreducible present. An inescapable past because the concepts by which experience is organized and communicated proceed from the received cultural scheme. An irreducible present because of the world-uniqueness of any action." For an application of such an approach to the study of diplomacy, see Neumann 2012.

20. For a fuller discussion, see Neumann 2002b.

study of the preconditions for action has to be complemented by the analysis of diplomatic practice, understood as the study of action itself.[21] Practices are discursive, both in the sense that some practices involve speech acts and in the sense that practice cannot be thought "outside of" discourse. Barnes (2001: 22) stresses that, just as rules do not contain rules for their own application, so practices do not contain rules for their use: "it is always necessary to ask what disposes people to enact the practices they do, how and when they do; and their aims, their lived experience and their inherited knowledge will surely figure amongst the factors of interest here." A central challenge for social analysis must be how to preserve the insights produced by the linguistic turn while adding the insights promised by practice theory, to combine the study of meaning and the study of the material (cf. Boyer 2005: 24–43). Ann Swidler's suggestion for doing so bears quoting at length:

> Practice theory moves the level of sociological attention "down" from conscious ideas and values to the physical and the habitual. But this move is complemented by a move "up," from ideas located in individual consciousness to the impersonal arena of "discourse." A focus on discourses, or on "semiotic codes" permits attention to meaning without having to focus on whether particular actors believe, think, or act on any specific ideas. Like language, discourse is conceived to be the impersonal medium through which (with which) thought occurs (Lévi-Strauss's notion that animals are "good to think with"). A focus on discourse then reintroduces the world of language, symbols, and meanings without making them anyone-in-particular's meanings. . . . The old terrain of ideas and actors thus split into two domains, that of practices and that of discourses. (Swidler 2001: 75)

Discourse may then be understood as a system for the formation of statements. Practices are "socially recognized forms of activity, done on the basis of what members learn from others, and capable of being done well

---

21. The linguistic turn has often been characterized as a turn back to the Sophists. If one wants to dabble in such parallels, it is indeed noteworthy that Sophists such as Isocrates (2000) consistently stressed the importance of language *as well as* practice—as did the early pragmatists some twenty-three hundred years later.

or badly, correctly or incorrectly" (Barnes 2001: 19).[22] The latter aspect is important because it pinpoints that practice is something more than habit.

Bringing de Certeau Back In

When a new turn in knowledge production is heralded, it is always possible to find precursors. Already in his *Arts de faire,* published in 1974 (*The Practice of Everyday Life,* 1984: 67), Michel de Certeau staked the claim for reversing the hierarchy between discourse and practice. Like Foucault, de Certeau moved away from structuralism, in the sense that he was not interested in analyzing "manifest" structures in order to establish a set of "latent" structures that undergirds the manifest ones. To understand everyday actions, de Certeau focused on the tacit knowledge that goes into performing them and perhaps altering them, all the tricks and improvisations which come into play and which are traditionally read out of social analyses (de Certeau 1984: 20).

Such a program immediately runs up against the problem of how to establish the area of validity of the findings—of how to generalize. The social analyst is, after all, not interested in one particular action as such, but in what that action can tell us about something wide-reaching. De Certeau's answer is that

> one must suppose that to these ways of operating correspond a finite number of procedures (invention is not unlimited and, like improvisations on the piano or on the guitar, it presupposes the knowledge and application

---

22. Other notable definitions are Anthony Giddens's conceptualization of practice as "rules and resources" which play a key role in what he calls structuration, whereby "the structural properties of social systems are both medium and outcome of the practices they discursively organize" (Giddens 1984: 25) Bourdieu, for example, also stresses that practice is different from theory inasmuch as the embodiers of practice cannot necessarily describe what they are doing in language, which is to say that practices typically appear separate from language (Bourdieu 1977: 106). Bourdieu's view that practices are unconscious has been criticized by Brenda Farnell (Farnell 2000: 408). To her, Bourdieu's distinction between conscious and unconscious rests on an unwarranted if classic Christian dichotomy between body and soul. Farnell argues that even if actions are not self-conscious, that does not necessarily make them un-conscious. Note also that Swidler's bifurcation lies itself open to the same kind of critique that Margaret Archer (1995) has directed against Giddensian structuration theory.

of codes), and that they imply a logic of the operation of actions relative to
types of situations. This logic, which turns on circumstances, has as its precondition, contrary to the procedures of Western science, the non-autonomy
of its field of action. (de Certeau 1984: 21; cf. Tully [1983] 1988; Scott 1998)

This analysis allows De Certeau to make a suggestion about how history and ethnography are tied together (1984: 125). I have put that suggestion to work in this book by focusing on narrative, or what he calls
"stories": "stories 'go in a procession' ahead of social practices in order to
open a field for them." His key example comes from the realm of diplomacy and concerns the stories told by Roman ritual specialists known as
fetiales. The *fetiales* came into play as storytellers when the early Roman
city-state was about to take action involving another political unit, be
it by war or by diplomacy. By physically moving from the inside of
Rome's territory, then to its frontier, and then inside the other political unit, and by telling stories in each succeeding locus, they narrated
a social field inside which acts of war, alliance, and the like could take
place:

> The ritual was a procession with three centrifugal stages, the first within
> Roman territory but near the frontier, the second on the frontier, the third in
> foreign territory. The ritual action was carried out before every civil or mil-
> itary action because it is designed to create the field necessary for political or
> military activities. . . . As a general repetition before the actual representa-
> tion, the rite, a narration in acts, precedes the historical realization. The tour
> or procession of the *fetiales* opens a space and provides a foundation for the
> operations of the military men, diplomats, or merchants who dare to cross
> the frontier. (de Certeau 1984: 124)

One may rephrase this example by saying that the storytelling and physical movement of the *fetiales* make possible a practice. Things are ordered,
subject positions are created, and these and other phenomena are named
so that a practice that is new in the context of the rival polity with which
Rome has to deal may take shape. This practice is nested in other practices,
both in the sense that it emanates from a set of similar practices existing
elsewhere (in this case, in Rome) and in the sense that it has to fit in with
other practices that already play themselves out in the new field into which

they are being inserted (in this case, for example, the other's way of thinking about treaties). The new practice widens the field where Roman discourse, from which that practice emanates in the first place, is relevant, so that it alters the relationship between the Romans and the other. When the relationship between two agencies is being changed, power is at work. Let us call the kind of power that goes with extending the discourse of which you are a part by establishing new practices or maintaining already established ones conceptual power.[23]

As the new practice is being adopted, two things happen. First, since this new practice has to fit in with other already established practices, they are altered: there are omissions, additions, creations. These alterations are large enough for the practice to fit into the new domain, but not so large that it may no longer serve as a conduit between that domain and the domain from which it was extended in the first place (if that happens, then the practice is no longer socially tied to the discourse from which it emanated). Second, as the new practice is institutionalized in the sense of becoming regular and a more and more seamless part of the social, it is also naturalized. As a naturalized social force, it produces stories of what things should be like. The practice speaks: "This is how we have always done things around here." The social fact that things are ordered in a particular way and not another may be conceptualized as a story that tells specific people what to do in specific contexts. To foreshadow the discussion in the next chapter, the production of knowledge within MFAs happens according to practices that make the resulting texts look very similar.

A phenomenon that makes people do what they would not otherwise have done is a phenomenon of power. In this case, it is a power that makes it possible to govern people indirectly and from afar, by impinging on their schemes of action by instituting a new practice. Let us follow Foucault (2000) and call this form of power governmentality. As long as people act in accordance with established practices, they confirm a given discourse; seen from the governor's point of view, they are well governed. The possibility also exists, however, that people will not act in accordance with a given

---

23. I choose the term as a homage to the German conceptual historians; for an introduction, see Koselleck (1979) 1985. Koselleck was a student of Gadamer's, so one alternative would have been "hermeneutical power" (cf. Boyer 2003).

Figure 1. Social life understood as a circuit of practice, discourse, and stories, charged with specific types of power.

practice, in which case discourse will come under strain. The discussion so far may be modeled as shown in figure 1.

* * *

Diplomatic practices are integrative, inasmuch as they nudge human beings into relationships of amity and enmity. To quote Swidler once more, they "remain stable not only because habit engrains standard ways of doing things, but the need to engage one another forces people to return to common structures. Indeed, antagonistic interchanges may reproduce common structures more precisely than friendly alliances do" (Swidler 2001: 85). Diplomatic practices are improvisatory, inasmuch as they play themselves out in concrete situations for which people may be only partially prepared. They are reflective, inasmuch as they have to relate to the actions of other actors (to what extent they are conscious is, however, contested). They are quotidian, in the sense that they play themselves out every day, often in seemingly trivial ways, and are part of everybody's lives. Finally, diplomatic practices are performative—they *are* their use—and they are stylized (de Certeau's choice of a ritual example is apt in more senses than one). The challenge is to study these practices as they emerge out of historically given preconditions. The rest of this book attempts to study diplomacy by treating preconditions for action as discourse, and practices as socially recognized ways of acting that may be done well or badly.

3

THE BUREAUCRATIC MODE OF
KNOWLEDGE PRODUCTION

Power is everywhere: not that it engulfs everything, but that it comes from
everywhere.

MICHEL FOUCAULT, 1984

We know about the production of diplomatic knowledge at home;
it involves notes, memos, reports, white papers, op-eds and, not least,
speeches. When I arrived at the Norwegian MFA to work as a planner,
I was expected to pick up the skill of writing in the bureaucratic mode
with no delay. Since the ministry produces a large number of speeches for
its ministers, its state secretaries, and also its senior civil servants, it was
no coincidence that my first assignment was as a speechwriter. In terms
of learning the ropes, however, it would not have mattered much what
specific genre of text I had been given, for almost all texts are produced in
the same manner.

Textual production largely determines textual output, making each text
very similar to its predecessors, so that understanding ministerial textual
production is key to understanding the bureaucratic mode of knowledge
production at large. In this chapter, I invite the reader to follow my travails as an MFA rookie. Much like a twig thrown into a river and getting
stuck, I found myself first disturbing the steady flow of things, and then

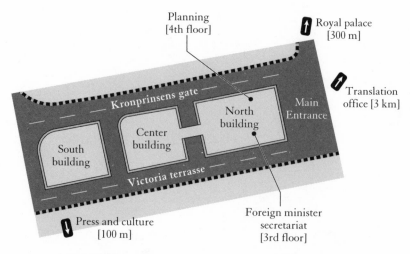

The Royal Norwegian Ministry of Foreign Affairs, Oslo, 1998. Scale: 1-1875.

experiencing how that flow simply swept me away, so that it could resume its accustomed course. I use my experience to detail how, through no fault of any one individual, a bureaucracy left to its own devices will produce texts that resemble their predecessors and one another. The main reasons are that texts are the result of teamwork; that the model for teamwork is previous texts; and that the (incidentally identity-producing) process of producing the text is inner-driven, so that little or no heed is paid to audience, circumstances of delivery, political effects, and other matters external to the ministry itself.

Scene-Setting: Generalists at Work

"The Asia adviser has ordered a speech in connection with the royal couple's visit to China. I thought this might be a good opportunity for you, Iver, to try your hand at speechwriting." We are at a morning meeting in the Planning and Evaluation Unit, an organ of the Norwegian Ministry of Foreign Affairs subordinated directly to the secretary general, on a par with the ministry's ten departments. The secretary general is the senior civil servant in the ministry, and outranked only by its politicians.

Like the ten departments, the Planning and Evaluation Unit is headed by a director general, and it is he who gives me a two-page order slip from the ministry's Asia adviser. He and the other regional advisers are all former ambassadors; with only eleven director general positions and around a hundred foreign postings headed by people with the status of ambassador, the ranks hold more ambassadors than there are regular jobs at the ambassadorial level, so positions like those of regional advisers are filled by ambassador-grade personnel. I am also an adviser, employed for a year and a half, brought in, or so I was told, to "furnish a different perspective" and be an intellectual jack of all trades. Speechwriting is an obvious task for the new adviser.

The speech turns out to be the king's, to be delivered in twenty minutes to a party of businessmen from Hong Kong gathered around a luncheon table by the Norwegian consulate general. Along with the order slip there is a half-page note from the consulate. It states that the consulate was established in 1907, as one of the first after Norway left the personal union with Sweden in 1905; that Norway and Hong Kong have always had good business relations; that Hong Kong is mentioned in particular in the Foreign Ministry's two-year-old Asia plan. There is also some advice on what the focus of the speech should be.[1]

The Planning Unit's number two is Assistant Director General Ranveig, a fellow Russianist whom I already know from working with her in Norway's Moscow embassy seventeen years previously. She has become my mentor. It so happened that she returned from a foreign posting to the second-highest position in the unit just as I joined it, and we have had ample opportunity to reestablish contact during my first weeks, when we

---

1. The advice is introduced with the words: "It is the opinion of the Consulate that . . ." One never uses the first person singular in internal documents or in any other connection, a fact that people who come to the MFA from the Norwegian developmental aid organization NORAD (which was then the MFA's only subordinate directorate and is now incorporated into the MFA) and other agencies have difficulty grasping. During my stay, an employee of the ministry with a NORAD background reported in the in-house magazine how she was initiated into fax writing at her foreign posting in the following terms: "—Using the first person singular or plural is not musical.—Aha! So I can write *one*?—That is not the correct language either. *One* is replaced by *the Embassy*. . . .—But how are they to know who has written this if I don't own up to the fact that it is I? . . .—That is not important, that's why we just sign *Noramb* [Norwegian embassy]" (Anon 1997: 13).

shared an office. Ranveig says that above all I have been given the task of writing this speech in order to familiarize myself with the workings of the ministry. She explains how I should proceed. I should "go and talk to" the various in-house sections to get their input. In this particular case it is of the essence to "establish rapport with" the Office of Foreign Economic Affairs, she explains. Why so? Because the office, and the department of which it is a part, are the closest in the regular organization grid to being directly responsible for the issue area concerned. Once I have "established rapport with" (*kommet i inngrep med*) them—that is, once I have spoken to them, received their input, and established a feeling of consensus—I may proceed to write the speech and put it in the director general's pigeon-hole. He will then read it, perhaps annotate it, and return it to me. I will subsequently correct it, send it to the Translation Section to be corrected (or "language washed," to use the Norwegian expression), and then it will finally be signed off on. Does that mean that I should send it to the archive? No, Ranveig explains, not entirely. I will deliver the finished speech to the unit's secretary, who will then write a covering note and make three copies (an original, a blue copy for the general archive, and a yellow copy for the unit's archive).[2] She will also, when necessary, make copies for the rest of the unit. In any case she will put a copy of the end product in my pigeon-hole. Finally, it may be wise for me to keep a copy of the processed text, and perhaps I should also make copies for colleagues who have contributed input and for the foreign minister's secretariat.

"So I'll find out who is the officer in charge of the case in the Office of Foreign Economic Affairs and send him or her an e-mail," I say. Well, says Ranveig, it would be a good thing if "you went and spoke to the officer in charge." The process, she seems to imply, should not be anonymous. Diplomats believe in the face-to-face. Of course I take her advice. I draw up an outline of the speech, print several copies, make additional copies of the order slip and the note from the consulate in Hong Kong, check who is the desk officer at Foreign Economic Affairs, call him to announce my arrival, and then walk the three hundred meters of corridor from the North Building on Victoria terrasse, home of the three main buildings of

---

2. When an electronic archive was introduced shortly afterwards, this procedure stayed the same.

the ministry, to the South Building, where the Foreign Economic Affairs Section is located.

I have a chat with the desk officer. Norway and its political community are tight-knit groups; I have never met the man before, but it soon turns out that a friend of mine was once his colleague. "When do you think you can send me the speech?" I say. "I think I can manage a little something for you in the mail by tomorrow," he replies. Two days later there is a brown envelope in my pigeonhole, containing half a page of text and a floppy disk. I sit down to write the speech, print it out, pick it up and head for the unit secretary. "I have this speech here," I say, "now what?" "Send it up to Harald," she says. Director General Harald's office is located next to the rest of the unit's offices, but his pigeonhole sits on top of a vertical stack of pigeonholes. Even in sections where the pigeonholes are organized horizontally, with the director general's always at the far left, one "sends up" drafts to be read through. The "up" refers to social space, not necessarily to the physical world of offices and mail slots.

Harald knocks on my open door as he steps over the threshold, putting the speech on my desk. I scramble to my feet. "This is fine," he says. "Just send it over to the Asia adviser when it's finished." Since it is the secretary who takes care of the practicalities when the speech is to be signed off on, I take his meaning to be that I should walk the two hundred meters over to the Center Building and deliver the cover note, the speech, and the floppy disk to the Asia adviser in person. We talk a little about something else, he leaves and I have a look at the draft, which he has annotated with a red pen. The corrections are what I would have called stylistic: word sequence, a certain weakening of the first person singular, an adjustment of a formulation about the expected HR (human rights) situation after the transfer of Hong Kong to Beijing's jurisdiction. I decide simply to implement the suggested corrections, finish the speech, store it on the ministry's central disk drive, and put the entire thing in the internal mail system. (This time I don't need to make a printout, because the secretary and I are among the younger generation in the ministry who use its new intranet.) The following day it is back in my pigeonhole all completed. I call the Asia adviser, and then I walk the 150 corridor-meters over to the Center Building and up to the attic, where his division is located. We talk a little about the possibility of a war between Taiwan and China and the consolidation of the regime after the generational shift in the Beijing leadership. He is going to accompany the royal couple, so I wish him a good trip. He thanks me for the speech. The following day I get a Norwegian-speaking but definitely English voice on the phone. She is calling from the translation office, which is situated in another part of town, so it is impractical for her to walk over and talk to me in person. No stylistic objections, she says, but there is an ambivalent point on page five. We resolve it, and the conversation comes to an end.

The speech is off and the job is done, but two things bother me. Although I have been brought into the ministry to be an all-rounder, the economic sphere is my Achilles heel as a political analyst, and one of the parts of the world I know least about is China. Seen in this light, the assignment was an odd one. I raise this in the canteen at lunch. At the table with me is an old friend from university, now a trusted civil servant, and a number of his colleagues. They all chuckle, and one of them says "welcome to the Foreign Ministry, that's how it is for all of us. Here in the foreign service our role model is that of the potato: we must be able to cover all needs and fit in with everything. You see, you have to be a generalist."[3] On later occasions I mention to people from the Foreign Ministry and also to foreign diplomats that my first experience of speechwriting came in an area where my expertise was at its weakest. They all react in similar fashion.[4]

The other thing that bothers me is that the writing job itself—that is, the thinking and writing up—took less than two hours, but everything else took ten hours. Counting input, reading, annotation, secretarial aid, translation, etc., it must have taken the ministry more than thirty hours

---

3. Being the staple of the Norwegian table, the potato is routinely used to connote jacks of all trades; Døving 2003.

4. Nils Ørvik et al.(1977: 92) report from a large questionnaire survey at the end of the 1960s: "The people in Defence, with their strong military attachments, and the ones in Commerce, with a corresponding concentration on economics, have a definite tradition of specialization, reinforced by the rate of horizontal mobility. Conversely, the trend at the Foreign Ministry is traditionally very generalized, although this has lately been tempered by the growing need for expert knowledge. Such was the picture as seen from the outside. Did it correspond to the images which the people inside the respective departments had of themselves? We checked this through our questionnaire: 'Would you regard yourself as a specialist (expert) on the tasks assigned to your office?' The results were quite the opposite of what we had expected. In the two 'expert ministries', Defense and Commerce, only half of the personnel (secretaries/chiefs of divisions) considered themselves experts. The other half replied *no*. The answers in the Department of Economic Affairs in the Foreign Ministry—notoriously the most generalized of them all—categorized themselves as experts!" (Cf. Barnett 1997).

to produce that twenty-minute luncheon speech. I pour out my soul about this to Ranveig. She says it is a totally reasonable and respectable allocation of resources. I ask her about the director general's corrections—is it common to receive stylistic corrections only? She takes a look at them and says that these are not only stylistic comments—human rights is a sensitive area where it is important to be consistent. "Yes," I say, "but there is not even a nuance of difference in meaning between the director general's formulation and mine." "Perhaps not," replies Ranveig, "but it is important that the ministry sends consistent signals, and the director general's formulations are more appropriate."

So, although the speech is not what diplomats call "operative"— meaning that it has no direct bearing on what they think of as day-to-day policy making—but rather decorative, this distinction is not of the essence. For all speeches, genre demands apply, and these demands are part of that stock of shared practices which may, as I suggested in the introduction, be said to constitute diplomatic culture (Bull 1977, Der Derian 1987). The distinction I have made between style and content does not necessarily apply as expected in my current working environment. My point, rather, is that the text is diplomatic, which is to say that it is adapted to the genre in general and adapted to the formulations that have been used previously about this cluster of issues in particular.

A few weeks later I come across a review of the speech in the Foreign Ministry's daily press clippings, taken from a commercial magazine. When I mention this at the morning meeting of the Planning Unit, however, I find that no one is interested.

Small We's, Large We's

A couple of weeks later the director general, the higher executive officer of the unit, and I are on our way to London for political talks with the Planning Unit of the British Foreign Office. "Political talks" recur at several different levels, at a political level between ministers, state secretaries, or political advisers, and on a civil servant level between heads of departments or, as in this case, between the heads of planning units. One meets to discuss affairs in general. Still, a list of more or less specific topics for discussion is often prepared in advance. In addition to discussions on current political affairs, talks at the civil service level are occasions for colleagues to exchange experiences regarding organizational planning. As a general knowledge-producing institution of diplomacy, the planning unit came into existence after the Second World War, when the British Foreign Office and also the U.S. State Department decided to resume the planning they had carried out in order to win the peace, but now in a more general form (Rostow 1964). The idea spread to other foreign ministries, with one of the channels of diffusion being political talks. The establishment of the Planning Unit in the Norwegian Foreign Ministry in 1973 was thus part of a trend. In a sense the three of us from the Planning Unit in the Norwegian Foreign Ministry are on our way to visit the mother ship.

The talks start with the head of Policy Planning giving a short account of the political and administrative adjustments that have resulted from the transition to a Labour government after seventeen years of Tory rule. She recounts that one of the first things the incoming foreign secretary, Robin Cook, did was to transfer speechwriting from Policy Planning to the Public Relations Section. When she has finished, as is the custom in all such contexts, both between foreign ministries and between their various subdivisions, her opposite number replies. In his reply, our director general laments the fact that Foreign Office Policy Planning, which is supposed to have a general overview of what is going on, has "lost" speeches to Public Relations and says that in Norway, speeches are being transferred from Planning to the foreign minister's secretariat. In her reply to the reply, the head of Foreign Office Policy Planning expresses the view that this is an unfortunate trend for "us." Here I entered the conversation and made the point that we do after all live in an information society, and that most speeches are given to groups where packaging and profiling of specific policies, institutions, and individuals are far more important than analytic content, and that it is therefore effective use of ministerial resources to place speechwriting in the part of the organization that specializes in its relationship to the general public. This point of view has little or no impact. The British side mentions that speeches, along with the hammering out of fact sheets on "British policy" in different areas, are the most important instrument "we" have for forming policy. My director general nods, and says half to our British interlocutors, half to me, that the foreign minister's speeches are decisive manifestations of policy, which it is important that "we" do not lose. The discussion moves on to other topics.

At the time I gave this conversation little thought—in retrospect, probably because at that point I noted how the contradictions between the various units of the Foreign Ministry were reflected in the most minute of details. Thus I understood "we" as referring to the planning units, in opposition to "the others" in the ministry and in particular to the Department of Public Relations in the British Foreign Office and the secretariat in the Norwegian Foreign Ministry. In accordance with political science notions about "bureaucratic infighting" (Allison 1971) and Michael Herzfeld's (1992) emphasis on the "interests" of various bureaucratic units, I saw the worry of the planners over the loss of speeches as yet another turf battle between various parts of an organization. However, the pronoun "we" is what linguists call a "shifter": what it signifies depends entirely upon context. In light of what came to light later on, I wonder whether the "we" in these talks should not rather be understood as the ministries in their aspect of unitary bureaucracies, as distinguished from the political leadership and their spin doctors.

This idea first occurred to me when I was working on another speech a month later. Speechwriting tasks were increasingly distributed by Principal Officer Hallgrim in the foreign minister's secretariat. Judged by size, tasks, and budget, the secretariat is a part of the Foreign Ministry that has increased greatly in importance in recent years. The transfer of speechwriting, which my director general had lamented during our visit to London, was in the Norwegian context part of a general concentration of business in the secretariat (and in meetings of the secretary general and his immediate entourage) rather than in the various offices (and in the regular morning meetings of the foreign minister).[5] In addition to its own head and spokesperson, the secretariat also has its own civil servants who cater exclusively to the needs of the foreign minister and the state secretaries. Personnel are handpicked from among the most promising late-thirties employees of the ministry. While I was at the ministry there was a change of government, and a new foreign minister who happened to be a career diplomat took office. One of those he summoned to the secretariat was a diplomat from

---

5. The tendency for speeches which were previously written in the Foreign Ministry to be written in the prime minister's office instead has subsequently escalated. An early example that was noted in the Foreign Ministry was an important speech on the Security Council that the prime minister gave at the UN General Assembly in 1995.

a foreign posting where he had been ambassador. The secretariat is thus the place where the current and future leaders of the ministry are found. Certain younger diplomats, and a few older ones, almost daily and seemingly incidentally pass by the third floor in the North Building, where the secretariat is located. The employees of the secretariat occasionally mentioned to me, always poker-faced, that so-and-so was often seen in the secretariat, but I never heard anyone explicitly saying why they might have been seen there.[6] It is a general trait of diplomatic communication that it is usually indirect.[7] The point was that Principal Officer Hallgrim in the secretariat was a man who could draw upon different resources to get things done, and he now had contacted my director general to inquire whether the Planning Unit could write a speech for the foreign minister to deliver to employees of the Department of Press, Culture, and Information.

At the Planning Unit's morning meeting, my director general asked whether I would like to write the speech. I was a little startled. The foreign minister, a career diplomat, is going to give a speech to colleagues most of whom he knows personally. Nonetheless, the task of writing the speech is given not to his secretariat but to the Planning Unit. This does not conform to the notion of "turf battles." Both the substance of giving such a speech—familiarity with the information habits of the Norwegian MFA—and the organizational aspect—the network and information between the minister and the section (the organizational unit of a department)—indicate that this speech should be written in the secretariat, and certainly not by an adviser brought in on a short-term contract. Still, I accept the offer, but add that it might be best for the number two in the unit, my mentor Ranveig, to supervise my work. This is accepted. My first draft is an account of how public relations units came into existence as a part of the democratization of diplomacy in the wake of the First World War, how one goes about image building, how the point is to get the population in one's own country and the elites and populations of other countries to accept the

---

6. Significantly, in the first half of the last century, there was a word (which dated back to the 17th century) in use for this practice, antechambering, whereas now, there is none. The practice is not acknowledged to the same degree as before, but it is alive and kicking nonetheless.

7. This is something that young people who are new to the system often remark on: "It's typical of the Foreign Ministry, one gives one's glass a light ring with the hand . . . ," as one trainee diplomat commented on the applause after the prime minister's welcome speech to the annual Christmas party.

representations or "pictures" of Norway that the Public Relations Section produces. Ranveig and I sit down together for the rewrite, we tighten it up and fill it in, and then we sign off on it. However, a few days later we hear that the foreign minister put our draft aside as "too analytical," and instead gave a loosely prepared feel-good speech. This is a format at which the foreign minister excels. A few weeks later I am present at the annual Christmas party (menu: smorgasbord) for members of the Foreign Ministry chapter of the academics' trade union. There the foreign minister gives a dazzling feel-good speech, this being his fourth of that day.

This incident taught me a bit more about speechwriting in the ministry. Not even feel-good speeches are treated as the minister's, or even the secretariat's, sole preserve. Every speech concerns the entire ministry, regardless of such considerations as form and place of delivery. Furthermore, when it comes to authorship, special competence is not essential, and even if people with such competence are at hand, normal procedures for speechwriting are not set aside. To this one may add that speed and efficiency are less important than right procedure, for a later incident illustrates how it is first and foremost politicians, and not the Foreign Ministry's own people, who treat speeches as something to be produced in a hurry. Half a year after the incident with the feel-good speech, when I and other colleagues were on vacation, one of the state secretaries found herself in acute need of a speech on the Foreign Office and cultural promotion. Her secretariat (in the shape of Hallgrim) tipped her off that there might be something in the Planning Unit's archive. My discredited speech for the foreign minister was excavated and used, clearly as an emergency solution. The state secretary herself was, I later heard from the secretariat, greatly satisfied with the speech, but I got the feeling that Hallgrim and the secretariat accepted this procedure only grudgingly and as an emergency solution. The unease caused both by the genesis of this particular speech and also on other occasions when a speech was simply fished out and delivered without being hatched specifically for the purpose was for me an analytical challenge. It showed that from the diplomat's perspective, it was not the quality of the speech as judged by the political leadership that was decisive—although that was what everybody said when one asked them the main criterion for judging speeches. Also, the incident demonstrated that things other than turf were at stake. The ministerial writing process involved a different logic, which came in addition to the desire to produce items that would

satisfy the political leadership and the desire to be better than other diplomats. What was the difference?

I started by thinking that this must have to do with the difference in the
degree of audience receptivity. The striking thing about the conversation
in London had been that neither the Norwegian nor the British diplomats
had any time for the argument that one had to start work on a speech by
thinking about the audience. This could not be due to a general insensitivity to the importance of targeting a speech, as shown by incidents within
the ministry: the foreign minister had chosen to give a feel-good rather
than an analytic speech to employees in the Office of Public Relations, and
in spite of an overwhelming workload he chose to tailor his own speech for
the annual Christmas party. Could there be a *partial* insensitivity to audience, which applied only to nondiplomats? This explanation did not satisfy
either. Diplomats themselves spend much time as audiences for speeches at
other foreign ministries and institutions, and in particular when they are
posted abroad and their main task is to report on the politics of the host
country. "The speeches were mostly of the Merry Christmas and Happy
New Year type," as one report from a foreign posting put matters, with
uncharacteristic lack of discretion.[8] As listeners to a speech, diplomats are
(at least) as irritated as others by lack of sensitivity to the audience.

My suspicion that audience targeting was not the clue was confirmed
a little later, when I attended a meeting between the Planning Unit and
the secretariat of the Foreign Ministry. Also in attendance was a political adviser. In this meeting, I suggested that the Foreign Ministry should
make a greater effort to identify the audiences of speeches and also of the
ministry's other output. I argued that it was one of the Foreign Ministry's main weaknesses that speeches were too similar and that they did not
differ significantly from other genres of writing in the ministry, such as
notes and reports. This was before Alexei Yurchak (2006: 75; cf. Boyer
2003) had published on hypernormalized speech in the Soviet Union—
"an unintended result of the attempts by great numbers of people who
were engaged in producing texts in authoritative language to minimize
the presence of their own authorial voice." This was just as well, or else

---

8. All unclassified "telegrams" (faxes from foreign postings to the Ministry) were collected in
folders and circulated in the Planning Unit.

I might have broken the unspoken MFA rule of never drawing parallels between the political practices of friendlies and less-friendlies. However, I did somewhat self-righteously point out that it was common to submit take-outs from already written texts belonging to other genres when one was asked to make a contribution to, or draft, a speech. The political adviser, whose background was in journalism, supported me enthusiastically on this point, but no one from the civil service picked up the gauntlet, the conversation took a different turn, and the topic was never raised again. The political adviser even caused a moment of embarrassment for members of the Foreign Ministry's regular staff who were present when she referred to the fact that the other minister within the MFA—the minister of development and human rights—had appointed a special speechwriter and made him a part of the secretariat. This was evidently an outcome of a trend much disliked by my colleagues in the Planning Unit and the civil servants in the secretariat. Thus aspects of speechwriting other than information and audience targeting were more important to them, and it was no longer obvious to me that this other aspect was turf battles.

Challenges Unfold a Previously Hidden Logic

Now I had become truly curious: what was the underlying, driving force of speechwriting in the ministry? When a new opportunity to participate arose, I grabbed it with both hands. This time it was the foreign minister's main domestic speech in Norway, the annual foreign policy accounting to Parliament. Principal Officer Hallgrim in the secretariat had given it to the Planning Unit, and the director general of the Planning Unit had delegated it to me. I suggested, and both the secretariat and my own unit accepted the idea, that we structure the speech around a uniting narrative, so that the speech itself would transmit a clear message. If things were done in this fashion, the ensuing speech would stand in stark contrast to previous speeches of this type. I noted that the previous annual accounts were indistinguishable from one another and indeed from other types of text the ministry produced, such as notes and white papers. So, with the aim of breaking the mold, I set to work. I asked for input from the offices, and read the statement of purpose put forth by the current governmental coalition upon accession to power, as well as the previous speeches of the ministry's political leadership. I found that the two topics that kept recurring in the recent documents were values and globalization. On this basis I decided to build the entire speech around the notion of "ethical globalization." This theme would allow me to include most of the topics and ideas that the various sections had come up with, but in forms that I could relate to the government's main message about the importance of values and the insistence of the foreign minister that Norway maintain a high ethical profile in its foreign policy. I submitted the draft to the morning meeting in the Planning Unit, and proceeded to tone down and edit in response to criticism. Then I passed it on to Hallgrim in the secretariat.

Two weeks later the phone rang. Hallgrim told me that the foreign minister had brought the draft along on two trips, but that he had had time to read it only the preceding day. When he had reached page two and the term "ethical globalization," he had put the speech aside as too analytical. Could I write a new draft more similar to previous speeches? I said I would discuss this with my director general. So I went and knocked on his door. "We had to expect this," he said. "This is not how things have been done before." "All right," I said, "but perhaps it would be wise if somebody else in the unit completed the task, so that we are certain to hit that ministerial slant." So it was done. The minister came before Parliament and made a speech similar to those of previous years. The speech did not start a debate in the press or in the foreign policy milieu, and the country's newspaper of record, *Aftenposten,* noted in an editorial that it contained nothing new. I never heard comments on this reaction in the ministry, and when I cautiously tried to get people in the canteen to express an opinion on *Aftenposten*'s editorial, they shrugged it off. The negative reception of the speech was simply not an interesting topic of conversation. I had confirmed that analysis was unimportant in the Foreign Ministry system, that the audience's reception was of little or no interest to the ministry, and that the established patterns were difficult to break. But I had learned little else.

It was difficult for me as an analyst to deal with the ministry's disavowal of analysis. The ministry's focus was everywhere but on the cohesion and vibrancy of the argument itself; it seemed more important to incorporate bits written by all and sundry than to say something that would actually have a bearing on political processes. When I let go the task of drafting the annual account to parliament, it was not least because the revised draft would specifically have to exclude any analytical aspect. Also, I let go of the task because I had another speech on the books.

This time it was in fact I who had taken the initiative, in the sense that I had established what the ancients called the *kairos*—an opportunity fixed in time and space to get something done. Soon after my entry into the Foreign Ministry, in a conversation about the relations between the ministry and the rest of Norway, my director general had complained that the ministry could produce policy speeches from only a small number of podiums during the year: a couple of times in parliament, the annual speech to the Oslo Military Society, and that was that. I immediately saw an opportunity to take on the role of entrepreneur. When former foreign minister, defense minister, and director of the Norwegian Institute of International Affairs (NUPI) Johan Jørgen Holst, passed away, NUPI, which happened to be my think tank employer at the time, initiated an annual memorial speech. The first two speeches had been given by Henry Kissinger and by the world's leading military historian, Sir Michael Howard. I suggested to my director general that considering Holst's role as foreign minister, it would be entirely appropriate for the current foreign minister to be next in the series of prestigious speakers, and that the topic of his speech should be Norwegian security policy. My ulterior motive was to see that the task of writing the speech ended up on my desk, and that I thereby might establish a new standard for speeches—an analytic standard, where the speech was a clean narrative with the red thread consistently on display. As Strathern (2004: 23) remarks about "knowledge workers" such as herself and myself:

> The knowledge that is attached to them goes with individuals when they leave one job for another, moving locations; insofar as their knowledge was originally created in the company of others, then it is the community from which they take. It is visible in being left behind. But in what sense can a person ever leave a previous community (so to speak) completely behind? To the extent that knowledge is embedded in what they do, it will in turn show traces of their training, occupation and the contexts in which they have used it.

Strathern also sums up one aspect of my own experience in the MFA here. In an agency perspective, I manipulated my affiliations. In a structural perspective, types of knowledge production were hybridizing, and that, to return to an agency perspective, provoked the MFA's hiring of me in the first place. I also thought it would be entertaining and personally satisfying to prepare such a memorial speech in a forum honoring Holst, for whom a colleague and I had once written a speech on our future security when he was minister.[9] The memorial speech was to be published in an academic journal for an audience of researchers and international diplomats. This time, I thought, an analytical perspective would be inevitable.

My director general, who was also on the NUPI board, took note of the suggestion. After a couple of days he came into my office, and asked me to probe the issue informally with the director of NUPI, and learn whether he might like the foreign minister to deliver the speech. I had expected this indirect approach, not only because of the general bent of diplomats toward indirect communication but in particular because it is a principle in the Foreign Ministry that as much as possible, cooperation with other actors should look as though initiated by others, who thereby appear to be the *demandeurs,* rather than by the Foreign Ministry itself. This practice causes a certain degree of irritation among the institutions that cooperate with the Foreign Ministry, and I have occasionally heard angry outbursts from people who have suggested things to the ministry. For example, Simon, a friend working for Telenor, the largest Norwegian telecom operator, remarked after a conversation with somebody responsible for information about Norway that "when you come along with Norway advertising worth big bucks (*millioner av kroner*), you still get the impression that it is *you* who are asking a favor of *them,* not the other way around." The practice recurs in the layout of programs of co-hosted events, where the Foreign Ministry always puts itself at the top, regardless of actual roles in preparing the events, alphabetical order, financing, and other factors.

The director of NUPI was positively inclined, and wrote a letter of invitation to the foreign minister. The Foreign Ministry secretariat sent an order to the Planning Unit, and, as anticipated, the order landed on my

---

9. That time the principal officer approached us, shook hands, and said with a certain uneasiness that we had managed to have most things of our work included. He had authored a competing draft, and could be seen comparing the speech delivered to his own written draft. In its comments on the speech that Holst gave at the time, and which was mainly written by researchers such as ourselves, *Aftenposten* noted that it was "the researcher Holst" who had been speaking, and not the foreign minister. Some journalists are in the know.

desk. I wrote a draft of which the purpose was to display some contradictions in Norwegian security policy after the Cold War, trace the causes back to the uneven adaptation of various aspects of our defense and security policy to the new geopolitical situation, and announce a few new moves that might reduce tensions within the policy and make it seem more proactive. After a discussion in the Planning Unit I once again sent a draft to the secretariat.

This time I had a response within a few hours. The draft had happened to end up in the hands of the ministry's assistant secretary general in charge of security policy. When he had finished reading, he had immediately walked over to Hallgrim in the secretariat, and said that he had "almost had *angina pectoris*" from reading the draft. "All right," I said, "what happens now?" Hallgrim's response to the ranking security officer had been to suggest a meeting in his office the following day, with someone from the Security Policy Section, himself, and me. The director general of the Department of Security Policy and a couple of his closest colleagues attended the meeting. It turned out that the department had two main objections to my draft.[10] First was a lack of detailed information about developments in certain areas, both their own and ones that were the responsibility of other sections of the ministry. Second was the direct language. I had thought that I had learned that diplomats think of style as content and of an indirect approach as a virtue, but clearly my draft was still much too direct. I immediately recognized the problem, but as far as details were concerned I decided to go for confrontation. "Who needs that information in this context?" I asked, and pointed out that the audience would be looking for an overview of the situation and the general drift of plans. We needed an eagle's view from above, and not a snake's view from below. "No," was the answer, it was not possible to give a speech on Norwegian security without mentioning the importance of the U.S. security guarantee, nuclear waste in the north, and so on. If such matters were not mentioned, it would be a signal that they were not given priority.

The policy had to be repeated. If not it would be weakened. This is of course an entirely valid argument. It takes hard discursive work to keep things

---

10. It is illegal to reproduce excerpts of internal drafts of Norwegian state documents, so, unfortunately, I cannot reproduce samples.

as they are (Garfinkel 1967; cf. Durkheim [1912] 1995). Making the world seem stable when it is in fact in constant flux means that wielding power involves the ability to freeze meaning. This has to be done by constantly repeating specific representations of things, actions, and identities, until what one repeats is naturalized to such an extent that it appears doxic. One can refrain from repeating representations only if they are already embedded in other representations that are repeated, so that they are confirmed indirectly. That was not the case on this occasion, so I did not feel that I could argue against the need to repeat the policy in general. Instead I argued that the occasion would be a closed forum for the informed, and that spending time on repeating the official line would be an ineffective use of resources. We should rather concentrate on saying something that would catch the interest of an audience consisting of academics and members of the *corps diplomatique*, and I thought that that something should be conceptual. This was rejected. It was not the "conceptual" but the "operational" that interested diplomats, and that should therefore be at the center.

This was also an unassailable argument. I was being subjected to diplomatic identity formation, according to the formula that "you academics" concentrate on the conceptual whereas "we diplomats" concentrate on the operative. The context of the speech was defined as being accidental and quite inconsequentially an academic arena; the arena was defined as mainly diplomatic. The space I had created for my innovative moves had thus been erased. I said that I had written thinking that the conceptual would be the main thing in a speech to academics, but that the speech would obviously have to be written differently if it were composed with a different function in mind. The director general leaned forward, and said "the draft is interesting enough, it is impressive that anyone would make an attempt at such a thing." The meeting died away, and I declined the invitation to coordinate the rest of the speech, giving as my reason that Hallgrim would be far better placed for the task. The conflict was resolved, but Hallgrim started a conversation with me about something else, and when the two other participants had left, he said smiling: "We might have avoided the risk of sick leave if we had polished the first draft a little."

I headed down the corridor for my own office. So if Hallgrim and I had sat down and polished the text before it had reached the assistant secretary general, both the risk of *angina pectoris* and the need for clarifying meetings would have been reduced. What was most interesting was the way the conflict had been handled: as soon as it was clear that the result would be what the assistant secretary general had decided, consensus-building and the reestablishment of collegial harmony were the main objectives. Instead of going straight to my own office, I knocked on my mentor Ranveig's door and told her the story. "Is it not this inclination toward consensus that eliminates the space for creativity and debate in the ministry?" I asked. "Well, is it better up at Blindern [the Oslo University campus], where people don't speak to one other at all?" came the question in response. No, I said, but in this case the result will be a less good speech. "It is important for everyone to be in on it, so that we get a speech that the entire ministry may stand behind," said Ranveig.

A Speech That the Entire Ministry May Stand Behind

At the following morning meeting I gave my account. The director general slumped back in his seat, and said that now the fate of another initiative taken by the unit, in which we depended on the goodwill of the Department of Security Policy, was open to doubt. No more was said about the speech, but I had finally found an answer to my question about what this "other" was that makes audience reception subsidiary. Of course the Foreign Ministry has a need to inform. It would be incorrect to claim that the Foreign Ministry is uninterested in the speeches it writes. But in addition a powerful imperative says that the entire ministry should be comfortable with what is written in its name. The fact that in this case it was our director general who emphasized how one turf battle might affect the next one, whereas our assistant director general emphasized consensus, is incidental. In no way was it due to a lack of awareness of the importance of turf battles on the part of the assistant director general. Only a few weeks before our conversation she had come to me to ask about something in connection with a speech she herself was writing, and had told me that "only an hour after Hallgrim had sent the draft to that office they were at his door complaining, but he has become so accustomed to it that he simply ignores them." Rather, by getting caught up in the importance of turf battles, as I did when I wrote my first speeches, I missed the importance of other practices that delimit how deep, comprehensive, and decisive diplomats let these turf battles become. Paramount was the practice of letting all implied parties have their say, and the practice of defining "implied" in as wide a manner as time allowed. The expectations inculcated by training in my academic discipline had blinded me to a lot of other things that were also going on.

I suddenly remembered how a diplomat friend once joked that he and his colleagues never fell out with one another, for they might end up as the only two Norwegian civil servants posted to Abidjan (most Norwegian posts have only two career diplomats). Indeed, there was no logical reason why this integrative and conflict-evasive way of organizing speechwriting should apply only between diplomats who work in different offices; it most likely applies within each office as well. That, after all, was the case in my own unit (see the organizational chart). One way of finding out whether this held true for other parts of the ministry would be to inquire about the writing of the new parts of the Holst memorial speech in the Department of Security Policy. So the next time I saw somebody familiar with that department, I asked him how much time it had taken to write the speech, and who had done it. He estimated the section's work on the speech at about twenty-two hours: he himself had spent eight hours on it, X had written about one field and Y about another, Z had written a few bits and the director general had read through the entire draft twice. The section as such had thus followed the same model as the ministry as a whole: everyone who was seen as having a claim to chime in had been invited to do so.

This mode of working takes time. The next time I met Hallgrim, I asked him for an estimate of how long the ministry as a whole had worked on the foreign minister's speech. He put the efforts of his colleagues and himself at about 40 hours, the foreign minister's at about 3 hours, that of the entire ministry at about 120 hours, "and in addition there are section meetings and canteen talk." As far as the most important speeches are concerned, it is not only in metaphorical terms that the entire ministry stands behind them.[11]

In fifteen years as a reader of politicians' speeches prior to my stint in the Foreign Ministry, I had not thought about the complexity of the

---

11. The speech was handed out in script form, with the usual "check against delivery" noted in the upper right hand corner—a convention for stating the fact that it is what is said and not what is written that is approved. The script was then polished once more, and published as Vollebæk (1998).

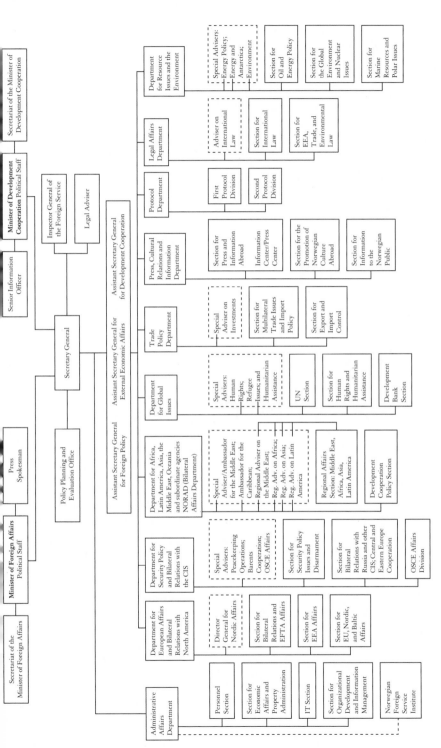

Organizational structure: The Norwegian Ministry of Foreign Affairs, 1998.

genesis of speeches. That blindness speaks volumes about how isolated academics are from the microphysics of power, even when they are seemingly in constant interaction with practitioners. It also says a good deal about the advantage of ethnography as a form of data collection about social processes, and about the enormous advantages of researchers who have personal experience in the field they are researching. An incident in connection with the foreign minister's delivery of the Holst memorial speech demonstrates this point. On that occasion a colleague who had been married to a top politician for many years came over, shook my hand with a grin, and said "congratulations on your parts" of the speech. He obviously knew how speeches emerged, but due to his training as a political scientist, he had probably never seen it as relevant to make his implicit knowledge explicit. Those who know a little about practical politics know that a foreign minister's speeches can seldom be read as the result of a simple tug of war. They are also the result of a process in which different points of view and emphases are patched together in a manner that everyone can live with.

It is the task of a foreign ministry, which by definition consists of widely different units, to join together in a higher unity in a way that renders the seams as invisible as possible. Each section mediates relations with various human collectives outside the ministry. If an MFA is to maintain its unity, like all organizations it must maintain its own integrative processes. In the case of the Norwegian MFA, speechwriting turned out to be one such process. It is among other things because speechwriting is so important as a common ministerial concern that informing and convincing the audience of the message in each speech is not held to be important. Speechwriting is first and foremost a question of ministerial identity building. Information and argumentation are important, of course, but the organization's self-confirmation and the confirmation of working relations among all parts of the organization and among all employees are of greater importance. When ministerial employees return from speechwriting courses, they relate that the lecturer—whether an employee of the prime minister's office or an American professional speechwriter (one effect of U.S. hegemony is that lecturers on such matters are usually American)—emphasizes the unity of the speech, and that it can be unitary only if there is one person who supervises its writing and has the final say. The customary expression holds that one person should "sit in the minister's lap" (that is, have his ear).[12] The American president has a crew of speechwriters consisting of a domestic and a foreign section. Roosevelt gave around eighty speeches a year, but Clinton averaged about five hundred, and thus he found it necessary to leave the writing to a dozen employees who worked directly for him, independently of the State Department. In the British Foreign and Commonwealth Office, speeches have also been torn away from the bureaucracy since the foreign secretary made them part of his political arsenal. If a future Norwegian foreign minister were to insist that his or her speeches should first and foremost be effective in relation to domestic and foreign political groupings, then the Norwegian foreign ministry would also have to give up its speechwriting procedures.[13] As noted, this has already happened to the British Foreign Office. It has also happened in other Norwegian ministries. To an increasing degree, it even happens in the secretariat of the human rights minister within the Foreign Ministry itself. These developments, however, seem to have no effect on how speechwriting proceeds inside the (rest of) the Norwegian Ministry of Foreign Affairs. One may conclude that as long as diplomats take care of speechwriting, their speeches will continue to look like the Foreign Ministry's notes and White Papers, for the simple reason that all such types of text are produced in the same manner. They are all texts that the entire ministry may stand behind, and thus they are not first and foremost expressions of the points of view of particular politicians or instantiations of particular fields, but rather instantiations of the ministry as such. What we observe here is nothing less than a ministerial mode of knowledge production.

When the entire ministry can stand behind a speech, it is because the speech *is* the ministry. The ministry exists among other things because it purports to speak with one voice, and it is therefore important that this voice rings out unequivocally, as often and as clearly as possible. Hence

---

12. Note the different indexing in English and Norwegian here; there is no sitting in the lap of the gods in Norwegian, so the reference is unequivocally to the parent-child relation.

13. A former foreign minister reported in an informal luncheon talk at the ministry in the autumn 2002 that when he had taken up the post, "I wanted a speechwriter in each department, but was immediately told that there could be no need for this when we had the secretariat. . . . I am certain that what we received [from the departments] was strong on substance (*faglig sterkt*), but actually, I could not always use it."

the number of speeches not written by the entire ministry is minimized, and notes that have no place in the bureaucratic scale are weeded out. As long as the politicians themselves do not intervene, nothing new will emanate from the Foreign Ministry. From the point of view of the bureaucrat, it is only when the system *does not work* that something new is produced, because the very fact that something new is produced shows that the system has failed. Civil servants in the Foreign Ministry do not find this paradoxical. On the contrary, they see it as evidence that the civil service functions as it is supposed to. To many people on the outside it is a mystery why the Foreign Ministry never produces anything that may serve to launch new departures in policy, when by continuing as previously, it increasingly and undeniably loses out in competition with other policy generators. Nonetheless, because of the structure of its discourse, the Foreign Ministry will continue to produce speeches that the entire ministry can stand behind until the political leadership forces through greater audience targeting by changing the routines. The change can come only from the outside.

If the Norwegian Foreign Ministry should follow the British Foreign Office in this regard, the diplomats' reaction to change will probably constitute no more than a lament that the old mode is being abandoned. The question whether there are in fact exogenous reasons for such a change of routine will likely go undiscussed. The British example indicates that diplomats do not learn lessons in this regard, but rather rest content with lamenting the loss of the speechwriting function. This is a historically overdetermined pattern, with overdetermined consequences. Commenting on Weber's classic adage from "Politics as a Vocation" (1968: 1404) that the bureaucrat who disagrees with a decision nonetheless has to "carry it out as if it corresponded to his innermost conviction," Minson (1998: 60) highlights how this involves the juggling of different social roles. In philosophical terms, he notes, civil servants act out an order of ethical life which places them foursquare in the neostoic tradition:

> It is not to the contemplative philosopher but the man of worldly rhetorical *paideia,* not to Aristotle but the historian/rhetor Tacitus that we should turn for guidance on the ethical capacities and comportments needed for state service, as did so many European soldiers, jurists, diplomats, court

officials and others in the seventeenth-century neo-stoic revival. (cf. Luce and Woodman 1993)

Institutional voice is achieved by drowning out the voices of specific diplomats. This may be said about many organizations and all bureaucracies. The glorious history of the diplomat is well known in its broad outlines, whereas the less glorious history of the home-based adviser is not thought of as pertaining to diplomacy. As we shall see in the next chapter, certainly diplomats themselves do not identify with bureaucracy. Far from it—in their negotiations of identity, they actively try to distance themselves from this part of their history and their work. For these reasons, it is somewhat *contre-courant* to point out how the bureaucratic mode of knowledge production informs diplomatic work, and points that are *contre-courant* always need to be stressed in order to register. I have tried to demonstrate how, on the level of practice, diplomats are, after all, willing accomplices in the kind of bureaucratization that they fight so doggedly on the conscious and even subconscious levels.

Anecdotal evidence suggests that the argument made here about how speeches are made may be generalized to other foreign ministries and foreign policy–making institutions in late modern states. Gunilla, a former Swedish diplomat who read an earlier draft of this chapter, commented that it could just as easily have been about his own Foreign Ministry. A senior British diplomat, Brigid, responded by saying that the account dovetailed not only with her own experience in Britain but also with what she had seen during her various postings abroad. A former American speechwriter comments on his experiences:

> Anyone with experience writing speeches—as I did for Jimmy Carter, during the campaign and in the White House, a quarter century ago—knows that composition is the easy part. . . . if the writer has, say, a couple of hours, he or she has a chance of batting out an interesting draft that advances one or two main themes. A full day might be better—but not a full week, because that leaves time for the hard part; fending off the countless advisers who want to "tune" and "improve" the speech. . . . the more time available to work on a presidential speech, the more complex and bogged down it becomes. The extreme example is a State of the Union address: everyone in the government has a year to see it coming and to try to work in his or her favorite causes. (Fallows 2001: 43–44)

A Mode of Knowledge Production

However, the argument may be broadened beyond speechwriting, to em-brace text production and hence MFA work in general. For example, in 2001, the Foreign Ministry set out to produce a so-called country strategy for the United States. Country strategies are relatively short documents (around ten pages) that outline and, ideally, rank the challenges to the bi-lateral relationship in order of importance, so that decision makers in spe-cific policy areas may have an opportunity to link the practical question of what to do in a specific situation to a wider and presumably official "line" on the overall relationship. In this case, the secretary of state (who was also a deputy foreign minister) in charge insisted that the initial work should be done by a task force of midlevel diplomats working independently of their heads of department. When I asked him why, he gave as his reason that recent work on other country strategies had been hampered by turf bat-tles among the departments on how to rank challenges, with each depart-ment holding out for its task to head the list. He wanted to postpone this part of the process, so that substance would be given a chance. As a mem-ber of the group, I was immediately made aware of two problems. First, the heads of department were not particularly sympathetic to the idea that work should be moved from the chain of command, and initiated a series of more or less subtle practices to extend their authority into the work of the task force. For example, when I bumped into another task force mem-ber on my way to the first meeting, she reported that her head of depart-ment had been on the phone twice in order to learn about and discuss the agenda of the meeting. Second, it quickly transpired that the midlevel diplomats, too, were intent on ranking the tasks of "their" departments highest. Furthermore, once the draft was made subject to the usual in-ternal hearing, ten stations, five departments, and two sections delivered written comments, and countless others weighed in with informal sug-gestions. The work was firmly back in the chain of command. As a result, when presented by the foreign minister to a group of Norwegian Ameri-cans meeting in Seattle, where I happened to be present, it was criticized for not being clear enough. Press coverage of the formal launch in Oslo fas-tened on the same point. The strategy document, which in the process had ended up looking very much like strategy documents on other countries, quietly disappeared, never to surface again. I asked the secretary in charge what he made of the experience. "That's the way the system works," he said, and shrugged (cf. Boyer 2005 on what he terms negative dialecticism). One year later, I was in charge of coordinating the announcement of funding for research. The announcement was supposed to include a list of topics that the MFA would be particularly eager to have investigated. The drawing up of the list, which was an affair that involved only the department in which I worked, followed the same logic. One head of section noted to one of her underlings that "we were able to have [topic X] included (*Vi fikk med. . .*)" The turn of phrase was also used by diplomats saying that they themselves or somebody else had their contributions included in a speech, as described above. When the head of department tried to shorten the list, a section or senior adviser who opined that "their" topics had to be included so that it would not look as if the MFA was not following events closely ("ikkje følger med i timen"), had done enough to rebuff him. Everybody should be heard, and everything should be included. At times, I felt as if I was trapped inside the fairy tale of Sleeping Beauty, with its lesson that the price for not including everybody in key activities may be death (one will recall that the reason the wicked fairy godmother wished her godchild to prick herself on a spindle with mortal effect was that she had not been invited to the girl's christening). The production of an MFA document, then, is in several ways diametrically opposite to the production of "I" genres like diaries and blogs (cf. Reed 2005: 226). When the diplomatic WikiLeaks of 2010 flooded onto the pages of the world's newspapers, the public was treated to a series of apt and entertaining reports from stations back to the State Department. Most commentators, and presumably most readers, seem to have taken these documents as representative of ministerial output. That is simply wrong. Such dispatches are the closest thing within a foreign ministry to the "I" genre. Their main function is to serve as one out of many inputs into the production of authoritative documents. The individual diplomat reporting on what she experiences is one of the beginnings of diplomatic knowledge production. She is never the end thereof. So it was with the research-funding exercise. It resulted in a list of topics that looked suspiciously similar to the list presented the year before. A speech, a strategy document, and a list of topics that the MFA would like to have researched by externals are different kinds of written material, but they are drawn up in similar ways. As a result, they tend to be vague and to resemble other examples of the same genre. Self-reflective diplomats acknowledge that this is the case, and has been for a long time. In 1985, heads of mission were asked to comment on the foreign minister's annual speech to Parliament. The ambassador to New Delhi responded dryly that "The parliamentarians expound their views on various issues raised by the foreign minister. A dialogue ensues. The format of the speech makes it an excellent hall stand on which the parliamentarians may hang a suitable number of hats."[14]

As reported attempts by the political leadership to revamp this process suggest, from the perspective of the top echelon of the organization the system sometimes does not do its job when it does its job in the way it always has. Politicians' expectations and ministry practice may be at cross-purposes. Politicians want priorities to be set and results to be achieved. The ministry wants its usual dog's breakfast, or rather dog's buffet, served according to the unto-each-his-own principle. As long as politicians do not intervene directly, bureaucratic practice rolls on. Michael Herzfeld has argued that

> As [Claude] Lefort has suggested, the paradox of bureaucracy is that the larger it grows, the more differentiated it becomes internally, and the more easily special interests are able to hide behind a mask of disinterested and objective rationality. Even at the top, then, despite Goody's account of the state as the primary agent of centralization, it is only the outer form of the discourse that is monolithic. It should hardly be a matter for surprise that the rhetoric of common interest sometimes turns out to be very thinly spread indeed. (Herzfeld 1992: 102)

The document-writing process in the Foreign Ministry is an example of this kind of invariance, and of how, in accordance with Herzfeld's main thesis, MFA civil servants are programmatically insensitive in relation to external parties, in this case the audiences for speeches. This insensitivity can be explained by pointing out that the discourse—in this case the system of genres, routines, and interactions that are preconditions for making

---

14. NNA, MFA 2 5/49 vol. 24, Ibsen to MFA 300985. In a diplomatic discursive setting, it is hard to avoid reading the comment as a dry put-down by a professional diplomat of a politician: The foreign minister himself is really no more than a hall tree, not only for parliamentarians, but also for the diplomats themselves.

a speech—has an inbuilt inertia that causes input from marginal elements such as myself to be repelled. Speeches remain as they were. Herzfeld's hypothesis that "even at the top [of the state] it is only the outer form of the discourse that is monolithic" is confirmed. However, it would underestimate the diplomat to think that speeches are not communicative at all. Speeches, at least the good ones, are communicative—for those who have the cultural competence to understand them, namely members of the *corps diplomatique* as well as a few highly specialized journalists and academics.

The drama in this story of speechwriting, as experienced by diplomats, was not about how the bureaucratic mode of production functions like a meat grinder that made standard-size hamburgers out of the most diverse raw materials. That was simply appropriate cooking. To them, the drama was rather how politicians in Great Britain, the United States and, as it turned out, Norway had to force through a greater degree of audience targeting as diplomacy's task increasingly involved mediating among actors other than the diplomats and political leaders of sovereign states. Diplomacy as an institution has altered but—and this is decisive—not from the inside, rather as the result of intervention by politicians. Inertia in the discourse is further underlined by the endless discussion in other contexts about how the Foreign Ministry has to relate to a steadily increasing number of nongovernmental actors. Note that there were frequent reminders that audience targeting might have been called for. Time and again, politicians and other outsiders reminded diplomats that they would have to fight for their own representations of reality, instead of taking for granted that their version of reality would win. The diplomats listened politely and then went on producing hamburgers. As a direct result, speechwriting in Norway has increasingly taken place outside the diplomatic system. That, too, has had no effect on the way other texts are produced. The rigidity of speechwriting was so great that diplomats did not see the shifts that were taking place as having any consequences for this discourse in particular. The only potential for change lay with the politicians. My fieldwork supports the claim of Mary Douglas (1986: 111) that "the individual tends to leave the important decisions to his institutions while busying himself with tactics and details." The MFA calmly watched as speeches disappeared and saw no reason to change the mode of production of other texts in order to ensure that the MFA would keep its other tasks. Going on as before was more important than changing in order to shore up the ministry.

Diplomatic common sense does not acknowledge an argument along these lines. "You write that there is no change in the Foreign Ministry, but there is," George commented after reading an earlier draft of this chapter, "it is just that it is more glacial." George is right. Diplomatic discourse has, in a long-term perspective, proved to be dynamic (cf. chapter 2). The point that change can be initiated only externally made little impression on him, because it is the nature of the job to leave initiative up to the political leadership.[15] As I spelled out in the previous chapter, a diplomat is among other things a bureaucrat who implements and upholds the policy of the political leadership at any given time. If one cannot accept that description of the job, one has to leave. A few prominent British diplomats did so after the Suez crisis in 1956, and again after the invasion of Iraq, when it became clear that they could not accept British policy. There have been several such cases in the United States, along with numerous examples of politicians who have found the diplomatic habit of following orders unbearably sheepish. For most diplomats, however, passivity is the hallmark of excellence, and Norwegian politicians have been far less critical of this tendency than have many of their American counterparts. This may also be the reason that diplomats did not take further action to keep speechwriting an exclusive part of diplomatic knowledge production. Diplomats may offer drawn-out and passive resistance to politically initiated change, but open resistance is very rare indeed. Besides, speechwriting is, after all, only one genre of text production. With speechwriting gone, the system may still go on producing other texts in the way it always has. The mode of knowledge production stays the same. As I will discuss in the next chapter, diplomats are required to be "actively expectant" (*aktivt avventende*) regarding developments in the world at large as well as in the profession. By doing nothing, diplomats may actually fulfill expectations.

* * *

In his work on the Ndembu, Victor Turner (1964: 41) observes that Ndembu mothers and their daughters have a lot to quarrel about, that

---

15. In organization studies, a debate ranged about this throughout the 1990s (see, for example, Olsen and Peters 1996). I do not want to make any claims about the general question of overall type and degree of change here. My claim is the more limited one of demonstrating how practice hampers innovation from within. This factor may or may not be decisive for the wider question of overall change.

these quarrels are in some degree understood by the Ndembu as what a social scientist would call role conflicts, but that "it is rather as though there existed in certain precisely defined public situations, usually of a ritual and ceremonial type, a norm obstructing the verbal statement of conflicts in any way connected with the principle and rules celebrated or dramatized in those situations." On the strength of my fieldwork, I suggest that speechwriting, and indeed knowledge production in general, at the Norwegian Ministry of Foreign Affairs is not only a practice but also a "certain precisely defined public situation."[16] Turner himself rightly generalizes in this direction when he writes that

> Social life in all organized groups appears to exhibit a cyclicality or oscillation between periods when one set of axiomatic norms are observed and periods when they give way to the dominance of another set. Thus since different norms govern different aspects or sectors of social behavior, and, more importantly, since the sectors overlap and interpenetrate in reality, causing norm-conflict, the validity of several major norms has to be reaffirmed in isolation from others, and outside the contexts in which struggles and conflicts arise in connection with them. This is why one so often finds in ritual that dogmatic and symbolic emphasis is laid on a single norm or on a cluster of closely, and on the whole harmoniously, interrelated norms in a single kind of ritual. (Turner 1964: 43)

Diplomats are no different. It has often been said that the credo of diplomatic work is "don't rock the boat." If that is an adage pertaining to how diplomats should behave vis-à-vis representatives of other states, then there is isomorphism between prescriptions for how diplomats should behave vis-à-vis those representatives and how they should live quotidian life inside the foreign ministry itself. Practices play out according to the stories that discourse holds out for them to play. When, as is usually the case, practices confirm these stories, they tell confirming stories of their own back to discourse. If all goes as it is set up to go, the result is social invariance.

---

16. In the context of celebrating economic anthropology, Ortner (1982: 132) shucks off symbolic anthropology as having an "underdeveloped sense of the politics of culture." Hardly. Ortner's understanding of politics must be widened to include processes that maintain a certain "we" at their very core, in which case Turner's insights seem central to *all* political processes.

4

To Be a Diplomat

When tracking down the self, an anthropologist is bound to be
a philosopher too.

MARTIN HOLLIS, 1985

The bureaucratic mode of production is the diplomat's main modus operandi when at home, as we have seen, and it is consistently undercommunicated by diplomats themselves. That begs the question how diplomats negotiate their own identities among themselves and vis-à-vis third parties like myself. That is the topic of this chapter. Broad historical comparison suggests that representing a polity, gathering information for that polity, and negotiating on its behalf are three basic diplomatic functions. Gathering of information by the diplomat abroad clashes with the bureaucratic mode of the diplomat at home, I suggest, and the juggling of the two tasks is central to how to be a diplomat. I also suggest that so many others gather information, with journalists key among them, that negotiation among states—a function that diplomats still tend to see as exclusive to their trade—takes on ever more weight as a marker of diplomatic identity.

When I begin this chapter about what it is like to be a diplomat by associating diplomacy with "the West," it is not only because the site of my work is the Norwegian Ministry of Foreign Affairs, but because diplomacy has a European history. One place to begin unpacking what it is to be a diplomat is to ask what it is to be a Westerner.

Two Stories

In a celebrated work, Charles Taylor (1989) identifies two scripts or stories for Western human beings in general. One concerns decency of everyday life, by which he means doing all the little things that are expected of you in a wide range of different contexts—being a "good man," "a nice woman," and the like. This story celebrates low-key, monotonous laboring life. It has no place for heroics in the sense of exceptionalism; it highlights the fact that you go on going on. It seems to be present in most professions (Abbott 1988). Even in prima donna professions like modeling or opera singing, individuals who refuse to follow the story are generally disliked by their colleagues and co-workers (*vide* Naomi Campbell, Maria Callas, et al.). Conversely, however, anyone who masters *only* this story will also come up a bit short. Perhaps the best novelistic treatment of diplomacy is William Boyd's *A Good Man in Africa* (1981), where the key point about the protagonist is exactly that he masters the story of everyday life while being wholly in the dark about any other story that may pertain to the status of "diplomat." He comes to work regularly, is a social presence, does not complain about his position, and does not complicate his colleagues' existence by forcing them to face new ideas. Still, he has no feel for the social and political context in which he is supposed to work and no quality that singles him out as anything other than an incidental presence. Outside the office, he comes across as rather anomic. This everyday story is the story of the clerk or the scribe—let us call it the "bureaucratic story." Chapter 2 may be read as an account of its historical emergence.

The other story that Taylor sees as particularly relevant for Western human beings in general concerns the deed. This is a hero story, involving exceptional individual braggadocio and/or leadership of men (and, increasingly, women). It is the story of the hero with a thousand faces, and like Taylor's other story, it is easy to spot its presence in diplomatic circles. In this context, the story is a career story where two of the thousand faces seem to be particularly relevant. First, there is the adviser, the robust, prudent and seemingly indefatigable analytical force who can muster a wide-ranging and high-powered network that guarantees access to as many sources of information and high-placed decision makers as possible. In Norwegian as well as in English, serving diplomats are often referred to as "career diplomats," ostensibly to underline that this is their full-time occupation, but also to underline the importance of this story. Advisers aim to be as close to the action as possible, which means that they thrive in secretariats and tend to complement their strictly diplomatic work with political work that extends their interface with politicians. Indeed, the full-grown face of a diplomatic adviser is the face of a politician; since the position of state secretary of the Foreign Ministry was established in 1947 (Stoltenberg 1983: 64), most individuals holding that position have been career diplomats, as have been three of Norway's foreign ministers.

If the face of the hero "at home" (*hjemme,* that is, in the ministry's Oslo buildings in Victoria terrasse) is that of the adviser, the face of the hero abroad (*ute*) is that of the field diplomat. The deed may be to found a new station in conditions of particular hardship, to undertake a particularly arduous fact-finding mission, or to mastermind and stage a political *fait accompli* such as a conference against the opposition of rival diplomats.[1]

Chapter 3 of this book described discursive preconditions for today's practices, and as an example of such preconditions, discussion of the life of the eighteenth-century scribe by the Danish historian Ole Feldbæk (2000: 331) is once again relevant:

> The administration's everyday life was characterized by their standard working routines. They had been deposited layer by layer through generations, and it was usually only the younger secretaries who had had to consult the office's Book of Wisdom in order to find out what was to be done in the case at hand. The older secretaries had had the procedures and the decisions

---

1. See Constantinou 1996. The diplomatic career is a variant on a theme of seminomadic rotation in the context of a sedentary society. As noted in the introduction, there are first two years at home and then two postings abroad. If you are considered good, you will be a head of section in your early forties, then something like number two at a large embassy, then deputy head of department and head of department, then an ambassador at a cream-puff station or two, and perhaps even permanent under secretary (the top bureaucratic job). If you do nothing wrong, your career peaks when you are somewhere around sixty, as Norwegian ambassador to Costa Rica or a variant thereof. Since there are many fewer top jobs at home than abroad, the end usually comes in the form of a final stint as special adviser on the arctics or the declassification of secret documents.

in the marrow of their bones for donkey's years. They had learned that old laws were good laws, and that uniformity and predictability were the very foundations of the management of the absolute state.

Routinization lives on. "My first ambassador always said that the best case work (*saksbehandling*) is to go to the dossiers," one head of department reminisced during a seminar. And indeed, when I was assigned my first task at Norway's Moscow embassy and asked a secretary for advice about how to go about it, her response was "you should look in the dossiers."[2] When Norwegian newspapers comment on diplomatic work, which they do at regular intervals, they invariably follow two variants of the hero story. The root metaphor of variant one is the pinstripe suit (with the champagne glass as an accoutrement), and of variant two is casual attire (the point being that the diplomat does *not* wear his usual pinstripe). The leading Norwegian newspaper *Aftenposten* runs regular anniversary interviews with successful career diplomats when they make it to sixty (and, in some cases, fifty), and the angle is always biographical, recounting their postings, with the journalist making comments about dapper suits and immaculate eating habits. I once heard a diplomat torpedoed in a political meeting by another participant who wanted to get across that he had not really grasped the issue at hand. He did it by charging that "he seemed to have a firm grasp of his champagne glass." However, the champagne glass plays a role not only in how others present diplomatic identity (what psychologists call alter-casting) but also in the presentation of self in everyday diplomatic life. Before I took up work with the ministry, I once arrived

---

2. In Norwegian, the advice "du får se etter på doss" is ambiguous; it may also mean "You will have to look in the loo." Since I misunderstood the utterance at the time, this story became a stock in trade of my self-presentation in diplomatic circles. Furthermore, since such memories cannot be trusted, I checked this story with the secretary in question as I was writing this text. She told me that when asked, she always told people to look in the dossiers. Small wonder, since modern bureaucracies are constituted amongst other things by their ability to build and run archives (Dery 1998). Actually, when precedents are not to be found in the dossiers, it is worthy of note, as when a speaker celebrating the MFA's seventy-fifth anniversary announced that, when he started work on his speech he went "twenty-five years back in time, to our fiftieth anniversary which was celebrated in the Aula [of Oslo University] and with a gala dinner at Akershus Castle, in order to gather material for today's celebration. However, no word about what was said then was to be found in the dossiers." NNA MFA 2 1/51, "Beretning om Udenrigets Stilstand tillige markeringen av den Ytre Etats 75-aars Jubileum" 151180 (initialed BP).

at a drinks reception that was slated to begin immediately after a conference, only to find that two diplomats had beaten me to the bar. "So," I said,
"you're already here." "Yes," one of them responded, smiling and raising
his champagne glass to his lips, "you know, we're the ones who know how
to do this!"

Conversely, when in December 2001 Norwegian newspapers covered
the exploratory mission to set up a Norwegian representation in Kabul,
much was made of how the key diplomat had considerable previous experience from a number of rough spots, and how his attire did not give him
away as a diplomat. When the mission was set up in the same building that
harbored the NGO Norwegian Church Aid, photos typically showed the
diplomat at work in everyday clothes, in unornamented rooms (for example, *Verdens gang,* 10 January 2001). In the autumn of 2002, *Aftenposten*
ran a story on how the diplomatic academy had introduced a new course in
leadership; the angle was that the training included challenges that could
not be tackled in a pinstripe suit.[3]

Diplomats still wear dark suits on a regular basis, though—in many
states, they still wear nothing but—and recruits are still fairly homogeneous in a number of respects. For reasons that have to do primarily with
changing Norwegian social mores and new recruiting patterns concerning
class and gender, however, "my" diplomats were rather more sartorially
diverse. Up to a point, that is. "I see it every year," our in-house French
teacher said to me. "They come wearing jeans and even with stripes in
their hair (she nodded toward a young woman sporting a black and purple
coiffure). And then they all end up the same."[4] It should also be said, however, that "they" have some additional key characteristics. They all have
academic degrees, typically in the social sciences, the humanities, or law.
They are all multilingual, and they are all (at least supposed to be) psycho-
logically robust. They are all interested in leading a life of travel, they are
all interested in public life, and most (but not all) are interested in politics.
They have all been sifted through written tests and interviews with people
who possess various social, psychological, and diplomatic skills. They are
typically in their late twenties, the legal upper limit being thirty-five years

---

3. *Aftenposten,* 22 September 2002.
4. She was almost right. That particular woman quit the service after a few years.

of age, and they have all been exposed to work in a bureaucracy. A number of people are recruited directly into a working post, bypassing the basic-rule trajectory that includes a year of case handling, academy training, and two postings abroad. They will typically be older, and they will typically have some kind of desired skill, as I did. Note, however, that I was fairly typical in that I had a wide academic training (in political science and Russian), that I had brushed shoulders with diplomats for years, and that I had even worked in an embassy (albeit at the tender age of nineteen).

Upon entering the service, this fairly homogeneous group of people is exposed to a diplomatic discourse that offers various stories of how to be a diplomat. These stories, and the practices that make them up, may be meaningfully read through the lenses of Taylor's general stories for the Western self. Taylor stresses that the two stories of the spectacular hero and the everyday hero are at loggerheads: in numerous contexts it may not be clear which story one should adhere to. Moreover, if a particular individual aims to make one of the two stories the grand narrative of her life, then it will necessarily be at the cost of the other. Both tensions run through diplomatic life. I begin with the second story.[5]

Overfulfillment of Stories

The ministry secretaries tend to know rather more about their bosses than the other way around. I once had dinner with a retired diplomat who had for three years worked with a secretary who was then arrested and given a steep sentence for spying for the Soviets. The matter was a *cause célèbre* at the time, and it is still important enough to be known to Scandinavians and Brits working in the field of intelligence. Although this was almost thirty years ago at the time, Harold was still besotted by the story, the key point of which was that he had really liked the woman and had not had the least inkling that she could have been a spy. When I started to ask him about her private life, however, it turned out that he did not know very much about her, except for her tastes in books and clothes. The relationship between

---

5. I will only incidentally focus on how a feel for these two scripts impinges on individual career planning, however. Suffice it to say that the key risk of the hero script is drawing too much attention from colleagues and politicians, and of the bureaucratic script, too little.

bosses and their secretaries has changed since then, but it is my impression that, even allowing for the obvious fact that a secretary spy is likely to be rather more reticent than her colleagues, and that MFA bosses may be better informed now than they were then, secretaries still know more about their bosses than vice versa. But I need not press that point. The only thing that must be granted for my argument to hold is that secretaries are more prone to talk about the private lives of their bosses than the other way around. I had secretaries telling me no end of stories, and the ones that were delivered with the greatest panache tended to revolve around diplomats who had made the hero story their lodestar. "Did you hear about X," one told me, "while he was away, his daughter took up with some no-good guys, and next week she's a key defendant in a drug case." X was a diplomat who had also been a politician, and who was known as a bit of a pompous ass. "Well Y came home from his posting and said to his family 'pack up! we're going to London'," Trine, a secretary in her late fifties, told me, "and they said no, you could have told us first, and then they refused to go. Guess he didn't watch his back, ha ha."

Secretaries were not, however, the only ones to come up with these stories "That [same] Y," a colleague told me during a tram ride home to the part of town where both she and I lived, "he went over my head once. He would stop at nothing (*gå over lik,* literally to step over corpses) if it would help his career." "Did you hear that Z had a heart attack?" I was asked by another colleague upon returning from my summer vacation. "And when he came to, the first thing he had said was that no one at the MFA must know." "Why so?" I asked her. "So that it wouldn't get in the way of his career" came the answer. In the ministry, I had frequently heard Z, who was always close to the political scene, referred to as "the climber." But the story that really drove home to me when one had crossed the fine line that makes you appear an overachiever in the eyes of your colleagues concerned a man who had word that he had been promoted. For senior personnel, promotions have to be confirmed by the king, which in practice means that they are read out at Friday cabinet meetings and then made public. The expression for this is *å gå i statsråd*—to be handled by (and presumably pass muster in) the cabinet—and it is used in such a way that your suggested promotion and you as a person are seen as interchangeable entities, as in "When will you be handled by the cabinet?" "I hear you were handled by the cabinet on Friday, congratulations." The verb used here literally means "to walk" or "to go to," so to the uninitiated, the seemingly perfectly clear meaning of these expressions is that the person has actually been to the cabinet meeting in the flesh. Not so—but his career has. Now, such announcements are made when the cabinet sitting is over and in this particular case, this happened relatively late in the afternoon. This being a Friday, most people had already left, but the one who was being "handled by the cabinet" was still at his post, sitting in his office behind his door, waiting for the verdict. This was in the early 1990s, when beside each door there was still a little rectangular glass case, inside which there was a wavy pillow of fake velvet to which were attached little white plastic digits giving your room number and little white plastic letters giving your name and your rank. When this man finally had word that he had passed Cabinet and been promoted, he immediately went on a scavenging rampage in the corridor, stealing letters here and there so as to be able to give his own little glass case the appropriate update. When his colleagues arrived on Monday morning, there was no need to ask if he had passed the cabinet—his new rank was already proudly announced beside his door. Of course, the operation had involved a bit of trespassing on other people's plastic self-presentations, so the story immediately made the rounds. I had it recounted to me on two different occasions, by two different people, and alluded to another time.

Not surprisingly, stories about people overfulfilling the career story tend to be told by others, usually their underlings. Stories about people overfulfilling the bureaucracy story are rarer. A lot of more or less sad stories tell about people who have basically gone to sleep on the job and, true to outside stereotype, dipsomania is frequently involved. For example, when ambassadors who were not considered high flyers come home, they might not be assigned a new position immediately. Rather, they were given the status *til disposisjon*—literally at (your) service—meaning that they were there to lend a hand while between specific jobs. Until recently, the fifth-floor corridor where these people had their offices was known as the drying loft (though what was being dried was diplomat dipsos rather than linen).

These cases are not ones of overfulfilling a specific story, however, but rather of losing your grip on all the stories that are available. A better example of reflection about overfulfillment of the bureaucratic story emerged over lunch one day, when Birger was reminiscing about his previous post: "When I was legal adviser, my Finnish colleague and I used to refer to one another as *Pilkunnussija,* comma-fucker." "Well," I said, "I suppose those exist in all MFAs." "Indeed," responded a third party, "that *is* the job." Some months later, this third party told me that he had just returned from a course in leadership. "I now know that I am not a comma-fucker," he said with a beam of relief; "I'm a semicolon-fucker."

Clash of Stories

If either of these stories may be said to be uppermost in the life of a specific diplomat, either by her colleagues or by herself, it is perhaps more instructive to examine how they clash in specific and varying contexts. Two particular types of context change may cause a switch in which story is seen as relevant. Diplomats refer to them as *hjemme/jobb*—that is "home" and "work," and *hjemme/ute*—"home" and "abroad." Two different but connected "homes" are at play here; the home as against the job is the private home (as in "home and hearth"), whereas "home" as against "abroad" means the national home (as in "my home country").[6]

The tension between home and job assumes forms that will be familiar from a whole gamut of studies of Western everyday life. In a department seminar, a head of section by the name of Gunnar took the floor during a discussion of ministry life and charged that, as a midlevel leader, he was stuck between a rock and a hard place. Above him were elderly men who no longer had small children; below him were desk officers with little kids to look after. The leadership could not acknowledge that his underlings were family people, he charged, for "if this had been understood, I would not have received new tasks at 3.45 p.m., for example. Small wonder that day after day, people who do an excellent job still have to go home with a feeling that they are not really up to covering all their bases."

The choice of 3.45 p.m. gives a clue to the earliest accepted time to leave on a daily basis, namely around 4 p.m. Like the other ministries, the Foreign Ministry has a punch clock (electronic then, digital now) where all employees have to register in the morning and the afternoon. This kind of surveillance, once typical of industrial society, now seems to survive mainly

---

6. For a study of the nation as an extended family and a new home for uprooted peasants living in the city, or indeed in the trenches, see Weber 1977.

in the few factories that are left and in bureaucratic organizations. At the beginning of every month, the electronic system presented each employee with a full yellow-colored printout of his or her comings and goings. Crucially, in addition to measuring total working time and holidays, surveillance is trained on whether you have or have not been present from 9 a.m. to 3 p.m., when presence is mandatory (the period is known as *kjernetid,* core hours). The time that you have not been present during core hours is prominently displayed and has to be made up. Gunnar's point was that, given this system, employees should reasonably expect to be able to leave with a clean conscience around 4 p.m. if they so desired. As we saw in the previous chapter, in the interwar years diplomats often returned to the ministry after eating supper at home. Changing spousal and familial responsibilities now make for intense cross-pressure on diplomats with a family. On Gunnar's account of the actual working routine, it may now formally be possible to leave—but informally a number of people could not do so with a clear conscience.

The head of department did not miss a beat. He shot right back that "My day is spent in meetings, and when I come back to my office, half the day is gone. . . . Every day is a landslide of tasks, and I spend it digging myself out of it all. And when I get back to my office, it is often 3:45 p.m., Gunnar. . . . The leadership role has changed, but the leadership responsibility has not."

Until some thirty years ago, colleagues told me, the ministry norm was that you stayed in your office until the boss went home (and in the interwar period you were frequently recalled). This norm survives in pockets of the ministry. Another head of department, a man in his late fifties who lived alone, once told me over dinner that "I keep my door open and expect people to pop their heads in and say goodbye before they leave, and there is no *rush* of people before around 6.30"—and then he laughed heartily. The exigencies of the bureaucratic story are not equally tough in every department, and there has been an upgrade of the home sphere. As of recently, female trainees may leave their academy cohort and join the next one after a spell of maternity leave. In the late 1980s, young male diplomats fought a brief but victorious campaign, against older males who outranked them, for informal confirmation of their formal right to take a month of paternity leave. The bureaucratic story may be less prominent now, and may be relevant in fewer specific contexts than before. Still, the basic contradiction lingers on. "There are other things that a man may do," Lars responded when I sympathized with how he had been slotted into an office that was really a walk-through to an archive and that indicated a sidelining of his career, "like spending time with his kids."

There is probably nothing uniquely diplomatic about any of these examples, but the tension between home life and job life has specific expressions. On my way to work one morning, I had just ordered the usual at my local café when my colleague Ludvig walked in. I had met him and his Balkan wife at a party some months before, and we had discussed the situation in the Balkans, where President Milošević had just launched yet another campaign in Kosovo. We chatted amiably, and he mentioned offhandedly that he was now in charge of the Balkan portfolio at the prime minister's office. Since job rotation is one of the key talking points in the ministry, I happened to know this already. I smiled and said that, given his situation, I was not quite certain whether that was such a good idea. He immediately rounded on me and asked in a rather imperious tone of voice what I meant by that? Well, I said, given that you are married to a national from one of the warring parties, I take it that you will be predisposed to see this conflict from that perspective. At this he raised his index finger and wagged it in my face and said, emphasizing every word. "That's not it at all. I make it a point of honor to be neutral. If I am not, I am finished (*Sånn er det ikke, altså. Jeg setter min ære i å være nøytral. Er jeg ikke det, er jeg ferdig*)." I mentioned Ludvig's reaction to a mutual colleague, who told me that Ludvig had reacted in the same way when he had made a similar point. There is no surprise that people react strongly when confronted with structural quotidian dilemmas. For example, Hugh Gusterson (1996) reports incidents from his fieldwork among weapons physicists at the Livermore laboratories. However, diplomats are famously indirect in their manner of communicating, and I cannot remember ever having interacted with one in this manner either before or after. That in itself demonstrates that, to Ludvig, the tension between his job responsibilities and his home life were tangible, and that he was very much alive to the possible repercussions of that tension. For these reasons, it is all the more interesting that his reaction to the tension was to deny its existence altogether. To Ludvig, managing the self in this case implied compartmentalizing how to behave at home and how to behave on the job in a decisive manner, and forcing that compartmentalization onto any skeptical interlocutors.

If tension between life at home and life on the job is not typical of diplomacy, tension between life at home and life abroad certainly is. There do, however, exist similarities between the two types of tension. At one point, my friend Miro had been appointed to a job in a particularly difficult situation abroad, where no school could cater to the varied needs of his five children. Miro was going nonetheless, opting to let his wife Petra stay behind and take care of the kids. I mentioned this to a mutual friend in the service, a man in his fifties, who told me in no uncertain terms that "I think Petra will do just fine, Iver, just fine" (*jeg tror Petra vil greie seg* helt *fint jeg, Iver*). The message was clear: this was how things were, and it was none of my business to worry about it. A man is a man, and a job is a job. If the two do not go together, it is nobody's business but his own (more on this in the following chapter).

Similarly, and this was one of the few times when I felt that one of my interlocutors made a real effort not to let his temper flare, at one point I met the Norwegian consul general to Murmansk, the Russian border town close to Norway. The general perception in the ministry was that life in Murmansk revolved around working during the day and drinking during the night. As we walked down the corridors, a mutual friend by the name of Finn greeted him and remarked to me, in a stage whisper, "he comes home every month for his detox (*avrusning*)" I could see that the taunt had its effect, but he shot right back: "did you say delousing or detoxing?" (*sa du avrusning eller avlusning?*). We trudged on together, and in an attempt to be sympathetic, I commented to the effect that his must be a lonely existence. "We are twenty people up there," he retorted. "Yes," said Finn, "but the work of the other nineteen is to prolong visas." The conversation had now definitely deteriorated. Finn took off, and the two of us continued on our way to lunch. In another attempt at sympathy, I remarked: "I'm impressed by the work that is done up there, I bet it's tough going." This seemed to aggravate him further: "There are so many misunderstandings about Murmansk. The tasks are very interesting indeed (*arbeidsoppgavene er kjempeinteresssante*)."[7] "Yes," I said, "but there are no schools and all

---

7. A year later, I found myself at lunch with the same man and a group of apprentice diplomats. In order to find out exactly what he held to be so interesting about Murmansk, I steered the conversation in that direction. He immediately repeated that it had been the most interesting of his three postings. "Why so," one aspiring diplomat asked. "You're alone up there?" "You aren't

that?" "That's exactly it. You can't be there with a family, that's true, but if you can separate your private life from your professional one, it's excellent. That is of course an artificial divide, but then again, it's only two years . . ." (*Men kan du dele mellom privatliv og jobb, er det flott. Det er selvfølgelig kunstig. Men for to år . . .*). We split up in order to join our respective lunch dates (lunch in the MFA canteen being the key networking event of the day), and the conversation turned to a colleague who had taken up a house loan that threatened to become too great. "Well, then he'll have to make the trip to Murmansk for a few years," one of my interlocutors remarked. Being consul general in Murmansk is the best-paid job in the Norwegian civil service. To find staff who are willing to work on this station, where the diplomat has to be away from her home country as well as from home and hearth, the Norwegian state offers substantial material compensation. Here the bureaucratic story deconstructs itself, for the suggestion that you go to Murmansk to provide materially for your family suggests that, in order to fulfill your everyday responsibility at home, you have to be away from that home, and so you cannot fulfill another part of the story, which is simply *being at home.*

This is an oft-observed paradox in the literature on the family and the workplace (for one key text, written by an author who grew up among diplomats, see Hochschild 1983), and so I will not pursue it further. Rather, I pursue the job/home split as a way into a question more specifically about how to be a diplomat, namely how this split is imbricated with the question of the relative weight of the two stories. Diplomats are highly reflective about this clash of stories (although of course not in the analytical terms used here). Since the mid-1990s, a Norwegian diplomat has been attached to the Norwegian mission to the country that holds the chairmanship of the EU. Since the chair rotates every six months, this job is particularly nomadic even for a diplomat. One result is that one ends up living in hotels even more often and for even longer periods than the average diplomat. When one of my superiors, Klara, held the job in Lisbon during the Portuguese presidency, she ended up in a hotel for the entire stay; her husband

---

going abroad to meet other diplomats, are you? Since you're alone, it means you have easier access to people in the local administration. . . . And one more thing: you have good rapport with the local officials on the Norwegian side." The opportunities for mediation are therefore ample, direct and, as it were, unmediated.

and fellow diplomat Gustav stayed behind in Oslo. She once told me over lunch, clearly displeased with herself, "I came home and I said to Gustav, 'Why haven't the bathroom towels been changed?'" Where Ludvig insisted on the possibility of keeping home away from work and the consulate general tried to celebrate the importance of work abroad even when it took him away from home, Klara conceded that she had caught herself trespassing by taking work (in the sense of the attitude of the workplace) home. What is at issue here is not the easy deconstruction of these boundaries, however, but the fact that admitting that they exist and need to be upheld make for tensions that structure the life of a diplomat.

Klara's reflections on her homecoming from Lisbon do not only exemplify the tension between home and work, they also throw light on the other tension between the bureaucratic and the hero stories mentioned earlier. This tension, it turned out, was also imbricated with the home/abroad dichotomy. To return to an episode noted in chapter 1, a little more than a year after Klara told me of her homecoming, I was having lunch with her and two other colleagues when the subject of Kaliningrad came up. I mentioned a research colleague who had followed the situation there for six years, and suggested that we invite him for lunch to get an informal briefing. When Klara hesitated, I remarked that it was a paradox to me that diplomats were always on the lookout for information and contacts when abroad, indeed that they actually saw it as a key part of the job to network and swap information, but that at home they seemed allergic to external contact. She answered that diplomats have a much freer position abroad, and that there is a bureaucracy shock when you come home.

Unwilling Bureaucrats

This generalization reproduces a general theme in research on stories of everyday life in other "Western" locations, namely that there is a hierarchy of stories in which the hero story is dominant and the bureaucracy story subordinate. This is relevant to the business at hand for at least two reasons. First, diplomats acknowledge that aspects of their work are bureaucratic and accept the factual correctness of being termed bureaucrats. Norwegian desk officers are referred to, formally and informally, as *saksbehandlere,* and this is also a term of self-description. Furthermore, tasks carried out by senior civil servants are also named by the term that refers to what a *saksbehandler* does, namely *saksbehandling,* "handling of cases." When the head of department canceled a meeting with our section without giving a specific reason, the head of section announced that "he won't come, supposedly he had to handle (*saksbehandle*) something." When the deputy head said that in fact he had to put snow tires on his car, the head's response was "handle the car's case, ha ha" (*saksbehandle bilen, he he*). When I started my second stint in the MFA and met my first boss again, one of his first questions was whether I had been able to get away from handling cases ("*du slipper vel saksbehandling?*"). A *saksbehandler* is definitely a bureaucrat. This term is used not only in other ministries but also of executive officers in other bureaucratic organizations such as social aid offices and regulatory bodies. In a Norwegian setting, Herzfeld's (1992) study of Greek bureaucrats would first and foremost be relevant to the study of the subset of bureaucrats known as *saksbehandlere.* Yet whereas *saksbehandler* is a ubiquitous term among diplomats, I never heard the terms *byråkrat* (bureaucrat) and *byråkrati* (bureaucracy) used as positive and nonironic self-referencing terms, even though both are everyday Norwegian terms. They are used frequently, but always in ways that imply distance.

Two examples. The first formal task for those who have been accepted into the diplomatic academy is to entertain at the ministry's annual Christmas Party. This is done through a team-building exercise: staging a variety show. If a sketch is of extraordinary quality, it may make it into the house magazine, which is distributed to all employees four times a year. In issue no. 1 for the year 2000, one may read an example:

The Promotion Phone Line

Sketch from the variety show 1999
   Author: Torunn Viste
   Setting: A gray bureaucrat is sitting at his desk amidst huge piles of documents and a telephone. He looks desolate.
   (*Ringing tone. The answering machine is activated.*)
   "You have reached the Department of Administration's promotion phone line. All lines are busy. Please hold."
   (*Beep*)
   "We are sorry that you will have to wait, but all lines are still busy . . ."

"To hear the foreign minister's brief in anticipation of the WTO summit in Seattle, press 1.

"For a pep talk from the secretary general of the MFA, press 2.

"For the minister of development's favorite speeches, press 3."

"For a reading of the Directive for Norwegian Foreign Service Employees by [well-known Norwegian actor] Kyrre Haugen Bakke, press 4. . . ."

(Hold music—Beethoven's Fifth [in Norwegian, the "Fate Symphony," *Skjebnesymfonien*]

"We apologize that you will have to wait. You are not moving ahead . . ."

(*Beep*)

"In order to move ahead in the queue, you may choose from the following vacant positions:

"For chancellor in Bogotá, press 1.

"For embassy secretary in Bujumbura, press 2.

"For minister in Ulan Bator, press 3."

(*Beep*)

"We would like to remind you that if you hang up, you will move down three salary brackets."

(*Busy signal*)

"We would like to remind you that the price of this call is one hour's salary per minute. The amount owed will be deducted from . . ." (*Finally a ringing tone breaks in, there is a sign of optimism in the bureaucrat's face*)

(*The answering machine is activated*)

"This is the Department of Administration. Our office hours are from 12.30 p.m. to 1 p.m. Please call back tomorrow."

(*The call is disconnected. Long dial tone*).

A second example. During banter at a weekly section meeting, the recurring question of how to guide a case through "the system" (*systemet,* that is, the MFA understood as a formal, line-based, hierarchical organization) came up.[8] "What is the rule in this case?" I asked. "Let's just take it straight to the political leadership, that's the easiest way to do it," said Wanda, who had good political connections and always tried to get a piece of the action.

---

8. Being a Teutonic country whose philosophical tradition closely followed Germany's up to, and partially even beyond, the 1940–45 occupation by Nazi Germany, German influences include a degree of domesticated Hegelianism, cf. Boyer 2005. One may speculate that trust in the system runs deeper than to mere politics, down to the ontic level. I note this here because approaches to systems in the more Lockean-oriented Anglo-American world seem rather different.

The chair immediately exclaimed "No, no!" "At least in practice," Wanda offered. "No, as many levels as possible," the chair said wryly, and a third colleague immediately added "Standard bureaucratic fashion." Indeed, referring to the MFA as "the system" already invites this kind of response, for it is seen as a vaguely negatively loaded term, to be distinguished from, for example, the frequently used term "in-house" (*her i huset* and *her på huset*), or "home" (*hjemme*). Heroic pitching of memos and ideas outside "the line" (that is, by bypassing parts of the formal chain of command) is to be kept to a minimum in favor of what is acknowledged as a bureaucratic story—but identification with this story is nonetheless kept at bay.

In keeping their distance from the terms "bureaucrat" and "bureaucracy," diplomats differ from, for example, employees in the Norwegian Ministry of Defence (MoD). During my stay in that ministry, I once approached the head of a section other than my own about the issue of money. The two sections, which were in different departments, had a vague history of enmity that seemed to be largely due to the fact that the other section had its hands on the purse strings in cases where "my" section had professional responsibility. I presented my request, and the man with the money asked to see the paper that empowered me to make it. When I did not produce a paper and simply referred to a conversation with the political leadership, he lost his temper and burst out: "No paper? What's that? We're bureaucrats, don't you forget!" The loss of temper, his appearance (tousled hair, shirt trailing over his trousers, tie askew), and his message all contrasted sharply with norms in the Ministry of Foreign Affairs. The internalization of the Weberian ideal type of what a bureaucrat should be, on display here, may serve as a reminder that although diplomats as civil servants are keenly aware that a subject position as bureaucrat is held out for them to fill and that they may be seen as actually filling it, they nonetheless keep their distance by refusing to adopt it as a self-description. Identification with "the system," understood as state bureaucracy, is simply weaker in the MFA.

Another incident concerns internal control. New Public Management is a rationality of government increasingly used for running states since the 1980s that uses cost-effective practices borrowed from private companies in order to benchmark bureaucratic output, as well as other ploys to heighten the level of governmentality throughout the public sector (Neumann and Sending 2010). In keeping with its principles, there is ever-increasing pressure on each and every public servant to report on his or her activities. This self-administration has come to take up a sizable part of the working day, on average perhaps 20 percent. Detailed sets of recommendations for a whole gamut of working operations have to be followed, and controllers check that self-supervision is conducted according to these recommendations. For example, tea and coffee, mineral water and food, may be provided only

a. At meetings and conferences where representatives of other public or private institutions participate.
b. At steering, council, board, and similar meetings where persons other than internals participate.
c. At the end of committee work that has had a long duration (Utenriks-departementet 2002: 40).

If you decide to go ahead and serve something, you have to fill in a special form beforehand and have it stamped by the department leadership. Then you have to order the food and check that the order has been registered. After the meeting, you have to write up a report on who actually participated. I went through with this in the MoD once, and complained bitterly about the amount of time it all took (all in all, about half a working day), only to be told that this was how things were, and how things should be. After this experience, I made it one of my goals never to administer food and drink inside a ministry again. This ambition was thwarted at the end of my second stay in the MFA, however. Sure enough, six weeks after my submission of a report on what was served, the report was returned to my section from Internal Control (*Regnskapsenheten*) with the note: "To be explained per refreshment expenditures schedule, see MFA management plan page 41." It turned out that "For meetings within regular working hours where it seems natural to serve food and drink," the tariff was NOK 65 per person, and I had spent somewhat more. My head of section wanted me to write a new memo, apologizing, so I did, offering to pay the trifling sum in question (NOK 600) out of pocket. This offer was summarily dismissed; I had to apologize and promise to be good from now on (*love bot og bedring*). So, gritting my teeth and reminding myself that I could not quit in the middle of fieldwork, I apologized. Between the three of us and the section's secretary, we spent some four or five hours on the operation.

The interesting thing, though, was that the head of section and my other colleagues, as well as casual MFA interlocutors to whom I wryly slipped the story, were feigning pious solemnty about the incident. Whereas in the MoD these matters were treated as serious by all concerned, the only one who seemed to take it seriously in the MFA was the person in Internal Control. Such typical bureaucratic chores were seen to with expert skill, but they were never talked about, rather they seemed to be tolerated as a necessary evil, never as constitutive of the diplomat's work.

Comparison with the MoD may be instructive more generally. In the MoD, the implicit baseline for lunch debates about general policy questions was that once the ministry had taken an official stance, loyalty demanded that this stance was binding on each individual employee. This was internalized, so there was also an expectation that questions of the type "don't you agree that . . . ?" should be answered in the affirmative. In the MFA, similarly, the expectation was that a dissenting point of view should not be explicitly brought up, but it nonetheless often emerged in conversation (albeit in characteristically understated terms). Furthermore, I never heard anybody demanding an active cheer for a specific policy, as I frequently did in the MoD.

Why this unwillingness to be counted as bureaucrats? Handelman and Leyton (1978: 12) ask a related question:

> To borrow from a concern of Victor Turner's, what are the "root metaphors" of bureaucracy in a particular society? We would suggest, as a working hypothesis, that in modern industrialized societies the bureaucrat is a prime symbol of "structure" of order, as against societal symbols of "communitas," or symbols that can be infused with communitas. . . . in comparison with other archetypal figures who have contact with the public (for example, the politician, the mass media personage, the religious personage), the bureaucrat is the least likely to have access to symbols of communitas, and hence, is the least likely to have opportunities to manipulate such symbols.

In the introduction to this book, I suggested that the champagne glass is the root metaphor of the diplomat. Drinking champagne—an eminent social solvent—is one way of gaining rapport, and a rather festive one at that. We are definitely in the realm of community here. Since at the global level order and society are less clearly organized and so less clearly separated than at less aggregated levels, it stands to reason that both functions need to be taken care of. Bureaucrats are, by definition, restrained by the order of which they are constitutive. If diplomats are only bureaucrats, they simply cannot participate in the continuing and precarious manifestations of *communitas* which are a precondition for structure to emerge. The reason for the diplomat's unwillingness to fulfill the bureaucratic story therefore transcends obvious questions about status and desire. There are also structural reasons to be taken into account.

Negotiation

He who seeketh shall find. I began this chapter by culling two scripted or storied selves from Taylor, and of course I found these two stories in the self-presentations of Norwegian diplomats. But something is missing. Little in what I have written so far is specific to diplomacy understood as a *practice*. What happens if, instead of investigating how stories of selves extracted from a broad "Western" discourse appear in the discourse of diplomacy, one begins by asking how diplomats present what they do? More specifically, one may ask how the presentation of self looks by seeking specific instances when diplomats present what they themselves think are the practices that form the key to or even the core of diplomacy.[9]

The one time I felt something that began to approach intimacy with one of my MFA bosses occurred at the end of an exhausting day of planning the department's work schedule for the upcoming year. We were tucked away in a lovely retreat at the edge of town and had just finished a rather good three-course meal. Some of the other participants had drifted off, and the three of us at our table were deep into our generous French brandies. The third person mentioned a meeting he had just attended, on development aid. "Mmm," the boss ruminated, and proceeded to recall how he had scuttled between his in-house job in Oslo and a particularly intricate and long-lasting UNCTAD negotiating game in Geneva concerning the afterglow of the New Economic World Order in the 1970s. "Those were the days. We negotiated around the clock, for months and months. I

---

9. I do not suggest that I am performing a shift here from etic to emic presentations of diplomatic selves, for as I have demonstrated above, diplomats are reflective about the bureaucratic and hero scripts.

remember we once kept a bracket for hours, way into the night (*En gang holdt vi en parentes til langt ut på natta*)." ("Keeping a bracket" means to stick to a negotiation point that has been separated from the draft text, and so is in danger of being sacrificed on the altar of consensus.) There was a pause, and then he looked up from his snifter and added that, of course, being away so much had cost him his marriage.

What stands out here is the clash of the everyday story of the home-bound good husband and the hero story of the nomadic diplomat. In terms of practices, however, what stands out is that the happy memory is encapsulated in "keeping a bracket." In negotiations, particularly in multilateral negotiations, it is common for the outcome to take the textual shape of a final communiqué. Following initial rounds, where positions are taken up, alliances formed, and tactics employed, one arrives at a stage when drafts are presented. Eventually, these drafts will be melded together, with the more or less explicit goal of a document that everybody will sign. Inevitably, there will be divergences over what to exclude and what to include, how points included should be formulated, how strongly they should be presented and in what order, how binding they should appear to be, and so on. If initial negotiations over these textual points do not result in immediate consensus, points may be literally bracketed, for example in the sense that a roundabout formulation will be agreed upon, and a more specific reading will be put in brackets (for an extended discussion, see Riles 2006). This is a dangerous moment for the side being bracketed, for everybody knows that there will be no end document if the bracketed issues are not settled, and the expectation all around will be that the final settlement will involve doing away with the brackets. There is no guarantee that any part of what has been bracketed will actually survive into the finished text. "To keep a bracket," then, means that you are holding out for what is (at least for the time being) a minority position. Inevitably, you will be pressured to capitulate, which implies that you will (again at least temporarily) be in the thick of things. "To keep a bracket" is to be in the thick of the practice of negotiation. The memory so dear to my boss that he put it across with uncharacteristic warmth concerned being a negotiator in full flight. And that memory was dear enough to be dear regardless of the steep personal price at which it had been acquired.

All five editions of Satow begin with the same definition: "Diplomacy is the application of intelligence and tact to the conduct of official relations between the governments of independent states, extending sometimes also to their relations with vassal states" (Satow [1917] 1979: 3).[10] Thus the authoritative handbook definition of diplomacy singles out one particular kind of negotiations—those that form part of the conduct of official relations between governments—as at the heart of diplomacy. This definition may be traced in the lived experience of diplomats, as when my boss looked back at what was for him a high point of his career.

To give an additional example, during an open staff meeting (*allmøte*) called by the foreign minister, Ole took the floor to plug the work of his department, describing an upcoming negotiation sequence as follows: "Those tasks are always the most interesting ones in the Royal Norwegian Ministry of Foreign Affairs when you are at home, and this is something that we really know how to do. We excel at it. . . . We will negotiate it tactically, [think about] how to time it correctly, how to pull off a linkage deal . . ."

My boss and Ole both celebrated negotiation as a practice they had lived. However, stories about negotiation are so compelling that they also leave an imprint on people who have not yet participated in this practice, but who would like to do so. As a result, they may act not upon lived practices but upon stories they have picked up about those practices. One day when the administration was in the midst of doing final interviews with applicants, I ran into Hattie, who had just finished her interview. We chatted, and she volunteered that "The psychologist asked if I had been in any conflicts in the workplace, and I said no, but to give him something I told him about the conflict in the family. I said that it had passed quickly, though, no need for him to think I come from this trouble-ridden family. He asked me how I related to that, and I said I took up the position of mediator (*meglerrolle*)."

An interview with a psychologist whose job it is to clear or reject you for prospective diplomatic work may be seen as an act of interpolation into a diplomatic subject position. Hattie, who knew the ministry from jobs in

---

10. This is a definition which purports to be universal, but which is highly culturally specific. As chapter 2 suggested, ancient Greek diplomats were *not* tactful. The sixth edition (2009: 3) has "dependent territories" instead of vassal states, and adds, significantly, "and between governments and international organisations; or, more briefly, the conduct of business between states by peaceful means." IO membership consists of states, so the definitional state-centrism continues.

agencies that had dealings with it, responded by "giving" the psychologist who interviewed her a presentation of herself as a mediator, that is, as an active facilitator of negotiations.

One defining trait of a negotiator is that he or she is in the thick of a negotiation game, that they incorporate a position in a game. Given this structural situation two things stand out as particularly important where the question of self-management is concerned. First, what kinds of positions are available to diplomats? Second, how do diplomats mediate their performance in those positions with their overall narrative of self?

Mediation as Diplomacy

A key feature of diplomats as negotiators is that they do not experience negotiation as something they do on their own behalf. Rather, they see their role as incorporating their minister, their ministry, their government, their state.[11] This explains a luncheon conversation during which Sam, who had just organized a large meeting, said that "The MFA does not know how to negotiate price (*UD kan ikke forhandle om pris*)." "Do you mean formally, or do you mean that we really aren't up to it?" I asked. "The latter. We get a four-hundred-kroner discount at the Radisson SAS Hotel, and we use it a lot. My wife gets a group discount of 1000 kroner, even though she doesn't really use it that much." "Isn't that a bit embarrassing," I ventured, "aren't the people in this building supposed to be expert negotiators?" (*Ække dette litt pinlig, skakke folk her i huset være spesialister på forhandlinger?*) At this stage my boss said, in the understated style that I had learnt to recognize as typical of the diplomat, "We are diplomats, you know." The implication seemed to be that this kind of negotiation was not really for the diplomat. There is a tension here, however, for like any organization, the MFA has an administration for which it is a key task to run things at the lowest possible cost. Furthermore, they take pride in doing so. "I'm just back from Singapore—got the rent [for the office building] down by 25 percent," one of their number bragged over

---

11. There are a range of other possibilities here, including the ones of representing a class, an ethnic group, an NGO, or humanity as such, but for this textual moment, I do not want to keep this bracket.

lunch one day. There is a tension here between an organizational necessity to haggle on behalf of your own organization on the one hand, and on
the other the idea that diplomacy should be about negotiation on behalf
of some other entity. It may be easier for somebody who is (always temporarily) based in the administration to solve that tension by bracketing
the exigencies of diplomacy (again temporarily). In a widely quoted work,
Raymond Aron tries to consecrate the diplomat's quality of being the representative of some other entity (as he sees it, typically and exclusively of
the state) as the essence of what is often if misleadingly called international
relations, when he states that

> Inter-state relations are expressed in and by specific action, those of indi-
> viduals whom I shall call symbolic, the *diplomat* and the *soldier.* Two men,
> and only two, no longer function as individual members but as *representa-
> tives* of the collectives to which they belong: the *ambassador,* in the exercise
> of his duties, *is* the political unit in whose name he speaks; the *soldier* on the
> battlefield *is* the political unit in whose name he kills his opposite number.
> (Aron [1962] 1966: 5)

In the days when the European states system had already evolved fairly
dense communications, with ambassadors far removed from their kings
in terms of travel time, and with messengers bringing written documents
that took days or even months to arrive—roughly from 1815 to the advent
of cable-based telegraphy in the 1860s—being the king's representative
often involved a high degree of freedom, for orders were short and few,
and the scope for running consultation was nonexistent (Nickels 2003).
Ambassadors were quite literally governed from afar (see the conclusion
to this book). Perhaps the time dimension of this may be captured by using
a parallel to the cultural translation of diplomacy, namely the translation
of a text from one language to another. In this period, the diplomat was
akin to the translator of a novel. He could sit in his study poring over the
text, consulting other texts and even other translators before he made his
move and translated this sentence or that paragraph. Today, the diplomat is closer to a simultaneous translator. She travels from place to place,
each time picking up something in one language through the ear and letting it come out in another through the mouth, but with infinitely less
time to shape it, and perhaps not even catching it all due to the speed of

the transaction.[12] Like global life generally, with the introduction of new communication technologies, the temporality of diplomatic life has accelerated. These are rather different economies of knowledge. Small wonder that diplomats look back wistfully to a golden age of diplomacy.

How relevant is this observation of historical change for today's situation? Today's diplomats may be more keenly aware of direct governance weighing in on their negotiating role, for in cases where the political interest of their superiors is high, direct interaction may be very dense indeed. Furthermore, inasmuch as general communications have become denser, the diplomat has a whole range of potential competitors as the local incarnation of the foreign state that he represents. There are more journalists, businesspeople, aid workers, tourists, military advisers, students, presidential representatives, and expats around than there used to be. This does not necessarily mean that the ability of diplomats to represent states has dwindled, for the amount of stuff to negotiate has mushroomed. But it means that more work will have to be spent on marking and demonstrating the ability of diplomats in more contexts than used to be the case. A Norwegian diplomat in Argentina still "is" Norway now, but she probably is Norway in fewer contexts and maybe in a lesser degree than her predecessor on the post was ninety years ago.

The current diplomat would still very much like to be Norway, though. As I demonstrate in chapter 5, the collective self-representation of the MFA still is that of "being Norway," and ideally the individual diplomat would like to see isomorphism between Norway, the MFA, and him- or herself. Norwegian ambassadors return home every summer to attend an annual gathering of all heads of station (now 103 of them), which is held at the end of August. The idea is to facilitate homecomings, which is nice for diplomats and their families, but which also ensures that they keep in constant touch with the country they represent, with the MFA, and with their colleagues. I met my old friend Vidar, who had gone through a rough patch at his station after the MFA ordered him in the spring to invite prominent local dissidents to official embassy functions. He was particularly miffed

---

12. At a conference in Costa Rica, I once asked a simultaneous translator from Spanish to English to clarify a point for me. She smiled and said that she never remembered anything of what she translated, that it just passed through her. For an excellent fictional account, see Brooke-Rose (1975).

that when he told a European colleague (a fellow ambassador) about this, the colleague had simply advised him to wait a bit before implementing that order. "That's easy for him to say," Vidar griped, "his national day is in the autumn." It turned out that the presence of the dissidents had cast a particularly dark shadow over the celebratory reception the embassy had thrown on 17 May, Norwegian Constitution Day. The guests from the Cuban MFA had not been pleased, and there had been sundry repercussions.

To the Norwegian ambassador Norwegian Constitution Day is "my" day. Here we have a naturalized identification with the country one represents as well as an example of how an ambassador can "be" Norway and think of himself in those terms. There are moments, then, when diplomats experience "being" Norway. In one particular sphere they may be Norway on a continuing basis without expending much in the way of resources, however, and that is in negotiations. True, diplomats may sometimes, and increasingly, have to vie with bureaucrats from other ministries for the role of key state representative, but this is a fight that they routinely win. "Scrambling to your feet and opening your intervention with 'Norway thinks' is really something," my lawyer (and nondiplomat) friend Simon reported from a trip to Brussels. Again, I never heard a diplomat foreground the experience in this way, which I take to indicate that this is something diplomats hold to be a natural part of the job—or at least think *should* be a natural part of the job, and so should not be singled out for comment.

Historical comparison suggests that, of the key diplomatic functions, the function of representation may be less important than it used to be. The same is true of the function of gathering information, because here, too, an increasing number of competitors have access to an increasingly varied and fast-operating gamut of media through which they may channel the information gathered (Neumann 2008b). It stands to reason that the third textbook function, negotiation, now carries more weight in determining what it is to be a diplomat. For both inherent and comparative reasons, then, negotiation stands out as a particularly characteristic part of what diplomats see as their portfolio.

If diplomats do not stand still for their portrait, however, neither do negotiators (cf. Clifford and Marcus 1986: 10; Der Derian 1996). The meaning of what it is to negotiate also seems to be changing. For the diplomat, the mediating aspect of negotiation, in the sense of moving information from one social and geographical locus to the other, seems to be of increasing importance. Three decades ago, my boss had shuttled between Oslo and negotiation sites, always with fresh positions in his portfolio. To him, negotiation was no longer strategic, that is, a question of long-term give and take where he himself could change parameters on a running basis, but tactical, that is, variations on a theme already given. "Keeping a bracket" is, after all, not a terribly varied activity. Nor does it involve sizing up the overall picture in order to plan for efficient ways in which to go about your business. When celebrating this activity as the most interesting part of the home-based diplomat's work, Ole stressed the *tactics* of negotiation, not its strategic aspects. Hattie presented herself as a *mediator,* a third party to a negotiation, but not as a fully fledged negotiator. It is the negotiating itself, the *doing* that is seen to be of key importance, not the *planning* of the doing. "Analysis seems to be a foul word around here," said a colleague offhandedly during a telephone conversation on which terms to use for a White Paper. This particular colleague happened to hold a doctorate in anthropology, and had once been warned by the ministry administration against taking a leave of absence to teach as an assistant professor for a year or so. The two of us had discussed the lack of a conceptual approach to policy making in the ministry at an earlier juncture, and now this colleague had just been told squarely that "analysis" was not a word to appear in a ministry document. The attitude was strong enough for the Planning unit, which was supposed to be the place in the organization for strategic planning, to be unceremoniously scrapped in 1999.

This willful situating in the here and now, epitomized in the role of the mediator, is a trait of the diplomat overall. In the Norwegian case, it ties in with overall foreign policy orientation. One key debate that ran through most of the 1990s and is still alive at the time of writing concerns to what extent Norwegian diplomacy should be about incarnating state interest and to what extent about being a *fredsmegler*—a mediator or facilitator of peace.[13] A jump from the level of diplomatic self-identification, where the stress is increasingly on the mediating aspect of negotiation, to the level of the diplomatic practice of a small state with a self-image as rich and

---

13. For a presentation of Norwegian global peace and reconciliation work, see Neumann, forthcoming.

secure, where the stress is increasingly on the mediating aspects of achieving world peace, is not wholly warranted. The differences in what is being mediated make for vast differences in context, in some respects too vast for the purely structural similarities to be very instructive. Still, when the question is what it means to be a diplomat, the structural point is that the third-party role, where you are more and more immediately tied up with the mediating aspect of diplomacy, is on the rise. "How does the [diplomatic] academy agree with you"? I asked Rudy during a drive up to the north of Oslo to fetch a newly slaughtered elk that he had gotten through his cousin and that we were going to split for winter provisions. "There are a lot of simulations and all that." "How so?" "You know, you have twenty minutes to prepare this position or the other." "You mean during language training?" "Yes." Sure enough, the academy's obligatory French course even stages a two-day simulation conference on a current topic every autumn, complete with a wrap-up reception where the simulated offerings are tea and biscuits. Before the October 2002 event, the language instructor circulated a long and richly annotated *Le Monde* article about the various positions of key states. Attached was the following message:

> A l'attention des participants à la simulation (mardi, mercredi). Thème: Irak—quelle résolution adopter? Document intéressant—chacun pourra y trouver "ses" arguments. Nicole. [For participants at the simulation (Tuesday, Wednesday). Theme: Which resolution to adopt on Iraq? You should each be able to find "your" position in this interesting document. Nicole.]

Seemingly as a sideshow to language training, Rudy and the other trainees are taught to simulate positions in order to simulate diplomacy. As trained diplomats, part of their work will be to simulate the positions of the ministry and the state that they and their ministry represent, mediating between that state and some other political entity. The substantial point is that diplomacy is about easing communication by turning yourself into an optimally functioning medium between other actors. One may see this at the level of negotiation itself, but one may also see it in the extreme degree to which diplomats make themselves available. One Friday evening, a centrally based diplomat and that diplomat's partner came over for a quiet dinner. In the middle of dinner, the diplomat's cell phone rang, and it took almost half an hour before order was restored at table. It turned out that the minister had wanted some telephone numbers in order to set up a meeting. It was quite normal for the minister to interrupt after hours, and it was a matter of course that the diplomat would interrupt a private dinner in order to respond. "It is part of the job to be available twenty-four hours a day" was the only comment made. Of course, in a neoliberal economy, such a degree of readiness is getting to be a prerequisite for more and more jobs. I think, however, that the apparent ease with which diplomats accept the increased encroachment into their spare time that the advent of the (invariably active) cell phone has brought, is at least partially due to an already established habitus as a mediator.

Methodologically, the key lesson here is that, from the point of view of the feedback loop between diplomatic practices and diplomatic discourse, there emerges a story of self that is different from both the bureaucratic story and the hero story. When seen in the light of "Western" discourse in general, negotiation and negotiation skills may simply appear as variants of bureaucratic activity, or perhaps as one face of the diplomat hero. Viewed up close, it looks different—a story fastened on mediation, a mediation where the role of the diplomat is to be self-effacing. In a famous discussion of how prescribed management of self varies culturally, Clifford Geertz (1983) evokes a recently widowed Javanese man whose wife had "been his life." We are offered a description of the widower as he hosts his wife's funeral service, smiling and making formal apologies for his wife's absence. Geertz quotes him as describing how he is in turmoil internally, and how he tries to smooth the waves in order to produce calm both internally and externally. Geertz then comments that this is to the Westerner a very foreign way of going about the management of self. At the generalized cultural level on which Charles Taylor discusses the Western formation of the self, Geertz is right. Still, the self-effacing host who sets aside his personal travails in order to put his guests at ease is a stock role, so much so that this kind of behavior is a widely held ideal of corporate man. It is routinely described as "acting professionally," not only when hosting, but for "soldiering on" after or in the midst of private turmoil. In the case of diplomacy, furthermore, I believe this kind of behavior is more than a "role." "Roles," according to a much-used definition like Boudon's (1979: 40), are "the group of norms to which the holder of a role is supposed to subscribe." The key point here is that roles are context-specific. Self-effacement in the case of diplomacy transcends particular context: it is relevant in so many contexts and is internalized in such a degree that I use the more pervasive term "story" (which, I take it, is a synonym of "narrative"). More precisely, in contemporary diplomatic discourse, it is one of three stories about how to fill the subject position of diplomat.

Self-effacement and passivity exist on the reflective level. In a vain attempt to get a somewhat critical memo on the turn for the worse in Euro-Atlantic relations after 9/11 "through the system" in the autumn of 2001, I once had an exchange with my deputy head of department, who was stonewalling what I and my head of section had "handed up" (*lagt opp*) to him. "You know" he pointed out, presumably as an explanation of why he was against forwarding the memo to the political leadership, "old [Ambassador] Johansen once told me that when [sometime Norwegian Foreign Minister] John Lyng took over, he said, 'I see you have a Political Department here. Why? I am supposed to make the policy.' And he was right!"

There is a fundamental tension between diplomat and statesman here, for politicians also have their moments of wanting advice. For example, as part of a study of the relationship between the Norwegian state and society regarding the issue of land mines, I once asked former Foreign Minister Thorvald Stoltenberg what the diplomats had thought about his hiring a man from "the third sector" (that is, an NGO) to work on this issue in the ministry. His response was that "You know you're asking the wrong man. If there were any negative reactions, I would rarely hear them, and then only after a long stretch of time. I understood that there were reactions to new ways of doing things, but that was one of the reasons I had asked him to come in the first place (*det var jo blant annet derfor jeg hadde bedt ham om å komme*)."

If statesmen do not get advice from diplomats when they feel they need it, their response may be to bypass them in favor of some other adviser. Indeed, the complaint is routinely made by politicians in other countries, sometimes in a generalized form, that diplomats cannot give advice of a strategic kind, as when John F. Kennedy complained about "Foggy Bottom" that "they never have any ideas over there . . . never come up with anything new . . . the State Department is a bowl of jelly" (Schlesinger 1967: 406; cf. Sofer 2000). There is a tension here between the politician wanting the hero diplomat's advice (and the story suggests that the hero diplomat should hang around the secretariat and the party organizations eagerly offering it), and the politician wanting the self-effacing story. Furthermore, diplomats actively bandy these stories about in their relations with one another, in order to maximize their importance in the organization. In this sense, the question of what it means to be a diplomat is also imbricated with the question of what it means to be at the dominant or the subordinate end of a set of strategic relationships inside "the system." This, however, does not amount to much more than an argument that relationships inside hierarchical organizations are themselves hierarchical—a trivial finding that takes us no nearer to answering the question of what it is to be a diplomat. Let us return to the level of self-descriptions.

Harold Nicolson ([1939] 1963: 117) makes a similar point when he writes that "the impassivity which characterizes the ideal diplomatist must render him much disliked by his friends." Alternatively, "You may only have one stone to throw," said my colleague Miro, "and what you do is you try to make damn sure that you throw it so that it will make a maximum of difference." And warming to the same theme in a later conversation: "I don't think the public realizes just how cynical we are. . . . If two governments seem to be on a reasonably good footing, then the best thing to do is to let them get on with it." "Let those who have a god take care of worrying about what we do," an elderly and respected colleague commented when our polite conversation turned to what was to him the subordinate role of analysis in diplomatic work as opposed to the need to know the specific context and the specific state of play on a specific question. It seems that the trick to being a diplomat is not to worry too much about what will come, and not to think too much about the consequences of your actions, but to concentrate on the here and now, on keeping the wheels turning and to intervene if and only if they seem to be slowing down. This may be summed up as *festina lente*—"make haste slowly." The key issue in debates within the ministry, however, is whether and to what extent one should be reactive as opposed to proactive. The paradoxical, and indeed seemingly impossible, self-description that usually surfaces at the conclusion of such debates is that one should be *aktivt avventende*—literally "actively awaiting." Summing up meetings, the chair will often say of some process outside of the ministry's grasp that it will have to be actively awaited. "You'll have to be actively awaiting" I said, tongue in cheek, to the trainee Hattie, who was fretting about a delayed piece of business for which she was responsible but which she was not in a position to speed up. "Yes," she said, "that's something I'm getting really good at."

***

This analysis has identified three fairly tightly narrated answers to the question what it is to be a diplomat. It is to do what is expected of you according to what is acknowledged to be a bureaucratic story (though it is not actually called bureaucratic). It is to manage alternate nomadic treks known as postings with stints at home in such a way that your superiors promote you and you appear to be a hero; a career diplomat worthy of the name. It is to incorporate a mediating function in such a degree that you do not spring into action unless it is deemed necessary by those on behalf of whom you mediate, i.e. when politicians think that action should be taken. Since the bureaucratic and hero stories are culled from what it is to manage the self in a broad Western tradition, whereas the third story seems to be specific to diplomacy, we are invited to conclude that to be a diplomat is to be a self-effacing mediator. This, however, would be to privilege one story for managing the self over two other and equally valid stories on the grounds that the two former stories may be found elsewhere. Yet what is at issue is the specific question of what it is to be a specific kind of human being, and not merely what it is to be specific. The answer to the question must be sought not in any one of the three stories but rather in how they are juggled in relation to one another.

One clue to how this is done emerged at a press conference at the Norwegian Atlantic Committee, a key interface between diplomats and others who take a professional interest in international relations.[14] A newly pensioned and successful career diplomat had done what a number of newly pensioned and successful diplomats do, namely publish his autobiography, increasing the number of such books by Norwegian diplomats of this type to thirty-two. His was primarily a tale of the end of the Cold War, and it was subtitled "A Personal Account." I had found nothing whatsoever of a personal nature in the book, only reports on corridor asides to

---

14. Bear in mind that, as discussed in Chapter 3, "international relations" is a discursive field of which diplomacy and war-fighting are key practices (cf. Aron [1962] 1966 above). It is a separate discursive field, among other reasons, because it tends to be discretely organized in relation to other discourses on global politics, such as the developmentalist or the economic discourse (cf. Shore 2000).

his ambassador colleagues during pauses in negotiations and the like. So in the Q&A at his book launch, I grasped the opportunity offered by the subtitle to prod him about how he himself had actually experienced what was going on, and what were his personal views on the course of events. "I haven't written about that," he shot back. "That's it," I said, "that's why I'm asking you about it here." "No," he said, "I've written what I have to say." At this, the chair weighed in and said that it would indeed be nice to hear his own assessments, and that we could make it an off-the-record thing. "I called it a personal account, not a private one," the diplomat insisted, and with that, the case was closed.

It was an intriguing move, for in the book, "personal" was used as a binary opposite to "official," and a reader might easily jump to the conclusion that this opposition was a riff on the private/public theme. But here he was, indicating that his division of the social was in fact tripartite: private/personal/public. "Personal" simply meant that part of business that was not specifically representative of official state policy, with "public" ostensibly being that official state policy. The clear implication was that, in the case of diplomats, the personal is indeed the public, but there also exists a third realm which does not come into play at all. The former UK representative on the UN Security Council, David Hannay (2008), heads off his account of that experience with a chapter called "A Personal Introduction." The diplomat, who prides himself on his negotiating skills, needs that personal touch in his work, so his performance takes place in two areas: on stage, and in the wings. Then there is the backstage (Goffman 1959).

Indeed, to judge by people in the Norwegian foreign milieu generally, if a diplomat does not master such a tripartite presentation of self, he or she is not a fully fledged diplomat and so not a fully operational *interlocuteur valable*. One of the favorite stories of a foreign policy analyst who was married to a top-rank Norwegian politician and had spent a lifetime around diplomats concerned how he had been sought out by a Chinese diplomat in the late 1960s. This is standard procedure; one information waterhole that any good diplomat posted to a foreign capital will seek out is the foreign policy think tanks. The way the foreign policy analyst told the story, after two visits the lack of exchange began to gnaw on him, and he insisted that if the Chinese diplomat came back, it would be for them to have an *exchange* of views. No problem, the Chinese diplomat retorted; he would just bring along some brochures explaining the Chinese "line" on the questions in point. At this, the foreign policy analyst opined that this was not what he had in mind, that he wanted the diplomat's *own* views. Bewildered, the diplomat asked, "do I have to have my own opinions?" (*Må jeg ha egne meninger?*) This story, which always drew gales of laughter, may serve as a parable of aloof democratic self-understanding, but that is not the aspect that I stress here. Another (and related) reason that this story sparked so much mirth was that the Chinese diplomat did not live up to Norwegian doxic ideas of how a diplomat should act. Since that is indeed the relevant measure for cultural competence in this setting, the Chinese diplomat confirmed the standard diplomatic presentation of self by blatantly breaching it. When asked about "private" views, the diplomat is *expected* to offer what he himself may describe as his "personal" views. A knock on the back door is expected to be answered by a reception not backstage, but in the wings.

In light of this, it makes sense that *only one* of the thirty-two autobiographies published by Norwegian diplomats actually talks about anything "private," and why the one exception is the privately published autobiography of a diplomat who, quite extraordinarily, lost her status in a court case (Taftø 1997). It also makes sense of why newspaper columns written by pensioned diplomats invariably come across as elaborations of official positions. Of course, diplomats still have a backstage. That backstage, however, seems to be tucked further back and presumably is visited less often and by fewer people than is the case for many nondiplomats in the same society. One theme that comes up frequently in ministry conversation is the uneasiness with which diplomats watch how retired diplomats take up menial jobs in the ministry that pay a fraction of their pensions. If you are posted at home, you may stay in the job until you are seventy; if you are abroad, you will have to step down on the very day when you reach sixty-eight. So you may give up your ambassadorial post on the day of your sixty-eighth birthday and go straight to a backroom job where the only story that counts is the bureaucratic one. "That's what happens to many people who have no network in Norway after all their time spent abroad," said Gordon, and shuddered visibly, "they are happy to hang around here doing that kind of thing."

Why the shudder? Presumably because the pensioner-diplomat has no career and no standing as an adviser, and so has lost access to the hero story. The negotiation story no longer applies, either. The pensioner-diplomat is left with only the bureaucratic story, and in the eyes of diplomats, to be a diplomat should be something more than being a bureaucrat. The pensioner-bureaucrat is a living reminder of what any diplomat may be reduced to. The bureaucracy story, after all, is already the master story: it weaves itself into the other stories, it is a key resource when senior diplomats set out to dominate junior diplomats, it dominates what the diplomat refers to as the "personal" sphere of life and looms over what she refers to as her "private" sphere.

At the risk of overinterpretation, I suggest that there is a home-and-hearth side to this on-the-job story of alienation. Gordon's shudder could not be in response only to what happens to the pensioner on the job, for on the job the pensioner still does have a network. Indeed, that is why he is there. The shudder must, therefore, also have to do with the diplomat-pensioner's situation in his private life. My guess at the scary prospect is that, not being permitted on stage as a pensioner, and after forty years of cordoning off their backstage, some diplomat-pensioners may have lost their way altogether. In that case, and with the stage itself inaccessible, the wings are the only place left to go. Perhaps old diplomats never die, they just fade into the wings.

In his lectures on governmentality, Foucault (2000) stresses that governmentality is a form of power where the king's head is chopped off, by which he means that from no one cerebral center does there emanate a master plan and a master's voice. Rather, it is the practices that hold out subject positions into which individuals are interpellated, as well as stories about what to do. To be a diplomat is to incorporate a set of practices (such as how to write a text that looks personal but that does not break with state policy; cf. the previous chapter). If socialization is about incorporation in the sense of mastering diplomatic stories so that one may gain fluency of practice, then governmentality is about acting out those stories fluently, which is to say in such a way that they confirm discourse. To be a diplomat is indeed to be self-effacing, but not only in the sense that the subject position of mediator effaces the diplomat as a third party between two actors. Self-effacing also means that, if you overfulfill your scripts or stories, you may experience anxiety about losing your entry pass to your own backstage.

5

DIPLOMATS GENDERED AND CLASSED

> In order for the individual to appear in liberal theory as a universal figure,
> who represents anyone and everyone, the individual must be disembodied
>
> CAROLE PATEMAN, 1986

Where the previous chapter asked what it is like to be a diplomat, this chapter discusses their differences and hierarchies.[1] Historically, diplomatic functions have tended to be performed by merchants, noblemen, and clergy. In medieval Europe, monks dominated. With the rise of the state and the coming of permanent diplomacy, the aristocracy took over diplomatic missions. As postings became permanent, the resident diplomat needed traits that were

> not contemplated at all in the older theory of diplomacy. He was the man
> counted upon to influence the policies, or perhaps simply the attitudes, of

---

1. The area where the areas of gender and that of diplomacy overlap has been little studied, but see Billig and Alvesson 1994, Enloe 1989: 93–123, and Clark 1984. The literature on women bureaucrats in Norway is slim, but see Hernes 1982 and Van der Roos 1996. Halford, Savage, and Witz 1996 discusses three approaches to organization and gender: contingent, essentialist and embedded. For a review of this literature see, for example, Martin and Collinson 2002.

the government to which he was sent in a sense favorable to his own; to minimize frictions, to win concessions, to achieve co-operation (or, what was sometimes just as valuable, the appearance of co-operation), and, if the worst came to the worst, to sound the first warning that things were getting out of hand, and that other pressures were required. (Mattingly 1955: 253)

Unlike monks, aristocrats had wives. In the Renaissance, these "were not expected to go on embassies, and by the Venetians not permitted to do so" (Hamilton and Langhorne 1995: 51).[2] From the eighteenth century onward, throughout Europe, the bourgeoisie began to fill the missions. They were usually ennobled for their service. Hamilton and Langhorn (1995: 103) point out, however, that this custom changed around the middle of the nineteenth century, so that "the early Victorian diplomatic service was no more, nor no less, aristocratic than the traditional British political élite as measured by membership of the House of Lords."[3]

Nonaristocrats needed to be trained. The best-known handbook on being a diplomat was written in the early eighteenth century, by an established writer introducing people to life at court, François de Callières. The earliest attempt at organized training also dates from this time (Keens-Soper 1972), although generally such training for diplomats began only in the midnineteenth century. Fully fledged diplomatic academies were a twentieth-century phenomenon. They strengthened the *cohort* as a key social trait of the diplomat. The cohort is the network on which one draws for rumors, particularly from home when abroad; it is the yardstick of how one's career progresses; and it is in some degree an in-group from which one watches other cohorts, for example to review career advancement.

Nonaristocrats needed to be paid. The first British attachés received payment in 1815, and about half were salaried by 1860 (Anderson 1993: 123). Only after the First World War, however, was the number of Etonian entries halved. Exclusion now came to center on "Jews, coloured men and infidels, who [were] British subjects" (Hamilton and Langhorne 1995:

---

2. The Venetians were also recommended to bring their own cooks, lest they be poisoned (Der Derian 1987). The *épouse problématique* is still an issue in postings like Kabul, and is well known in military discourse. From the mid-1970s to the mid-1980s, British troops in Northern Ireland were not allowed to have their wives with them in that country.

3. On the transition from aristocracy to bourgeoisie, see Der Derian 1987.

171). This thinking was more or less in evidence throughout Europe, and extended to wives:

> Before World War One the German government considered the social distinction of the ambassador's wife so important that when it wanted to name a certain Count von Hatzfeldt as ambassador to London, he was informed that before he could be appointed he would have to divorce his American commoner wife of Jewish extraction. Hatzfeldt refused, but eventually agreed to a legal separation for the duration of his assignment. (Thayer 1960: 231)

In Turkey, until the 1990s, diplomats who married foreigners had to quit the service.

With the arrival of the bourgeoisie came additional pressure for openness in the diplomatic and, even more strongly, in the consular service. Sweden published a list of its consuls as early as 1824, and a full annual list of serving diplomats and employees within the MFA from 1870 onward (Anderson 1993: 114). Other nations followed suit, although Russia, characteristically reclusive, has yet to publish such lists. The merging of diplomatic, consular, and MFA services, which started in Sweden in 1906, further undermined the grip of the aristocracy, for MFA employees had generally been bourgeois from the establishment of those organizations in the eighteenth century (see Hocking 1999; Neumann 2007). What of women diplomats? American women became legally entitled to be diplomatic and consular civil servants in 1922; Frenchwomen in 1929. The Scandinavian countries and Britain followed suit around the Second World War. This short sketch of key personnel shifts serves as a reminder of the similarities between personnel changes concerning class and those concerning gender.

Since it is human beings and not organizations who practice diplomacy, the social traits of diplomats are relevant to their work. For example, Meinecke points out that "It was the diplomat, sending in his reports, who was the acknowledged discoverer of the interests of states. . . . he found himself compelled to try and bring events, plans, and the possibilities at any particular time, over one common denominator" (Meinecke quoted in Der Derian 1987: 103; cf. Watson [1982] 1984). One way of understanding the field diplomat's work is as the producer of reason of state. Different people, with different social traits, will report different things, so one key issue concerns in what measure such differences result in different outcomes. It may be that organizational structure and others' expectations about how persons will act are so strong that they cancel out the importance of personality traits. Organizations inculcate discipline, bodily comportment, action register. Like all professions, diplomats try to hold their turf against all comers. For example, they dislike the spoils system, by which ambassadorial posts are filled from outside the service (this is the rule rather than the exception in the United States).[4]

When Norway formed its Foreign Ministry in 1905, women were barred from holding professional positions, as they were in all other MFAs (Towns 2010). The MFA of the newly sovereign Norwegian state had a handful of recent female arrivals who worked as typists. A woman was first listed in the MFA's annual calendar in 1918; she was working as an archivist. By 1960, of the 417 persons permanently employed, 124 were women. However, only one was a diplomat, that is, a permanently employed civil servant in the foreign service with a duty to take up any post at home or abroad to which he (not she) was ordered. Today, the ratio of men to women is roughly 1:1, but women dominate as typists and men as service personnel.[5] About one-third of the diplomats are women.

Two things are immediately clear: the Norwegian MFA is a gendered organization, and its gendering has undergone changes during the organization's history. Furthermore, the gendering is not atypical for a European country. The first female diplomat ever to head a foreign post was Alexandra Kollontai, appointed to Kristiania (now Oslo) by the Soviet Union in

---

4. It is a trait of professions, not least of that other key profession of international life, the military, that commonalities in organization, training, and practices everywhere make for a certain professional uniformity throughout the globe. In this sense, Hitler was right in his complaint about diplomats representing "an international Society clique" (quoted in Irving 1978: 166).

5. Typists, not secretaries; secretaries were the lowest professional grade for permanently hired consular and diplomatic personnel. Since the late 1960s, "secretary" has been used in the MFA informally in its society-wide meaning as typists and their successors, but it has also still been used for professional personnel at posts abroad. The former category remains strongly female-gendered. To avoid confusion and highlight gendered function, I use "typist" throughout. The title formally used is "assistant." There were also some washerwomen. "Service personnel" refers to messengers, janitors, superintendents, chauffeurs, etc.

1923.[6] Women were still barred from serving as diplomats in several countries by the time of the Second World War, and the arrival of female diplomats took place within living memory. Indeed, as part of my research, I
was able to interview the third and fourth female diplomats in Norwegian
history; both were recently retired. Given this state of affairs, and given
that the literature is very sparse, any exploration of the gender of the diplomat should begin with the empirical question "Where are the women?"
(Enloe 1989). In our case, we begin with an account of the breakdown of
diplomatic homosociality.[7]

Stories are told about the diplomat as hero, as the previous chapter suggested. The hero story is a gendered one. Consider, for example, Anne
Campbell's (1993: 30) argument that "It is men, not women, who slay drag-
ons and fight in defense of the innocent. The literary heroes of boys' worlds
are fearless worriers, flying aces, crime fighters. From Tom and Jerry to
the Teenage Mutant Ninja Turtles, from Superman to Indiana Jones, it is
males who both use and receive violence."

Although the number of female heroes is rising, this argument still
holds true. For every Lara Croft there are ten Conan the Barbarians, for
every Lyra ten Harry Potters. And although, in diplomacy, you become a
hero by making violence subside rather than by perpetrating it, the diplomatic hero is definitely coded as male. How are heroic stories gendered,
and what effect does it have on the diplomats involved and on the MFA
as a whole? Discourse offers certain gendered stories for how to live a
(diplomatic) life. Gender is then performed as a practice (West and Zimmermann 1987, Butler 1993, Martin 2003). Individuals are interpolated
into gendered subject positions and held accountable for them on the basis
of whether social interlocutors hold them to be either physically male or
physically female. The key fact here is that the circle of recognition involved tends to be universal. Few people think of themselves as being, and

---

6. In IR literature as well as in lexical works, Alexandra Kollontai is often referred to as
the first female "ambassador." This is not correct. Russia, and its successor state the USSR, was
amongst the five powers that, since the Congress of Vienna, had the right to appoint ambassadors,
but this title was reserved for envoys to other great powers exclusively. Since Norway was a small
power, Kollontai was simply a plenipotentiary. Conversely, all Norwegian heads of postings had
the title of minister until the Allied small powers were granted the right to appoint ambassadors
to the great power Allies in 1942.

7. I.e. preferring the company of the same sex (Kanter 1977, Lipman-Blumen 1984).

even fewer are "beyond" or "above" ascribing gender to themselves and others.[8] Any one story or set of stories may be gendered, and diplomatic stories are no exception.

In highly differentiated societies such as Norway, discussions of gender that do not relate to matters of class have little purchase. Class involves questions of status, material inequality, and group agency (Crompton 1998: 10–12). In a setting where the wage differential is fairly low, as is group agency (the key MFA union organizes all employees, from secretary general to janitor), the emphasis falls on status.[9] Within the MFA, class is important in at least two ways. First, being a foreign ministry employee usually has a consolidating or furthering effect on one's social status in society at large. Civil servants in general, and diplomats in particular, form a social elite. Traditionally, Europe's ruling class ruled by dint of dominating top positions within the state (the aristocracy until the mideighteenth century, the bourgeoisie thereafter). Conversely, attaining top positions secured membership in the ruling class for those who did not start there. In the eighteenth century, people without rank routinely had nobility bestowed upon them as part of reaching these positions. One may see a social remnant of this practice when senior civil servants today are routinely made commanders of the Norwegian state's Order of St. Olav.[10] In some degree, the nimbus of state employment also surrounded nonprofessionals. In Norway, employment in the central state administration traditionally carries a social premium regardless of occupation. At least until the 1970s, being a chauffeur in the Foreign Ministry was considered socially attractive within the working class, and typist in the Foreign Ministry was a socially acceptable career for a bourgeois woman whereas a similar job in a large private firm was not. As these two examples suggest, the class

---

8. The question here is not the physiological and analytical one of whether there exist more than one biological gender (see Laqueur 1990), but the ethnographic fact that my informants assume that there are two genders, and categorize people accordingly.

9. I follow Warner et al.'s definition (1963): "By social class is meant two or more orders of people who are believed to be, and are accordingly ranked by the members of the community, in socially superior and inferior positions. Members of a class tend to marry within their own order, but the values of the society permit marriage up and down. A class system also provides that children are born into the same status as their parents. A class society distributes rights and privileges, duties and obligations, unequally among its inferior and superior grades."

10. The British equivalent to Order of St. Olav would be the Order of St. Michael and St. George.

narratives of employment were highly gendered (no female chauffeurs in the foreign ministry, and very few male typists). By the same token, the gender narratives were highly classed. For example, to ask whether it was socially acceptable for a bourgeois male to work as a typist in the Foreign Ministry is historically superfluous. Although men had manned the lower echelons of foreign ministries from their inception at the end of the nineteenth century, in the early twentieth century the idea of a male typist was so unacceptable that the question did not even arise.

A second reason that class is key to a discussion of the diplomat's gender concerns the multiple and hierarchical nature of performing gender (Mauss [1936] 1979, Csordas 1994). Recent research on masculinities in modern and postmodern societies has highlighted how there are several ways of being a man, and how these ways are hierarchically ordered (the *locus classicus* is Pleck 1981). R. Connell (1987: 183, 1995: 77) understands hegemonic masculinities as discursively specific and idealized forms of masculinity. Research on femininities has not foregrounded hierarchies in the same degree (but see Eisenstein 1994, Chowdhry and Nair 2002). Generally, in any sizable organization, where more than one class is represented, performance of gender will meld with questions of class. Where diplomats are concerned, class becomes even more interesting as a social marker because of the lack of differentiation regarding ability and, particularly since the 1970s, material wealth. Since the 1920s, nearly all hired diplomats have had academic training, and their evolving life income has been roughly similar. In terms of differentiation, the result has been a historical weakening of material factors and strengthening of status as a differentiating mechanism. To put the point more technically: as secondary socialization processes have become homogenized, the heterogeneous effect of primary socialization in the family home and childhood neighborhood and the habitus it inscribes in the gendered body have become more important for social differentiation.

The world, and particularly social scientists, seem to think that class is less important in Scandinavia than elsewhere. In terms of income differentials, this is true. If we turn to Bourdieu rather than to Marx for our understanding of class, however, then we focus not on absolute but on relative difference, and on questions of consumption as much as on questions of production. In the world of diplomacy, with its emphasis on etiquette, protocol, and convention, the question of style pervades the social, and this claim includes the performance of gender. Bourdieu ([1979] 1984) observes that questions of style and taste are not only highly class-sensitive but key to the constitution of class. As material discrepancies lose importance in the constitution of class, habitus takes over.

The Arrival of Women: Wives, Typists, Diplomats

Embassies used to be itinerant affairs that could last for years. Wives were usually not present, and as already noted, the Venetians even forbade them from accompanying their husbands. As permanent diplomacy became institutionalized, however, women entered the world of diplomacy as wives. A sizable amount of diplomatic work revolves around representation, which takes place in a class-specific format, particularly receptions and dinner parties. Until the end of the 1960s, it was invariably expected that the host's wife should be present. Then a culture war broke out between older women who identified with the role of hostess, and younger spouses—women and a few men—who did not wish to preside at social occasions (Heiberg 1983; Knudsen 1998: 100). In 1973, the MFA issued a statement to the effect that "The spouse is not employed in the foreign service, so cannot be ordered to serve either by the MFA or by the heads of station."[11] The expectation survives informally, however.[12]

Before the nineteenth century and in a lesser degree since, some women have helped their spouses by carrying out work that was socially marked as male. Diplomacy is no exception. When the salon was a key meeting place, diplomats' wives played important roles as administrators of events and facilitators of communication. To take but one example, when the Norwegian vice consul to Kobe left town in 1906, a local English-language newspaper wrote that "Mr. Koren was very popular in Kobe, and Mrs. Koren had a very large circle of admirers and friends. A number of people came

---

11. NNA MFA, 2.5/10, Circular 13/73.

12. The spouses tried to gain remuneration for this kind of work, but their campaign failed due to two groups of women; women who thought diplomats were privileged and that the campaign for women's rights should focus on what they saw as more important issues, and housewives who insisted that "Throughout Norway, 'representation' means energy for activities which makes the home and the immediate environment into resource-rich places to grow up" (*Aftenposten,* 13 July 1976).

to Yokohama to see them off, they having charmed every one by their quiet desire to please and [by their] warm appreciation. Mrs. Koren is so unconsciously attractive that she is a natural help to her diplomat husband."[13]

There are also examples of wives who not only seconded their husband's work but took it over on a temporary basis. For example, half a century after her departure from Kobe, Ms. Koren recalled that during their posting to Montreal, it happened that her husband would be gone for a week at a time. She then took over as de facto head of the consulate.[14] On postings abroad, where tasks were varied and the number of personnel small, relations between foreign service employees and spouses were particularly multiplex.[15] A minister's wife could sometimes make or break a man's career. In 1900, for example, a young attaché wrote to his superior about how the wife of the consul general, Christophersen, had broken one of his colleagues: "He is nervous, and feels invaded by the treatment he has suffered at the hands of Mrs. Christophersen, which was nasty beyond belief."[16] However, diplomacy was never among the professions where widows inherited their deceased husband's posts. Even by contemporary standards, the exclusion of women from the Foreign Ministry and its predecessors was particularly strict.

By the end of the nineteenth century, a few women worked as typists and on menial chores. As elsewhere in working life (cf. Kessler-Harris 1982, cf. Kittler [1986] 1999), the typewriter is a symbol for an almost complete regendering of the lower writing ranks of the organization. As long as writing was an integral part of diplomatic work, it was treated as the handling of secrets, and women were not admitted. With the emerging practice of typewriting, which led to a separation of authorship and preparation of documents, a new but marginal social space opened up for women.[17] As a result, when the Norwegian minister in Berlin petitioned

---

13. NNA MFA, K1C 2/06, box 3514, *Japan Gazette,* 26 December 1906.

14. Given the gendering of the early-19th-century state as masculine (Towns 2010), this was quite remarkable.

15. These structural factors are still in place. see Enloe (1989: 93–123). Historically, the diplomat's wife is a particularly acute instantiation of the being-in-the-world of the noncareer upper middle-class wife (cf. Finch 1983).

16. NNA MFA, K5G1B/ÆS Belgia, box 3517, Boch to Ibsen 17 February 1900. Mrs. Christophersen's side of the story is unknown.

17. The break between document authorship and preparation should not be overemphasized, since before the typewriter, documents were often dictated (Jespersen 2000).

the foreign minister for more hands, the minister simply suggested that he employ women: "This labor power is cheap and has proven to be wholly satisfactory."[18] His answer brings out the newness of having women in the organization; the assessment is presented as an evaluation of a fresh phenomenon. It also led to something historically new, namely that typists—which is to say women—came under a regime structurally similar to that for male employees: it was part of the legal job description to take up any post not only at home but also abroad.[19] These were bourgeois women, often recruited by word of mouth, within closed and perhaps charmed social circles. For example, one recounts how "In 1946, I had a phone call from my friend Ragnhild . . . in the MFA. A position was falling vacant, so if I wanted to, I should go and see Intendant Berg and apply immediately" (Jacobsen 1994: 1). After the Second World War, some of these women went on to become civil servants and took care of specific portfolios in the organization (notably, culture and the legal questions concerning inheritances left by Norwegian Americans to Norwegian relatives). They did not receive diplomatic training, however, and were under no obligation to move. They spent their working careers permanently employed in the MFA, but they were neither diplomats nor typists. By 1960, of 215 people permanently employed but with no obligation to move, 123 were women (Galtung and Ruge 1965: 171). At the same time, of the 202 permanently employed with an obligation to move, only one was a woman.

The immediate reason was legal. Norwegian women became legal persons only in 1888 (Hernes 1982: 16), and only thereafter could they become civil servants. This was the normal European state of affairs. Formal laws need a specific rationality. When parts of the discursive order are consecrated in formal laws, there exist deep-rooted and often more or less explicit discursive elements on which legal rationality exists. Pateman (1989), Towns (2010), and others argue convincingly that by the nineteenth century, "woman" and "state" were constituted in mutually exclusive terms:

---

18. Løvland to von Ditten, quoted in Omang 1958: 57–58.

19. In a wider social perspective, we have here a partial and transformed return of a much wider social practice that was legally binding for all but civil service families and town dwellers until 1854, whereby unmarried school leavers were legally obliged to go into domestic service (see Sogner and Telste 2005).

Nineteenth century "woman" thus consolidated as a being with characteristics and capacities for action that were in direct opposition to those
of the state itself: as the state became one of reason and force, woman became entrenched with emotion and weakness; as the state became one of
science, women became fused with faith and religion; as the state turned
self-interested, woman was cast as selfless. In the bifurcation of rule of
the nineteenth century—depersonalized rational-legal authority and co-
ercive power—woman became the object of both forms of rule. (Towns
2004: 71)

The exclusion of women from the state was thus grounded not only in
factors such as lack of training or general appropriateness but in a meta-
physics. This has significance for our argument, for discourses do not
change in perfect sync with the legal orders embedded in them. When a
law or set of laws is changed, even if this happens as a result of erosion of
the social and metaphysical grounds upon which it rests, those grounds
may linger in discourse and so remain a precondition for action even in
lieu of legal purchase. The emergence of the female diplomat illustrates
this tendency.

The question of female civil servants was broached for the first time in
Parliament in 1891 and was kept on the agenda by women's organizations
(Stendal 2003: 54–58). The breakthrough came in 1912, as part of a whole-
sale upgrading of women's rights (the following year, Norway would become the first European state to introduce the women's vote).[20] Whereas
equality was made the general principle for state employment, however,
there were five exceptions: members of the king's council (i.e., ministers of
state), ministers of the state church, "diplomatic and consular positions,"
military officers, and new areas that might be deemed sensitive. Of course,
such exceptions were ready targets for a continuation of the campaign for
women's rights. In the MFA archive, one finds letters from sundry organizations.[21] A new breakthrough came in 1928, when the Norwegian Wom-
en's National Council launched a campaign in favor of female ministers of
state. Whereas the target was the first of the five exceptions, the Ministry
for Law and Police conceded on the third as well: "with no hesitation [we]

---

20. Finland, then a grand duchy of the Russian empire, had already done so, however.
21. See NNA MFA, A1A 1/30.

may take one more step . . . so that women may be allowed to be diplomatic and consular civil servants."[22] As the case moved from the cabinet to the Storting, however, it became a question of removing *all* exceptions to state employment. In a country with a Protestant state church and a well-organized Christian lobby, the attempt to change the law foundered on resistance not to female diplomats but to female state-employed church ministers. A comparative perspective brings out the contingency of the religious factor even more clearly, however, for in the same year (1934), a parliamentary bill permitting female diplomats passed in Denmark and was narrowly defeated in the United Kingdom. Once the issue was decoupled from the question of female church ministers, however, Norwegian women won the legal right to become diplomatic and consular civil servants on 24 June 1938. In France, this had happened in 1929; in Britain, it happened in the wake of the Second World War.[23] During the following decades, the legal barrier to female diplomats was dismantled throughout Europe.

Social resistance inside and outside the MFA was another matter. In 1916, a women's organization petitioned the cabinet to increase the number of women serving on state committees and in state commissions, giving as their reason that with the current state of affairs, "No matter how clever she may be, a woman cannot expect to wield influence on the outcome of a case."[24] News coverage of the petition was distributed within the MFA, where a major new commission was in the offing, and it attracted ridiculing annotations. "Why should she serve in the commission, then?" read one, and another answered: "In order to keep silence in the churches (*tie i forsamlingen*)."[25]

Individual women who queried the MFA about the possibility of becoming diplomats were told in no uncertain terms that their chances were slim.[26] When the secretary general was asked by a journalist whether any

---

22. Ot.prp. (Proposal to a chamber of the Norwegian Parliament) no. 47 (1930). Printed parliamentary paper.

23. As already noted the U. S. roughly fits the European pattern; there, the year was 1922.

24. Christiania Women's Council covered in undated newspaper clip, NNA MFA, A1A 1/30.

25. The reference is to Corinthians I, 14:34: "Let your women keep silence in the churches: for it is not permitted unto them to speak; but they are commanded to be under obedience as also saith the law."

26. NNA MFA, 1G11, box 8836, MFA to Sørensen 15 May 1933; MFA to Tank, 16 May 1933.

of his female employees were suited for a diplomatic career, he answered in the negative.[27] After two years of roaming in the archives of the Norwegian MFA and five years of listening to the MFA lore, I have yet to come across anything to indicate that a single male Norwegian diplomat did anything to lift the legal bar against female diplomats.

Female Diplomat No. 1: Gudrun M.

Once it was clear that the parliamentary bill would succeed, however, the foreign minister decided to act, and saw to it that one of the typists in the organization, Gudrun M., was accepted into the diplomatic academy in the spring of 1938, which gave her the rank of temporary secretary. There was immediate resistance from within the ministry. In the 1930s, training usually began with a short stint abroad, where the new secretary served as an attaché. The foreign minister turned to Norway's legation in Italy and asked "whether it had any objections."[28] The head of the legation had five of them, one of which is of particular interest:

> As seen from Italy, it would appear utterly strange for a lady to be registered (*anmeldt*) as an attaché. Amongst the many hundred names in the Italian diplomatic list, there is no lady. . . . From an administrative point of view, it seems unfortunate to have a younger assistant outrank an older person at the same legation.[29]

The latter point is of particular interest, for it draws on the discursive precondition that "female diplomat" is an oxymoron, and it also implies that it would be ill-advised and, ultimately, uncivilized (cf. Towns 2010) to permit such a phenomenon. In a word, the point demonstrates resistance to recategorization. The head of legation denies that the woman in question is a secretary. The category of assistants consisted of female typists and was obviously outranked by the category of secretaries, which consisted of male diplomats. The head of legation tries to deny the very possibility that

27. *Morgenbladet,* 19 February 1934.
28. NNA MFA, 1G11, box 8836, Koht to Irgens, 30 April 1938
29. NNA MFA, 1G11, box 8838, Irgens to Koht 9 May 1938.

a woman may leave "her" category, and explicitly points to the "unfortunate" consequence that a female would then outrank a male.

The foreign minister dealt summarily with this objection, pointing out
that the woman in question was a secretary. On the other hand, he accepted
that it would "seem foreign" to Italians to receive a female attaché. Since
this might "cause problems for the legation's work," he withdrew his suggestion.[30] Gudrun M. served abroad in London instead. It emerges from
her autobiography that the Italy incident was not isolated. For example,
it was customary for the new hands to be congratulated by the secretary
general. Rather than being congratulated, she was given the cold shoulder:
"He was an old bachelor, with no feel for new trends. He advertised in no
uncertain terms that he found my budding career to be an abnormality"
(Ræder 1975: 112).

Like many pioneer women, the first Norwegian female diplomat was
treated as matter out of place (cf. Douglas 1996). She passed her exam in
April 1939 and served with distinction at the MFA in exile during the
Second World War. Gudrun M. eventually married a male Norwegian
diplomat, became Gudrun R., and left the service at the end of the war.
Her obituary details what followed: "After the war, she became Norway's
hostess. First in Brussels, where J. G. Ræder [her husband] became head of
legation in 1949, then in Madrid from 1953 on. As of 1958, she was the permanent under secretary's wife here at home, and from 1965 to 1973 she was
the ambassador's wife [ambassadrise] in Rome."[31] So the first Norwegian
female diplomat did eventually arrive in Rome, but as "the ambassador's
wife," not as a diplomat in her own right.

Female Diplomat No. 2: Kirsten O.

From 1945 to 1958, the situation was as it had been before 1938: there were
no Norwegian female diplomats. Again, circumstances changed as a result of political intervention, not because of any move taken within the
MFA. In 1954, a Labour MP who headed Parliament's Foreign Affairs

---

30. NNA MFA, 1G11, box 8838, Koht to Irgens 28 May 1938.
31. *Aftenposten,* 1 October 1998.

Committee, Finn Moe, raised the issue there. Although Moe did not get the backing of the foreign minister, pressure mounted. Once again, the diplomats resisted change. In 1957 a journalist asked the MFA's head of administration why there were no female diplomats. He stated that he was not opposed on principle (an untenable position anyway, given that female access was now the letter of the law) but added: "A woman may leave a nice position and become her husband's wife, but what man would give up his calling and become his wife's husband? . . . The Americans have a woman career diplomat [in Oslo] today, Miss Willis. But . . . mark this: *Miss* Willis."[32]

The form may seem dated, but the *problématique* is not. A female diplomat who was doing quite well left the service in 2005 for the express reason that her partner did not want to accompany her abroad. Coming from her interview with the admissions board, Kathrine, who was living with a foreigner, told me that "they asked me if I would ditch my partner, I thought that was rather cheeky." I asked Hattie, who also lived with a foreigner and had been up before the board the previous year, if she had been asked that question. She first said no, but then it turned out that they had indeed asked what her partner thought of her application. I have met a handful of foreign female diplomats posted to Oslo who have brought their husbands, a Canadian ambassador included. Without exception, the issue comes up in conversation and obviously makes for social complications.

The acceptance of Kirsten O. as Norway's second female diplomat in 1958 followed a political campaign that was covered by the newspapers. She had a successful career, peaking as Norway's first female ambassador in 1975 (to the European Council in Strasbourg, a minor European posting). The considerable literature on lesbians in traditional male professions contains nothing on diplomats, and a study of Kirsten O. would be apposite. For decades, she lived with one of the leading Norwegian foreign correspondents of her day. To ask the question whether they lived in an "open" lesbian relationship would be to miss the point, for although the question of "openness" was raised by Norwegian lesbian activists in the 1970s, the issue was too new to have social purchase in a discussion of

---

32. *Arbeiderbladet,* 7 February 1957. There was substantial newspaper coverage at the time, see in particular the op-ed in *Dagbladet,* 27 July 1957.

the social significance of the relationship. Norway recognizes a long tradition of bourgeois women living together (Hellesund 2003). As long as the relationship was not advertised, it was not problematized in polite society, of which diplomacy was still definitely a part. My (highly conventional) maternal grandmother counted amongst her friends a female couple, and I cannot recall her commenting on their living arrangement during my childhood. My paternal aunt lived with a woman for over twenty years, with few questions asked. Furthermore, the MFA had its own tradition of homosexuality. The ministry's *grand seigneur* in the decades following 1905, Fritz Wedel-Jarlsberg, makes a thinly disguised appearance in Proust's *Remembrance of Things Past* as "Le prince de Faffenheim-Munsterburg-Weinigen." That work's Norwegian translator highlights the obvious similarities between person and persona, "from obvious vanity and diplomatic skill to suggested interest in young men, from royal acquaintances (Wedel-Jarlsberg *was* actually a friend of the British queen) to grand receptions and shining cars" (Amadou 1973: 315).

Anecdotes about this homosexual tradition form part of ministry lore to this day. For example, my interlocutor Jarle told how a young attaché passed the *grand seigneur*'s house as he was overseeing the arrival of crates of champagne. "Ah," the young attaché said, "champagne is such a noble drink." "Yes," the *grand seigneur* replied, "too bad that it gives you such a sore behind." Lore also has it that the *grand seigneur* played favorites among the young secretaries and helped in their careers. It is hard to find written sources on this tradition, but in his day and even in the decades after his death, the *grand seigneur* was held up as a role model not only as a diplomat but also as a man about town and the "oldest son" of the "MFA father-house," to use the metaphors employed in a celebratory cantata written for the MFA's twenty-fifth anniversary.[33] At the very least, homosexuality was not an active hindrance to a diplomatic career. At present, several gay and lesbian Norwegian diplomats are in active service, with few questions asked. At the academy ball a few years back, a male graduate made a hit by turning up in a ball gown. Academy briefings on how to cope with life abroad include meetings with diplomat partners, and since the late 1990s

---

33. NNA MFA, 2.25/62, box 10060; note that the cantata assumes that all the employees are "sons."

gay and lesbian partners have been asked to address the attachés on their experiences. Such relationships are not advertised, however, and to date there has been no case of outing. There has also been little activism beyond calls on the administration to help in cases where same-sex cohabitants want to register as part of a diplomatic household with the host country authorities. The administration has taken a sympathetic but cautious line regarding such requests.

Female Diplomat No. 3, Beate M., and Successors

Following further pressure from politicians and newspapers, a third woman was accepted by the diplomatic academy in 1963. Beate M. had a successful career, finishing as ambassador. There were complications, however. She married in 1965, to a student, and had a child. The situation was new three times over: a married female diplomat who was a mother and a breadwinner. When diplomats go on a new tour, they are entitled to certain standardized payments, all of which since the 1970s have been specified in a detailed agreement between the Norwegian state and MFA employees. The drawing up of these rules has a long and thoroughly gendered history. Before 1919, neither salaries nor reimbursements were standardized. When standardization began in that year, it was on the principle that married diplomats ranking as ministers should receive more than unmarried, and those with children more than those with no children. This principle was contested throughout the interwar period, and the debates give us a fairly detailed picture of a key aspect of the gendered male diplomat, namely the breadwinner. The line of argument in favor of paying the father more was as follows:

> Ministers with children have more mouths to feed and are in need of more space. The children should be fed, and as long as they are little, more servants are needed. The situation becomes still more challenging as the children grow up. The minister will have to give his daughters an upbringing equivalent to his position, and doing this abroad usually means incurring high costs. When they reach the age when it is time to come out as a debutante, money spent on clothes will increase significantly. Where the sons are concerned, the minister will naturally wish to have them raised as good

Norwegian citizens, which means either hiring a Norwegian teacher or sending them to school in Norway. Either way, it costs góod money.[34]

Beate M. faced a double challenge. First was the letter of the laws and regulations. Whereas the social democratic welfare state paid its married male diplomats abroad for their wives' keep and no questions asked, a married female diplomat would be paid only if the husband were unable to work for medical reasons. If the husband was able-bodied, the wife was treated legally as if she were unmarried—and being single meant not being entitled to a whole string of extra payments. Beate M. petitioned a key female Labour MP about this matter. She proved to be no sister, answering baldly after three and a half months that "it was fair enough that there was a specified foreign service payment for the wife, who has to move and take on extensive duties of representation. Perhaps it would be even harder getting more women employed in the foreign service, if we were to be totally schematic in our approach to equality?"[35]

A second problem was how the administration proceeded. A sustained series of reminders and creative suggestions for handling the case notwithstanding, the administration did not make any effort to interpret the regulations in a way that would be advantageous for the one married Norwegian female diplomat. Furthermore, once her husband ended his studies and gained employment, the administration promptly moved to take away those payments that had actually been permitted.[36] We may draw a historical line here, from the passive resistance of male diplomats to the idea of female diplomats, via the cold welcome extended to the pioneer, to this lack of interest in making homosocial rules and regulations fit an actual heterosocial situation.[37] Yet once the case became widely known, it led to a change in the rules in the direction of full equality between the sexes.[38]

---

34. Eckell and Bjercke, report, NNA MFA, A1B I/33, box 6780.

35. Beate Mo Alvegård's private archive, Seweriin to Alvegård, 22 June 1966.

36. Beate Mo Alvegård's private archive, Alvegård to Adm. dep., 13 October 1972. The administration's handling of the case is typical of Western approaches to incoming women employees, as discussed by Acker 1993.

37. Not too much should be made of this, however, for like any bureaucracy, the MFA administration is usually uncreative in the application of rules in all fields, not only where gender is concerned.

38. In the mid-1990s, Norwegian maternity leave rules were changed so that five weeks of the twelve months available had to be used by the father, or else they were lost. Yet again, general

Furthermore, the loose "secretary group" that organized young diplomats petitioned the administrative department on her behalf. It was a rearguard action, limited to pointing out that it would be "unfair" to deny her equal treatment given that "decisions that establish the principle of full equality in the service" were about to come into force.[39] This happened in 1971, and it is the first instance I have found of male diplomats making an effort to ease structural conditions for female diplomats. As will be seen, it took place *post festum*.

The early 1970s mark the arrival of female diplomats in earnest. It was a small part of the breakthrough for women's rights that accompanied the massive entry of female baby boomers into the work force. A fourth female diplomat was accepted into the academy in 1969, a fifth in 1971, and a sixth in 1972. With the exception of No. 6, who quit soon after joining, they all made the rank of ambassador. In 1974, three women were accepted; all went on to brilliant careers peaking as ambassadors, head of department, and assistant permanent under secretary. They sometimes had a cold welcome, however. One of them told me how, while in the academy, she and the rest of her academy cohort attached a conference, meaning that they were each assigned as a temporary attaché to a single participant, to assist with sundry problems.[40] At the luncheon, there were empty chairs, and word went out to the attachés that they should fill them (diplomats are sticklers for form; empty chairs at a meal are not done). When the three women attempted to follow orders, however, they were held back with a "not you." One of them, Brigid E., arriving at her first posting in Latin America, was told by the head of legation that "she would not be taken

---

state-society relations changed life in the organization, as young male diplomats availed themselves of this opportunity. "It is nice to see Stein and the others taking up that fight," Sisela said to me. "What's the cost?" I asked. "The old guard indulges in a bit of ridicule during lunch" (*Den eldre garde latterliggjør dem litt i kantinepraten*). Ridicule was, as we have seen, an important part of the social resistance to the early attempt to introduce female diplomats; now male diplomats were getting the same treatment. The heterosocialization of the practices of p/maternity leave and ridicule against males served to further destabilize the dichotomy of breadwinner/caregiver. The cumulative change in practices here is bringing about a discursive shift, where it is no longer clear that women are caregivers simply by dint of being women.

39. Beate Mo Alvegård's private archive, Graham to Adm.dep., 14 January 1971.

40. There is no limit to when you stop acting as attaché to foreign guests, for the simple reason that the only thing it takes to qualify is for the diplomat to have a lower diplomatic rank than the guest.

seriously," whereupon she was, in her own words, "locked into my office for three months."

In 1976, one woman was accepted into the academy, and then from 1977 on, about one-third of each academy cohort were women. From the early 1990s, about half were women, with women making up the majority for the first time in 2003. In the 2007 cohort, 13 out of 19—68 percent—were women. In total, female diplomats now make up more than one-third of the entire corps. During the last couple of years, the percentage of women becoming head of section has been roughly the same as for men, and it has taken about the same time for women to advance to that position as it has for men (ten to twelve years). The number of female heads of department has, however, been low, and there has yet to be a female ambassador in any of the key postings (which, as seen from Norway, are London, Washington, Berlin, the EU, NATO, Paris, Stockholm, and Copenhagen). At regular intervals, the Storting distributes letters to Norwegian ministries about the importance of female representation, with at least 40 percent being a declared goal for each unit. The newspapers take up the call, publishing articles about underrepresentation of women among Norwegian ambassadors. At the time of writing, one-fourth of those with ambassadorial rank are women.

To sum up: at no point has the impetus for gender change come from within the MFA itself (although, as we will see, from the late 1960s onward, some of the newly recruited personnel were quite creative). Changes have come due to the involvement of the MFA in general state-society relations. Furthermore, change has been regularly resisted. Specific efforts have always been undertaken only when the key decisions have already been made elsewhere, and so must be classified as face-saving.

An analysis of the gender of the diplomat should ideally look at how the social, physiological, and psychological systems come together in the body (Mauss [1936] 1979).[41] For such an analysis, I think we may take male and

---

41. I would argue with Skeggs that "Bodies are the physical sites where the relations of class, gender, race, sexuality and age come together" (1997: 82; cf. Moore 1994). According to Acker (2006: 5–6), "*Gender* is best understood as pervasive patterns of difference, in advantage and disadvantage, work and reward, emotion and sexuality, image and identity, between female and male, created through practical activities and representations that justify these patterns that result in the social categories of women and men." A feminist like Butler would emphasize how these are all to be understood discursively, with materiality being "power in its formative and constituting

female as physiological givens and then trace the changing content of these categories in the context of diplomacy. So far it seems clear that the resulting subject positions will not be dependent on the discourse of diplomacy as such, but will emerge from changes in general state-society relations. It follows that the gendering of diplomats will vary not only historically but also among states. On the other hand, the analysis so far also suggests that the relevant state-society relations are broadly similar throughout Europe. The validity of this analysis may be extended from Norway to Europe as such, perhaps even to that elusive entity known as "the West." Building on these premises, I now attempt to specify the multiple gendered subject positions at play.

The Rearguard Action of the Homosocial Diplomat

As already noted, the diplomat of "old diplomacy"—the European-based diplomacy which dominated from the emergence of the European states system to the First World War—began life as a homosocial diplomat. As women entered the world of diplomacy as wives, typists, and eventually diplomats, he was enmeshed in an increasingly complex web of heterosocial relations. His reaction was to salvage as much as possible of the homosocial arena. Only in the mid-1990s did young male diplomats start availing themselves of the new social possibilities afforded by the increasing heterosocial space available (though male spouses had done so since the 1970s). Older males continue the hunt for homosocial space to this day, however. I have already noted one constitutive practice in this regard, namely ridiculing young male diplomats who take the paternity leave to which they are legally entitled. This example pales besides the exclusionary practices that older males still use vis-à-vis female diplomats.

In 2005, I was invited to present the findings of my centenary history of the MFA to a lunch meeting of the "group of pensioners," which consists

---

effects" (Butler 1993: 34). Yet when I have quoted Whitehead's claim that "Masculinity is not a product or an entity that can be grasped by hand" to diplomat interlocutors, the result has invariably been raucous laughter (Whitehead 2002: 34). Everything is malleable to representation, but physiological entities less so than psychological and social ones. For analytical purposes, there are gains to handling these three systems separately.

of people who reached the rank of ambassadors during their active service. Of the thirty people present, two were women—nos. 3 and 4 to be accepted into the service. I interviewed them. A key theme was how they had felt socially isolated on their postings abroad. Then No. 4 said:

> *So we had a weaker network, you weren't automatically included, you didn't go out for a beer, no, then we weren't there, it was nice enough, at official functions, always, but never in a pub, then they wanted to be by themselves. . . . After that luncheon thing, then there were people going out for a beer afterwards, but we weren't asked* (men vi ble jo ikke spurt).
> *IN:* So the boys still do it like that?
> *No. 4:* . . . the men stick together . . . they meet with their spouses and I don't have a spouse.[42]

It is widely known that the academy year remains important to diplomats until death do them part. George once told me that he had come across the academy class of forty-four years earlier, in a little seaside resort. Everyone still standing had come for the weekend. In the nomadic world of diplomacy, where the group of people with whom you work changes every third year or so, the cohort of your academy year is your social home. It is a group on which you depend for information, gossip (very important in the world of diplomacy), social support, and even support when you apply for new postings. As a result of homosocial rearguard action, early women diplomats were cut off from this vital resource throughout their careers.

Yet their social exclusion does not seem to have remained constant throughout their professional lives. Both underlined how they had been taken well care of during their early years, not least by older male colleagues. "What happened?" I asked. "Perhaps it was easier to relate to us when we were only a few." Once tokenism gave way to block recruitment of female diplomats, however, the rearguard action increased.[43] Despite a possible weakness for tokenism, male diplomats who are now pensioners

---

42. Taped interview, Bristol Hotel, Oslo, 22 November 2005. The point was repeated later in the interview: the only place they had access to gossip was in the lunch canteen, "and then it was supposed to be a big thing (og da var det liksom noe)."

43. For an incisive discussion of tokenism, see Kanter 1977: 206–42.

have, it seems, not experienced significant changes in their relationship to women diplomats beyond the standard changes incurred by getting older. Where this cohort is concerned, changes in patterns of masculinity are due to internal changes in the hierarchy of masculinities.

Masculinity before the Second World War

What to say about this masculinity? Although closer scrutiny would probably yield historical and social specification, the ideal of masculinity in Norwegian diplomacy before the Second World War was the standard European bourgeois "manliness" of the day, which was hierarchically superior to all other masculinities (not to mention femininities). This masculinity stressed physicality, virility, morality, and civility (Whitehead 2002: 14–23). On a European plane, however, this masculinity was arguably still hierarchically subordinate to noble and devil-may-care masculinity, toward which it strove.[44] In Norway, where the aristocracy was very weak, bourgeois masculinity was in a proportionally stronger position. As noted in chapter 2, the present Norwegian state apparatus hails from the time when Norway was part of the Danish composite state. Absolutism arrived in 1661 and was followed by intense state-building. On the county and commune levels, the state representatives were lawyers, ministers, and officers. The lion's share were imported from German-speaking areas and from Denmark in the later 1600s, with a sprinkling of Norwegian-born elite families (a very few of them noble) and a strong element of upwardly mobile burghers. The three to four hundred families involved, making up perhaps 1 percent of the population (Seip [1974] 1997: 64; Try 1979: 31), tended toward endogamy. By 1814, when Norway was attached to Sweden, this elite had become a self-aware stratum, arguably a class. In 1814, the Norwegian civil servants called a congress (with some token

---

44. Again, this is of course an oversimplification for political purposes. Consider, for example, the impact of Romanticism: Lord Byron's aristocratic masculinity was obviously different from, say, the aristocratic masculinity of his contemporary, thrice foreign minister Lord Clarendon. The stricter confines of bourgeois masculinities as compared to aristocratic ones are paralleled in Bourdieu's contrasting of present-day bourgeois and petit-bourgeois masculinities (Bourdieu [1979] 1984).

representatives of the freeholding peasantry) and drew up a constitution, which was accepted by the Swedish king. Norway had become a modern state. Noble privileges were abolished in 1821 (Neumann 2002c). The civil servant families were also leaders in society at large, the business world included. A reader of Bourdieu's ([1979] 1984) *Distinction* with this kind of class background immediately recognizes himself and his forebears in Bourdieu's social portrait of the upper middle classes. Since nobility is virtually absent from today's Norway, this is the top rung of the class ladder.

The model of masculinity in these circles was the standard European bourgeois one, with aspirations to emulate the nobility. (Of the three key founders of the Norwegian MFA on the diplomatic side, two were noble and the third was the son of Henrik Ibsen, another solid source on this type of masculinity.) Bodily comportment should be relaxedly authoritative, hair should be short and slightly pomaded, with no facial hair except an optional moustache, the shirt should be white and made of the best materials, to be worn with a tie or a bow tie, the shoes black and shining, the suit dark with optional pinstripes. Social life centered on the dinner party, the visit, and the outing; a male bourgeois was taught from boyhood how to perform at these occasions. The inheritor of this form of masculinity is still hegemonic in diplomacy, perhaps more so than in many other contemporary social settings, because diplomatic social life is still formatted in this way. A measured and easy use of the body at meals and during introductions, a measured dose of interest in topics under discussion, and an ability to ease the flow of conversation are at a premium. Great attention was and is paid to language. Using the wrong case for personal pronouns is a key marker.[45] Crucially, an integral part of claims to higher status is a thoroughly lived understanding of the relevant and hair-splitting social distinguishing marks. Subordinate males will often not even know which diacritica are in play, and fail to understand their importance if alerted to them. This hampers their ability to rise in the social scale.

The bourgeois male was expected to treat women underlings on the basis of respect rather than of rights. As one key diplomat reports from the 1930s in his autobiography: "It happened that [my personal assistant

---

45. Particularly for the third person plural (*de/dem*). A linguistic parallel may be drawn to the American English usage "between he and I" etc., but the Norwegian equivalent is an even stronger social marker of class inferiority.

typist] Miss Nicolaysen and I worked in the ministry into the wee hours of the morning. Head of Section Waldemar Foss criticized me and said that I mistreated the assistants. My answer was that they liked working for me. I know they did" (Colban 1952: 44).

As long as the façade was untainted, social and sexual life could take any form. However, the wife should be bourgeois and divorce was frowned upon. All this remained the case through the Second World War. When one senior diplomat divorced in the 1950s, according to one of his heirs and two of his colleagues, social pressure at the ministry was a key reason that he remarried his estranged wife. The effortlessly self-centeredness of this masculinity was in evidence as late as in 1962, when the after-dinner speaker at the annual Christmas party announced that "modern methods will be used in the recruitment of typists. The advertising for ladies will get a sharp and fun edge, centered on the following slogan: Why lonely? You too may have daily intercourse with young Norwegian diplomats. Seek your fortune now or later."[46]

For reasons that should be obvious from this brief sketch, nationalism in Norway took the form of freeholding peasants demanding more parliamentary representation and better social positions, which meant that civil servant families—usually easily identifiable by their names, which were either foreign-sounding (like Neumann) or the names of well-known native elites (like Galtung)—came under attack. State personnel changed, beginning with the new class of schoolteachers and then spreading up through the ranks (Slagstad 1998).

Post–Second World War: Three Masculinities

I suggest three sorts of masculinity amongst present-day diplomats: civil servant, petit bourgeois, and troublemaking. The first of these has already been discussed. The second arrived at the MFA around the time of the Second World War. With the coming of a social democratic government in the 1930s and the nation-building experience of war, the change of state personnel begun from below finally reached the apex of the state structure,

---

46. NNA MFA, 2.25/62.

as a handful of men from a rural or working-class backgrounds were accepted by the diplomatic academy. They embarked on a class journey, but
their habitus often continued to mark them as hierarchically subordinate.
Consider this autobiographical account of how one of the first of these men
arrived in Cairo, his first post abroad, in 1956:

> My new boss told me during our first interview that "you will address me
> as *De* [the polite form of you, like French *vous*] or Minister"[47] . . . I told him
> about myself and my experiences, among other things as a small farmer and
> a sailor, a background that was very foreign to him. A lot of what he consid-
> ered his birthright and wholly natural, were things that I had to learn. After
> a while he nodded and said: "So everything may be learned!" He took it as
> his task to teach me as much as possible, major things as well as minor ones.
> He usually did not do it directly, but rather by telling a story. Once he lit my
> cigarette. I let him do it, and thanked him. Then he told me a story from his
> posting in Cairo. The local British governor had been in conversation with
> a young secretary. When the secretary brought out a cigarette, the governor
> lit a match. But when the secretary stooped to light up, the governor let go
> of the match, which fell to the floor. Moral: When an older person of higher
> rank lights a match for you, you should not let him light your cigarette, but
> rather take the match and light his! When I appeared at the office unshaven,
> he used the same pedagogical method. (Svennevig 1996: 35–36)

A diplomat from rural western Norway, a part of the country that remains
distinct in terms of language and social mores like religion, told me that
when he entered the MFA in the mid-1960s, there was only one person
"from my milieu" there. He told me how, as late as in 1993, when the foreign minister wanted the MFA to put on a populist face with a view to
the upcoming referendum on the EU, the minister had summoned him
and three other senior dialect speakers to his office, greeting them with
the words: "and here come the peripheries (*og her kommer distriktene*)."
By then, however, "the peripheries" and other non–civil servant social

---

47. It was the breaking down of traditional class distinctions that made it possible for a person
such as this one to become a diplomat, which necessitated spelling out what the form of address
should be; any bourgeois would have used the polite form of address as a matter of course. From
the 1970s onward, however, the polite form became increasingly rare in colloquial Norwegian. At
present, using it has become a statement, either of extreme politeness or of hostility. In 1956, a few
Norwegian legations, Egypt amongst them, were still not headed by ambassadors.

locations were well represented in the lower and middle echelons of the organization. In 1998, I was on a trip to the NATO headquarters in Brussels with a couple of colleagues from Planning and a diplomat from another department. When I came down for breakfast, the latter was already there, wearing a suit and a colored shirt, deep in his newspaper. I sat down and said good morning. He looked up, said good morning—and continued to read. One Monday upon my return to the MFA I chanced upon three males in their early fifties in one of the corridors, and joined their conversation. They were all wearing colored shirts. One of them recounted how he had spent a long weekend "at home on the farm" (*på hjemgården;* it is a tell-tale distinguishing feature of the upwardly mobile that they go "home" to farms which either have not been their home since their teens or on which they have never lived but have spent summers from childhood due to their fathers having been born there). The other two reciprocated with stories about "their" farms. "There we are," my colleague Bernhard said and looked at me, "yeomen all" (*Se der, bønder alle sammen*).

Class is something of a taboo in Norwegian public conversation. When raised, which is rarely, it almost always happens implicitly. The best example I have of an exception—the most striking one I have come across either in conversation or in reading—concerns how the dean of Norwegian foreign policy journalists characterized the secretary general in connection with a personnel conflict in the MFA. The secretary general had been one of the first to break into the academy from the lowest ranks of the MFA, where he worked as a messenger. He was an extremely capable man with no university education and little polite conversation who favored colored shirts. The journalist wrote:

> When Bjarne Lindstrøm was appointed in the spring of 1996, he came from administration, with broad experience from budget and personnel work. This was his base. Regarding the profession of diplomacy, his only field experiences were a lowly UN job and a posting as consul general to South Africa, a thinner and narrower base than that enjoyed by any of his Norwegian predecessors or European counterparts. (*Aftenposten,* 22 April 2005)

The number of people with this class background in Norwegian diplomacy began to increase in the mid-1960s (when at least one person changed surname to fit in). By 2002, a universal structured interview with the

academy cohort showed them to be in a clear majority. The best charac-
terization I have come across of these two masculinities, highly culturally
specific and, in line with the point made above, highly implicit, was delivered by a Norwegian foreign policy journalist, who stated that people
who were accepted into the diplomatic academy were "either rovers or the
brightest young things from the Oslo West End."[48] Rovers are senior boy
and girl scouts who diligently lead youngsters. The reference is to straight-
lacedness, lack of frivolity; small-town, the countryside or Oslo's East End
rather than the West End, and not West End at all on the level of social
fact. (Oslo remains sharply socially divided between an East End of apartment blocks and small houses, and a West End of roomy apartments and
villas.) In a word, the bookish but multiple-talented from the middle lay-
ers as well as the upper layer of society.

Bookishness may take you in many directions, however. If we follow
Bourdieu, the habitus of the upwardly mobile class discussed here, which
he refers to as the *petite bourgeoisie,* is first of all characterized by a certain
rigidity:

> It is no accident that the adjective small (*petit*) or one of its synonyms can be
> applied to everything the petit bourgeois says, thinks, does, has or is, even
> to his morality, although that is his strong point: strong, and rigorous, its
> formalism and scruples always make it somewhat tense, susceptible and
> rigid. With his petty cares and petty needs, the petit bourgeois is indeed a
> bourgeois "writ small." Even his bodily hexis, which expresses his whole
> objective relation to the social world, is that of a man who has to make
> himself small to pass through the strait gate which leads to the bourgeoisie:
> strict and sober, discreet and severe, in his dress, his speech, his gestures and
> his whole being, he always lacks something in stature, breadth, substance,
> largesse. (Bourdieu [1979] 1984: 338)

This is due to a stronger socialization from childhood, and is intensified by
a contextual factor: There is more to learn, and more to lose. The upper
middle class, however, can take more for granted. To repeat a quoted passage, "A lot of what he [the person born to a civil servant family] considered

---

48. *"Enten rovere eller preceterister fra Persbråten,"* Kjetil Wiedsvang in conversation with the
author, 13 November 1999.

his birthright and wholly natural, were things that I [the person born to a small farmer family] had to learn" (Svennevig 1996: 35–36). Lamont (1992: xxiii–xxiv) found the same in her comparative study of French and American upper middle-class milieux; those firmly established over generations practiced "cultural standards such as intelligence, refinement, curiosity, and aesthetic sophistication," whereas the newcomers were after sincerity and/or material goods. Bourdieu's class stories and Connell's masculinity stories pair up nicely in the MFA of the early postwar years, where the confluence between class and masculinity was high. The hierarchy of class was also a hierarchy of masculinities.

We may speculate how these stories map onto the specific social world of diplomacy. In the previous chapter I argued that two hierarchically ordered hero stories are at work in the world of diplomacy; one about the diplomat who stands out by doing something exemplary in exceptional circumstances, the other about the bureaucrat who stands out by doing something exemplary again and again in everyday circumstances. Then there is the story of the mediator. Doing something exceptional while mediating is the ultimate ticket. It stands to reason that the upper middle-class male will be drawn to and more effortlessly live out the story of the mediator, whereas the rigidity of the upwardly mobile will fit better with the story of the bureaucrat. It is, for example, not surprising that the only secretary general to reach that position as a result of a class voyage also stands out among both Norwegian and European permanent under secretaries as being highly bureaucratic.[49]

The hierarchy of the two masculinities has been somewhat destabilized over the last quarter of a century by the arrival of a third masculinity at the MFA. In Connell's terms, we have here a troublemaking masculinity. Consider a speech delivered in celebration of the MFA's seventy-fifth anniversary in 1980. The speaker reminisced about the plurality of fresh diplomats that he had had under his wing as an MFA head of section. He began by describing a straightlaced, square fellow in well-ironed pants and polished brown shoes with a military background—clearly a petit bourgeois rover.

---

49. There is a limit to how far we may take this argument—scripts are social facts that exist at the level of analytical abstraction, whereas the persons who live them are persons with a physical, psychological, and social existence. The more stable the hierarchies involved, the harder it is for a person to get out of the habitus.

In Norway as elsewhere, brown shoes were then a class marker (but only when worn after regular office hours). He then described his first meeting with this fellow's

> diametrical opposite. He was by the standards of those days—I repeat, those days—rather unkempt, wearing an old turtleneck, with hair straggling here and there below eyes and ears. He didn't knock on my door, but rushed in, surrounded by the sour smell of his pipe, poised himself at the edge of my desk and said something like "Listen. The administration has decided that you are going to work with me, well, that I will be in your section. I have spoken to Thorvald [the first name of the state secretary of the day]. What we have to do now is get the European question onto a progressive and political track. Which political youth organization did you belong to in your student days?"[50]

If it is clear that the military man was petit bourgeois, it is equally clear that the unkempt one was a baby boomer and a child of the student movement of the 1960s—what is known in Norwegian as a "68-er." The 68-er had his predecessors—the beatniks of the 1950s and the cultural radicals of the interwar period, even certain literati before the First World War—but in the context of the MFA, he was definitely new and definitely trouble. He had a destabilizing effect. First, since intellectuals emerged as a self-conscious group in Poland and Russia in the early nineteenth century, their self-understanding has been as a many-classed group. Intellectual 68-ers, who dominated among those who entered the MFA, were no exception. By embodying a mix of the habitus that separated the other two masculinities, they brought disorder to a clear hierarchy of masculinities. For example, as in the case of the fellow described above, they wore colored shirts that were definitely not rich in cotton but at the same time they hailed from traditional civil servant families. As Alice, a librarian, reminisced to me about him: "And the *clothes* he was wearing! I don't think he ever washed them." Upon further questioning, it turned out that Alice, who had an upper middle-class background, was not troubled by the clothes as such, but by the fact that this particular man with his civil servant family background should have known better than to wear them in the MFA. To her,

---

50. NNA MFA, 2 1/51, speech by Huslid, 15 November 1980.

it was a case of letting the side down. To me, it is a case of hierarchy desta-
bilization between classed masculinities.

A second destabilizing effect of the male 68-ers on the MFA was that
they were the first to support their female colleagues. They broadly refused
the homosociality described above, and it was they who initiated the campaign in support of No. 3.[51] These new recruits became agents of internal
change, refusing to be fully pacified by the organizational grind.

To sum up, three masculinities may now be broadly identified within
the Norwegian MFA. The dominant one is what we may refer to as traditional civil servant masculinity. The subordinate one is the more rigidly
bureaucratic variety of the upwardly mobile male, the rover. The third,
the potentially troublemaking one, was pioneered by 68-ers and has, with
the passing of that cohort from the scene, transmuted into a more generalized intellectual and many-classed masculinity. These masculinities basically sustain one another. There are interesting overlaps between these
diplomatic masculinities and the nondiplomatic masculinity of the service
worker, also present in the MFA. The dominant masculinity relates to the
latter on the basis of *noblesse oblige*. The subordinate bureaucrat masculinity, with his humbler class background, has an easier rapport with it
but also a need to differentiate himself from the service worker. To the
intellectual masculinity, the service worker is an object of (more or less
patronizing) solidarity. But whereas diplomatic masculinities emerge from
society at large, on a day-to-day basis, they are first and foremost related
to and hence sustained by one another, with nondiplomatic masculinities
playing a decidedly minor role. Where the hierarchy of femininities is concerned, however, this is very different.

Three Femininities

All of the early Norwegian female diplomats shared an upper middle-class
background, but as female diplomats began entering in numbers in the

---

51. A third major destabilizing effect of the MFA 68-ers kicked in when, from the early 1980s
onwards, the MFA incorporated the personnel working with development policy. Norwegian development specialists were 68-ers almost to a person. Nomadic like the diplomat, but "improperly dressed and improperly opinionated" (to quote a part-time ministry employee, Gorm, who

latter half of the 1970s, the class hierarchy within the MFA was already changing. Class still seems to be an important ordering principle of femininities within the MFA, working in the same way as for masculinities, but other factors seem to be equally if not more important. Women's class voyages in Europe in the twentieth century have generally been significantly more frictionless than those of males. My evidence points to two factors in particular: the degree to which women pitch their imperative status as *either* woman *or* diplomat, and relations among the three subject positions of diplomat, spouse, and typist.[52] Regarding the former, consider the following clash between Nos. 3 and 4, reminiscing about their careers. No. 3 has cropped gray hair and wears a turtleneck, corduroys, and sensible shoes. No. 4, who wears a bob, a necklace, a business suit, stockings, and pumps, has just brought up her experience as ambassador to Morocco in the early 1980s.

> *No. 4:* Moroccans are really very hospitable and empathetic, and I had some respect for how the gents (*herrene*) retreated after a supper, so there I stood, fidgeting a bit and talking to my Nordics [my Nordic opposite numbers] and tried to get something out of the conversation, but then they, too, had to join the gents . . . and I thought once a lady, always a lady.
>
> *No. 3 (frowning):* Even as ambassador you had to join the ladies?
>
> *No. 4 (throwing her hair to one side):* Yes, but I did it a little out of respect for the culture, like, and then I could meet ladies who said "are you an ambassador, then you must meet my husband who is a governor" and then they fetched the governor and we were introduced . . .
>
> *No. 3 (leaning forward):* But if you had marched in on the men, what would have happened then?
>
> *No. 4:* Well, then I think I would have turned many against me, and if you get the women against you, then you get the men against you as well.
>
> *No. 3 (clearly engaged):* Really, you mean the spouses, these ambassadors' women, then? (*kvinnene til disse ambassadørene, da?*)

---

worked on development himself), the development specialist (or, in MFA parlance, "well digger") was an Other from which diplomats needed to keep their social distance. This was harder than it would have otherwise been given the existence of 68-ers within already established MFA ranks. The MFA 68-ers thus became liminal, a dedifferentiating group with a dual potential of making even more trouble and becoming a meshing force.

52. Note that the claim about imperative status is pitched at the level of diplomats' self-reflection, and *not* on the analytical level, where I programmatically think it should be left open.

No. 4: Yes, I shouldn't, like, be with their men—they have this man/woman aspect.

No. 3: But that is still rather hair-raising?

Pause (three seconds)

No. 3 (with finality): Your rank as ambassador wasn't respected at all.

No. 4: Yes, but here we have to draw a line between when you are in contexts where you are clearly marked as ambassador, then of course you were with the men, with your colleagues, but when it was a bit social . . . (*shooting her chest forward and bobbing her shoulders lightly from side to side*) I both bowed and curtseyed for the king, no problem there.

No. 3: But then it was Norway that bowed and curtseyed.

No. 4: I thought why not curtsey, and then I added a little bow (chuckles mutedly).

No. 3: As long as you didn't make a full reverence, I suppose we'll have to let it pass (*så får det være i orden*).[53]

Here we have juxtaposed two different strategies. To No. 4, gender is a given and imperative status: "once a lady, always a lady." This goes not only for self but also for other. She privileges relations with other women and deems relations with males as derivative of those all-feminine relations: "I would have turned many against me, and if you get the women against you, then you get the men against you." This makes for a clear self-ascriptive role hierarchy: woman first, diplomat next.[54] She pitches herself as a woman who happens to be a diplomat. Where No. 3 is concerned, all these points may be reversed. The main self-ascription is diplomat (more specifically, ambassador), who relates to others first and foremost in their role of ranked fellow diplomats. Diplomat first, woman next. She pitches herself as a diplomat who happens to be a woman. The issue here is not whether these strategies are more or less professional or more or

---

53. Taped interview, Bristol hotel, Oslo, 22 November 2005. When I read this out to her afterwards, Beate M. commented spontaneously about no. 4: "Yes, she was more of a woman (*Ja, hun var mer kvinne*)."

54. Note that we are at the level of folk models here. Ortner & Whitehead (1984: 8) were amongst the first to comment on "the general cultural tendency to define men in terms of status and role categories ('warrior,' 'hunter,' 'statesman,' 'elder,' and the like) that have little to do with men's relations with women. Women, by contrast, tend to be defined almost entirely in relational terms—typically in terms pertaining to kin roles." I note that, a quarter century on, I still find traces of this in my material—but only traces.

less gendered; both are aimed at getting the job done, and both are self-reflexively gendered. But we have two different femininities: the woman-first-diplomat-next and the diplomat-first-woman-next. The finding confirms Spike Peterson's (1992: 17) basic structuralist argument that

> what appears at first to be simply "adding women" (as an empirical ges-ture) turns out to be more complicated. To the extent that "adding women" means adding "that which constitutes femininity" to categories constituted by their masculinity (the exclusion of femininity), a contradiction is exposed. Either women as feminine cannot be added (i.e. women must become men) or the category must be transformed to accommodate the inclusion of women (as feminine). The (masculine) gender of the original category . . . is exposed. Because the categories of masculine and feminine are mutually constituted, a new category accommodating women/feminine necessarily reconfigures the gendered meaning of the original category—including the construction of masculinity it presupposed. Therefore, not only is under-standing of the public sphere and politics transposed, but . . . the meaning of masculinity is also altered.

Since there was an inherent tension between the statuses "women" and "diplomat," the strategic choices made by individual women in the MFA were over-determined. They had no choice but to privilege one status over another. For this reason, we may probably generalize the finding to other MFAs and even more widely. Indeed, Billig and Alvesson inter-viewed a female Danish MFA employee who reported from service in the UN that

> if you were too business-like and not feminine you were uninteresting, but if you were too feminine and not sufficiently business-like, well, then you were just a woman and were not respected as far as work was con-cerned. Clearly, it was a balancing act, and I think the same applies here in the ministry.[55]

These strategies may be treated as stories emanating from discourse. Since the immediate "circle of recognition" (Ringmar 1996) of the woman-first-diplomat-next femininity consists of other women, and its general circle

---

55. Billig and Alvesson 1994: 160.

of recognition is gendered persons generally, this story ascribes a lot of action to relations with nondiplomats. What wives say and do, for instance,
is held to be crucially important. In earlier evidence, the woman-first-diplomat-next also ascribes her informal social inclusion or lack thereof to
the actions of diplomats' wives. Logically, the woman-first-diplomat-next
tends to have "sister"-based relationships with feminine nondiplomatic
personnel. If gender holds imperative status, it follows that common gender affiliation is more socially meaningful than workplace hierarchy. It also
follows that such women will seek social recognition in the relationships
they privilege—with wives and nondiplomatic personnel. I worked with
a woman-first-diplomat-next for two years. She used to call me into her
office to show me particularly dramatic sunrises (in the Oslo winter, they
occur around the start of the working day). Always smiling, her conversation was about her children, travels, shopping, and other topics marked
feminine in general discourse. When she applied for a posting that she did
not get, she immediately ascribed it to her being a woman. I heard her discuss this with our typist at length. It also came up during one luncheon,
when I was the only male present. My impression is that she discussed this
with all her woman acquaintances in the organization, and with males
who she felt respected her as a woman. When, in compensation for the
posting she did not get, she was offered another one by the administration, she turned it down, telling me that she did not take just *anything* that
was on offer (*jeg lar meg ikke by hva som helst*). I asked George in administration why she did not get the job she had applied for, and was told that
another diplomat with similar credentials had stayed longer at home and
hence took precedence. And then he added: "We offered her something
else, and she did not take it. You know, that does not work. It's unprofes-
sional." This woman-first-diplomat-second had evoked and confirmed a
male expectation about the emotional, choosey, moody woman.[56] Western
men, Victor Seidler (1994: 19) argues, "learn to live as if our emotional lives
do not exist, at least as far as the 'public world' is concerned." The civil servant male was secure in his gendered professionalism, for it permeates the
organization as well as the culture.

---

56. She eventually became an ambassador.

It is no surprise that a femininity premised on stuff marked female in discourse will evoke reactions marked male in that same discourse. If male and female are mutually constitutive categories, this is a necessity for discourse to have any permanence (and we know that it does). There may be hefty career costs attached to the femininity "woman-first-diplomat-next." First, as seen in the exchange quoted above, it evokes the ire of a competing femininity, the diplomat-first-woman-next, who may see her actions as letting the side down, by acting so that one's diplomatic rank is bracketed. There is logic to this reaction, for by privileging gender as her imperative social status, the woman-first-diplomat-next necessarily disprivileges not only her own professional status but also the professional status of other women. When, for the first time in history, two Norwegian female diplomats served at the same post abroad, one as an ambassador, the other being on her first post, something happened that was unprecedented in the history of Norwegian diplomacy. The junior woman sent a long and damning memo on her boss to the MFA, and when the memo did not have the desired effect, she left in a huff. I asked the head of administration at the time how this could be, and he said "You know, women." One obvious reading is that the incident reproduced a male (and arguably a general) stereotype, namely that women will quarrel (cf. Kanter 1977: 220).

A second cost of woman-first-diplomat-next concerns how it is premised on social recognition from nondiplomats inside and outside the organization. The time and social capital used on gaining the recognition of nondiplomats may not be relevant to gaining the recognition of fellow diplomats, so such behavior may be professionally wasted and even counterproductive. A third cost, evident in the recounted reaction by George in administration, is that the acting out of a femininity premised on general social discourse on gender invites typical masculine reactions. Given that general social discourse operates on a hierarchical principle where males are privileged, the woman-first-diplomat-next confirms and perpetuates that hierarchy, to her own loss as well as to the loss of women who embody other femininities. This, however, is an analytical point that the woman-first-diplomat-next would contest. I was talking to a group of women in the academy about these things during French classes. "It is nice to be a woman," said Ginny M., "women have more to play on" (*mer å spille på*). This as she tilted her head slightly to one side and slightly back, showed all her upper teeth and let her lower shoulder swing discreetly back. In the short run, perhaps Ginny is right. In the long run, probably not.

There are also costs to being diplomat-first-woman-next, however, for making male diplomats your circle of recognition and insisting that you are just one of the boys means playing and being umpired on terms that are male, and so not your own. There is an inevitable gap between the person of a male and the impersonation of a male-based representation of diplomat which puts the diplomat-first-woman-next at a disadvantage.

Since the late 1970s, there has been a third femininity in the MFA. Where dress, hair, and make-up are concerned, these women are much more understated than the woman-first-diplomat-next, but they tend to be more dressed up than the diplomat-first-woman-next. Where the woman-first activates her status as woman on a continual basis and the diplomat-first is equally persistent in toning it down, this new femininity activates the status "woman" on a tactical basis, due to situational demands. Witness Ginny M. This femininity relates to wives and secretaries on a "sister" basis, but it privileges relations with other diplomats, male or female. Their relations are not "sister" based; gender solidarity is valuable only for its instrumental uses. For example, when asked explicitly whether any of the two hundred female diplomats who had been accepted into the MFA after them had sought their advice on how to be a woman in the diplomat service, female diplomats nos. 3 and 4 answered with a firm "no." The new femininity's circle of recognition is diplomats, regardless of gender. I worked with one such female diplomat for two years. One day, she came beaming back from a course on leadership. I asked what the good news was. "They gave me a male mentor. I am not interested in these women's networks, I have women contacts already. What I need are male contacts." This is the femininity that dominates committee work on equality within the MFA administration as well as in its trade organizations. It is self-consciously instrumental and career oriented, and so makes for tensions with other femininities. For example, Brigid, a diplomat-first-woman-next who was about to receive her first ambassadorship, complained to me that "some of the younger women" used the trade unions to boost the number of women ambassadors. When I retorted that boosting the number of female ambassadors was a state goal, she readily agreed, but pointed out that this would happen by itself in due course. This conflict has logic. It is not surprising that, upon reaching her goal of becoming an ambassador, this diplomat-first-woman-next, who had bided her time and not fielded the issue of gender, would find it awkward to share the honor with others whom she saw as having reached the same goal on a quota basis.

If we compare the three diplomat femininities in the MFA to its three masculinities, one striking feature is the degree to which they are differently classed. Whereas only one of the masculinities, the intellectual, is many-classed, this is true of all three femininities. The femininity of woman-first-diplomat-next, for example, comes in upper middle, petty bourgeois, and even working class variants. Take Tracy, a woman who favored tight pants, large belts, a lot of make up, and brightly colored hair. She hailed from a small countryside community, and introduced herself on the phone by the name of that community. We were talking about her work as a supervisor in the academy, and she said: "Many of these new ones are so clever, some of them have doctoral degrees and things. What I think is important for them to learn is to be nice and kind (*god og snill*)."

We may now ask the same question of the MFA's three femininities that we asked of its masculinities, namely, what is their hierarchical order? Since the difference between the woman-first and the diplomat-first turns on the grounds on which female diplomats should be judged—as women or as diplomats—it is undecidable on its own terms. The stories invite recognition from different groups on different terms. The new femininity aims to combine the advantages of the other two femininities and cut the costs. A dialectician would argue that it is a synthesis of the other two. At the beginning of its life cycle, this new femininity had the marks of a troublemaking story, but the demands it fielded were met, and so it spelled success rather than trouble for those who made this story their own. It is a subject position that fits the concept of the person held out by the neo-liberal discourse in which Norwegian diplomacy is embedded. Small wonder that it seems to be gaining ground at the cost of the other two, and comes across as increasingly dominant. Perhaps we should call it "designer femininity."

* * *

How do the six gendered scripts or stories map onto the stories discussed in the previous chapter? I focus on only two of these, namely the story of the hero mediator and the story of the everyday hero bureaucrat—which also provide a way of establishing the hierarchy of gendered stories overall. All six stories lend themselves to the bureaucratic story, but two of them less so: the story of intellectual masculinity, which may be too troublemaking to fit in with the bureaucratic story's demands for conforming blandness, and the new femininity story, which may be too tactical. To bring out the point, let me go back to Anne Campbell's remark to the effect that heroes are basically male. A Swedish female diplomat once responded to my suggestion that there are two hero stories for the diplomat by rightly pointing out that "the hero script applies much more to men, to Western men," than it does to women (Gudmundson 2004: 98). On second thought, however, she made the following point: "I sometimes ask myself if I am acting out a female story in the Baudrillard sense that women tend to work as guerrilla warriors outside to the inside of the institutions, if so it seems to work very well" (Gudmundson 2004: 122). This describes moves characteristic of what I have labeled designer femininity—but note that the guerrilla warrior is an irregular. She may score the odd victory, but she does not have access to all the paraphernalia of a regular army like a general staff, an orderly line of command, and a fortified base, so her forays are always high-risk.

Where the story of the mediating hero is concerned, only three of the six seem to fit. The upwardly mobile male story seems too derivatively rigid, the woman-first-diplomat-second story too professionally unfocused, and the diplomat-first-woman-next story too self-effacing. That leaves the stories of traditional civil servant masculinity, intellectual masculinity, and new femininity.

The traditional civil servant masculinity story has the unbeatable advantage of being the only gendered diplomatic story to be fully compatible with both hero stories. Perhaps shifting from military to musical metaphors may serve to bring out the point. Like the hero jazz musician, the masculine civil servant can keep up the basic beat on an everyday basis, and then soar above his peers when room opens up for a solo. Intellectual masculinity and new femininity have greater difficulty combining the steady beat of the everyday with the effortless solo. The intellectual male values opposition too much, and so has problems keeping up the beat. The new female is too tactical and so has problems with the timing. Since she is not able to take the continuation of the music for granted in the way that the masculine civil servant is, she is not "loose" in the same way. As a result, trying a solo will be more risky and the chances of failure will be higher. As she is uncertain of support from the rest of the band, it may also prove difficult to fall back into her normal rhythm when she has finished her solo.

On this score, the new femininity resembles subordinate masculinity. Consider the case of Bjorn, a diplomat who had seemingly done everything right. He was getting out of the subordinate habitus by marrying up, always dressing sharply, handling himself with the proper comportment, and establishing a deserved reputation as an incisive analyst. When he was appointed to a major station where diplomatic uniforms were still in use, he decided to don the traditional Norwegian ostrich-feather cap and saber for his audience with the royal head of state. The uniform had not been in general use for generations. The incident found its way to the press, and the other males of the organization seized the opportunity. "But I always found his judgment to be sound," I piped up in his defense to George. "Ostrich feathers! How intelligent is that! (*Strutsefjær! Hvor smart er det'a!*)," he shot back. Coming home, Bjorn, who was widely expected to be the new secretary general, ended up in the doldrums. Victor summed it up: "If you lose your reputation in the MFA, you're finished." Bjorn attempted to soar above the band, but he had struck a false note.

Since gender is relational, the entry of women diplomats beyond the threshold of tokenism was certain to bring about changes in all the organization's gendered stories. The gendered stories of intellectual masculinity and new or designer femininity have destabilized traditional gender hierarchies for decades, and have the potential to reconfigure them still further. Over the last three years, a handful of people of ethnically non-Norwegian parentage, all women, have been accepted into the service. Their number is bound to rise, and eventually there are bound to be male diplomats with this background as well. These developments will probably have some transformative potential. So far, however, civil servant masculinity still rules the roost. If organizational divisions in the setup of the diplomatic service are added to the dividing lines concerned with class and gender, it is clear how the everyday practices of Norwegian diplomats, far from being as uniform as they seem from the outside, are actually quite diverse and dispersed.

Conclusion: Diplomatic Knowledge

Anthropologists claim that the more primitive the community the stricter
are its conventions. . . . Most diplomats would perhaps resist being classified
as anthropologically primitive, but in a sense their community is just that.
Outside the local law, beyond the jurisdiction of the courts, the diplomatic
corps would be a lawless community were it not for its self-imposed ethics
and rules which together comprise protocol.

CHARLES W. THAYER, diplomat, 1960

Traditional stories about how diplomacy emerged have not taken ad-
equate note of the fact that *all* polities need mediation. While it is true that
today's diplomacy is the successor to the diplomacies of ancient Greek *polis,*
Italian city-states, and Westphalian territorial states, diplomacy may also
be found before these versions, in between them, and elsewhere. Moreover,
since they focus on representation abroad, traditional stories about contemporary diplomacy routinely omit those origins of contemporary diplomacy
that are to be found at home. In the institutionalization of court advisers in
the thirteenth century, the emergence of foreign ministries toward the end
of the eighteenth century, and the amalgamation of these ministries with
consular and diplomatic services beginning only a century ago, we have a
second set of origins for today's diplomacy. The direct predecessor of the
diplomat working at home is the bureaucratic scribe.

The diplomat working abroad and the diplomat working at home are
engaged in two different modes of knowledge production. The practice
that anchors the knowledge production of field diplomats is the gathering

and processing of information. In contrast, diplomats at home are caught up in a web of text-producing practices that ensure that, when not interfered with by politicians, they produce nothing new. A central drama for the individual diplomat is how best to switch between these two modes of knowledge production. Another is how to handle the fact that the diplomat's work is about mediating between other people's positions. A third is how to integrate one's public persona with one's personal life, when representing one's country plays such an important role in both spheres. Ideally, diplomats should be heroes in two senses of that word; they should be immaculate in shouldering the burdens of everyday work, and they should do exceptional things, such as negotiating a peace. Given the discursive obstacles of class and gender that structure diplomatic life, despite the large changes in recruitment patterns over the last half-century or so, the upper middle-class male is still best placed to pull off this feat.

The Norwegian Ministry of Foreign Affairs sprang into existence in 1905, and like other MFAs depends for its organization and its form on diplomatic discourse. Diplomatic knowledge production is also dependent on specific discursive practices. Consider the story told by diplomatic discourse about how to draw up a document. The story is made up of concepts, and the story's power depends on the resonance of those concepts (Koselleck [1979] 1985). Documents become instantiations of the ministry because the whole ministry is, at least implicitly, active in producing them. Discourses have what we may call conceptual power.

When practices do not change, they tell confirming stories back to discourse. Sometimes, however, there is no positive feedback. Established discourse may reassert itself, as it did when I tried to write speeches different from the speeches that had been written before. Alternatively, and probably as a result of political intervention, discourse may change. The Chicago anthropologist Marshall Sahlins (1981: 8) once observed that "The great challenge to an historical anthropology is not merely to know how events are ordered by culture, but how, in that process, the culture is reordered. How does the reproduction of a structure become its transformation?" Leaving aside the unwieldy aggregate of culture and focusing on diplomatic practices, my aim has been to specify how this happens on a quotidian basis.

If it is the case that diplomats do, and go on doing, things they would not otherwise have done because of the way diplomatic discourse is set up, we are dealing with relations laden with power. To determine what kind of power is at work, it is helpful to consult Michel Foucault (particularly 1994). According to Foucault, there are three modes of power relations: strategy, dominance, and governmentality. Strategy is a game between wills where it is unclear who will win. Strategy is ever-present, but because it sees no further than the acting individual, it cannot help us understand how practices perpetuate themselves. Dominance is a direct type of power, whereby individuals are molded to serve the needs of power (Ransom 1997: 57; Neumann and Sending 2010). Diplomats are certainly molded. Regardless of what a woman diplomat did before the mid-1980s, she could not escape the choice between two, and only two, identities: diplomat-first-woman-next, or woman-first-diplomat-next. Either way, the woman diplomat was at a disadvantage vis-à-vis her male colleagues, whose gender identities were not at loggerheads with their professional identity.[1] Most of the time, however, diplomats are not molded directly by people but rather indirectly, by discourse. In the form of power that Foucault calls governmentality, people monitor and govern their own practices by drawing on the stories that discourse holds out. This is the sort of power that permeates the diplomatic discourse of which I was a part for almost six years. The way in which my attempts to change the making of MFA speeches were thwarted is, I think, a typical example of governmentality. I was up against practices that were firmly anchored and that amounted to one of diplomacy's central modes of knowledge production (the other being the information gathering conducted when the diplomat is abroad).

Over the last century, the sheer amount of diplomatic business has increased manifold, and so have the number of diplomats and the size of foreign ministries. Diplomats both metaphorically and literally enable the state to "govern from afar"; they may still be seen as a, I would even say the, key embodiment of the state beyond its own borders. Crucially, however, one consequence of the exponential growth in international, transnational, and nongovernmental organizations is the number of people who, though not diplomats traditionally understood, are nonetheless engaged in practices akin to diplomatic ones. Such people are producing knowledge that is often in direct competition with the kind of knowledge that diplomats

---

1. Furthermore, dominance kicks in when governmentality does not work. If indirect governing of diplomats does not work, the diplomat is taken off the task, or, in extreme cases, is asked to leave or even stripped of his or her job in a lawsuit (see Taftø 1997).

traditionally attempted to monopolize. "Globalization" describes what we are talking about.

Broad social change offers challenges and opportunities, and quantitative change can spell qualitative change. As I reflect on how diplomacy has changed during the thirty years since I served as a guard and interpreter at Norway's Moscow Embassy, I am struck by the increased number of interlocutors that diplomats have to face. The importance of the media and the existence of competing knowledge producers and brokers puts considerable pressure on diplomacy's meandering style. More technically, the temporality of diplomatic practices is at loggerheads with that of other practices in which diplomatic practices are imbricated. One result may be a speeding up of diplomatic practices (Neumann 2008b). Another seems to be that state diplomatic practices are changing in a networking direction, but in particular senses: more bilateral state diplomacy is becoming multilateral, and the network is evolving more nodes that are not states but local (parastate), state-transcending (transstate), and nonstate.

Here is a concrete example. When the end of the 1980s brought an apparently system-transforming change in the Soviet Union and the Cold War ended, the possibility of forging new practices opened up for neighboring states. In Norway, the key attempt to establish a new practice concerning its relationship with Russia focused on the 196-kilometer border in the high north and the possibility of building some kind of regional structure for cooperation. Following input from research institutions, the MFA's Department of Policy Planning and Research initiated an attempt to establish a "Barents Region," a region of transborder cooperation between Norwegian and Russian authorities. The planners brought Foreign Minister Stoltenberg on board and set up a small retreat to go over the details. As Kvistad (1995: 11) points out, "the Barents project was conducted and promoted on a relatively independent basis in the early stages, detached from the ordinary hierarchical line of administration in the ministry. A small group of people took care of most of the communication with foreign embassies including meetings and lunches to prepare the Kirkenes conference. All along, there was close informal contact with the Russian embassy in Oslo."[2]

---

2. As a diplomat would say, "I will not omit to point out (*vil ikke unnlate å peke på*)" both that I was the supervisor for the political science M.Phil. thesis on which the quoted source was based,

Within the repertoire of available practices (from various cross-border cooperation schemes, from the Nordic region, and from the newly established Baltic Sea Region), and on the margins of established institutions (first and foremost the Norwegian MFA), a small group improvised the building of a new region. This process fits nicely with de Certeau's (1984: 125) insight into how stories, in this case about a Barents Region, "go in a procession" ahead of practices that may then make such a region materialize. In this case, MFA planners commissioned a think tank to tell detailed stories about the area in question and ordered two reports, one from a historian and one from a political scientist, on how relations between Norway and Russia had "always" been friendly at the grassroots level—with the incidental exception of seventy years of communism. The lesson produced was that, with communism gone, building a region would be not a new undertaking but a reestablishing of what was historically "natural." With this story in place, new practices could be initiated.

In terms of diplomatic discourse, however, the stories about a Barents Region contained a concept that was new and hence unwanted. The suggestion was that the institutional structure of the Barents Region should have two tiers: a council for foreign ministers and a regional council headed by elected local representatives. To give regional politicians a diplomatic function was the one piece of the initiative that was innovative, so bureaucratic resistance focused on it. Some cautious diplomats wanted the state's representatives to take the lead in the proposed regional council, not the elected local representatives. This change would secure MFA control of foreign policy (Kvistad 1995: 11–12). Faced with a new idea, a foreign minister must choose when to follow bureaucratic practice and kill it, when to follow the statesman's practice and back it. In this case, the minister chose the latter. I asked the foreign minister to recount how he had gone about it, and the answer is worth quoting at length:

> When I came back as foreign minister in November 1990, one of the first questions I raised was how we could take advantage of the end of the Cold War. The natural place to look was where there had been tensions, namely in the North. The planning staff responded, Sverre Jervell was a key person,

---

nor that its author subsequently embarked on a successful diplomatic career. The Norwegian foreign policy–oriented milieu is a close-knit affair.

and it was his idea to involve the counties and the local politicians, at least he was the one to suggest it to me. This turned out to be the beginning of a trend where counties and regions work with one another across borders throughout Europe. I launched the plan 25 April 1992, at the annual meeting of the Labour Party in Troms. I had already talked with [Russian Foreign Minister] Kozyrev, he was so keen he even decided to run for his Duma seat in Murmansk, I also spoke to [Finnish Foreign Minister] Väyrynen, [Swedish Foreign Minister] Margareta af Ugglas, and to [Danish Foreign Minister] Uffe Ellemann-Jensen, and we all met in Kirkenes on 13 January 1993. The regional council grew out of two factors. First was the very idea that the motor of the cooperation should be tended to by the people in the North themselves, for the people in the North themselves. . . . Secondly, a general move towards involving regional politicians in transborder activities was afoot, around the Baltic Sea, the Skagerrak, around the North Sea, and so on. Whatever we say officially, the reality is that our relationship to borders has changed rather dramatically. As seen by the civil servants, it was an unusual thing that the counties were involved.[3]

It was unusual, in the sense of breaking with bureaucratic practice. One also notes how meetings between opposite numbers pushed the initiative through, and how stories about local initiative "go in a procession" toward the broad public before the practice is introduced.

With stories in place and the political decision made, it was time to change working practices inside the MFA. This involved some improvisation. In part to insulate the initiative from extinction by established practices, most of the early work was carried out at the political level, flanked by the Department of Policy Planning and Research, which had been partially detached from the standard chain of command. In this way, the initiative could be normalized as part of the ministry's routine before it was actually slotted into ministry working practices. Once the project was going according to schedule, a working group of twelve to fifteen people from different offices and departments was established and met on a weekly basis. This loose grouping was then turned into

---

3. Interview with Thorvald Stoltenberg, 29 February 2000. For an analysis that was done immediately after the event and contains more details, see Tunander 1994. For the record, I know the early stages of the case first hand, and participated in the public discussion of it until it became a routine part of Norwegian diplomacy.

a Barents secretariat, consisting of two employees, that took care of the daily business. Only when the Barents Region had been formally established was the project fully integrated into the normal bureaucratic procedures of the Ministry of Foreign Affairs (see Kvistad 1995: 13). The incremental character of the actions taken by politicians vis-à-vis the bureaucracy suggest how strong they held the power of established practices to be. Innovation had to come from the very top, and its normalization as part of a changed practice had to be overseen every step of the way. In this case, the chain of sustained actions resulted in the innovation being accepted, and diplomacy changed accordingly. When I arrived in the ministry three years later, to work in the very same Department of Policy Planning and Research that had been responsible for hatching the innovation, colleagues from other departments would still occasionally complain about how "my" department had breached the chain of command to push through the innovation. When the department was closed down in 2000, several people found the explanation in this chain of events.[4]

Local administrators and politicians thrived on their new foreign policy role. The chair of the Nordland County Cabinet and head of the Barents Council of the Regions told me:

> Our experiences from the Barents Region prove that the two-pillar system of cross-border cooperation is successful. It is my most exciting political experience so far. The division of labor is that we look after the people-to-people contacts, while the Foreign Ministry handles foreign policy overall. They are not able to handle the hands-on culture and business contacts. . . . Each year the two county mayors and I have a meeting with the foreign minister, to discuss the division of labor, financing of projects, and so on. Before meetings in the Regional Council, we often initiate informal contact. Before the last meeting, I had a conversation with [Norwegian Foreign Minister] Jagland. We don't feel instructed, but rather that we work our way through an agenda. They are present, but we don't feel them breathing down our necks. It's a functioning two-pillar system.[5]

---

4. One of them was the head of that department at the time of the Barents initiative; interview with Kåre Hauge, 19 August 2001.

5. Interview with Geir Knutson, 15 December 2000.

Not only regional bureaucrats but also regional politicians have become heavily involved in practices of a diplomatic kind. From the perspective of the MFA, the cooption of local politicians succeeds to the extent that local politicians re-present foreign policy and diplomatic practices isomorphically, by playing out the exchange of notes with Russian opposite numbers, by having the leading local politicians go before their local assemblies to inform them about their foreign policy activities, and so on. Where diplomatic practice is concerned, then, there was a need to change the internal practices of the MFA and a need to establish new practices for cooperating with substate actors.

We have here a successful example of governmentality, as shown in Figure 2. To sum up: changes in the overall political discourse opened up the possibility of new practices. Key personnel at the Norwegian MFA responded by improvising a new practice. Stories of historic friendship between Russians and Norwegians, cut short by Soviet power, were written by researchers at the behest of the Norwegian MFA, and created a social field inside which the new practice could emerge. By producing and fielding new knowledge, the MFA wielded conceptual power that made possible the establishment of a new practice. This new practice was then established in the face of opposition from the "discourse police," particularly inside the Norwegian MFA. As a result, Norwegian diplomatic discourse changed.

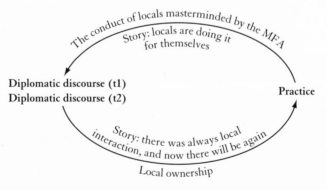

Figure 2. Change in diplomatic culture, Norway, 1991 (t₁)—1995 (t₂).

A Spread of Diplomatic Practices

This change in diplomatic culture demonstrates how the MFA interpolated local bureaucrats and politicians into the diplomatic process in order to increase action capacity. As a result, local bureaucrats became agents of diplomacy. They are only one such new group. We are witnessing a "diplomatization" (cf. Jönsson and Hall 2005) of other discourses. Present preconditions for knowledge production, with its intense networking and often real-time communication, are making other professions and other fields of expertise more similar to the diplomacy and the diplomat's way of being in the world. One such sphere that immediately comes to mind is the military. Recall Raymond Aron's ([1962] 1966: 5) insistence that interstate relations are expressed in action by two kinds of individuals that are symbolic of the state, the diplomat and the soldier (see chapter 4). The military attaché has been a staple of embassy life for one and a half centuries or so. At Norway's delegation to the European Union, we now find attachés from all state ministries, but the military attaché still "takes precedence over other Service Attachés at the post" (Satow [1917] 1979: 169).

Since the globalization of social life is a general phenomenon, bureaucrats of all stripes deal increasingly with the transnational and so are diplomatized. For diplomats, who are very particular about being different from and something more than bureaucrats, this poses a problem. If (other) bureaucrats are diplomatized, then the challenge is not only to limit the amount of bureaucratic work done by diplomats but also to limit the degree to which other bureaucrats may claim that they are representing Norway and to innovate ways of doing this effectively. Not long after I left the MFA, I was on the phone with Lieutenant Colonel Even J., who headed the military headquarters office responsible for military attachés. He knew that I had recently been working in the MFA, and volunteered a story of what happened when he heard about the MFA's work on its first spousal policy. The military had been quicker to respond in the early 1970s on, when Norwegian women entered the workforce in earnest. One result was that the military had years before drawn up a plan on how to take care of spouses accompanying military attachés. Even J. had called on the MFA administration and offered his help. The response was not what he had hoped for. As Even told me: "they did not welcome my call, to put it mildly" (*de var svært avvisende, for å si det mildt*).

Other state representatives, such as development specialists, are also diplomatized. In Norway, what was previously the Norwegian Development Agency has now become part of the Ministry of Foreign Affairs. Another group, business and NGO expatriates, do not represent the state as such, but given the ever denser interfaces between the state on the one hand and large transnational corporations and nongovernmental organizations on the other, diplomatization takes place directly, and these groups copy diplomatic practices in such areas as establishing missions abroad, information gathering, reporting between those missions and home headquarters, and turnover of personnel. Key examples of such organizations in Norway's case include developmental organizations (the five largest understand themselves as nongovernmental although the state has at times funded more than 90 percent of their work) and the oil company Statoil (which is quoted on the U.S. stock market but whose board still consists solely of the Norwegian minister for oil and energy). I know of their diplomatization because I have been instrumental in it, having been invited to brief the company on how diplomacy and diplomats work.

In other social spheres, aspects of work increasingly resemble the work of the diplomat. For example, Boyer (2005: 96, emphasis in the original) draws attention to how journalists may, in certain social settings, be seen as *"an anthropomorphism of epistemic mediation itself."* When mediation is transnational, isomorphism between the diplomat's and the journalist's modes of knowledge production seems particularly strong. Ethnographic work on foreign correspondents draws attention to their forging of networks, their production of knowledge, their use of international hotels and restaurants as "switchboards," and their nomadic treks between home and abroad (Hannerz 2003; Hannerz 1996: 102–12). All this looks quite familiar to the student of diplomats.

Isomorphism makes for competition. Since the telegraph wire was introduced in the 1860s, communication over long distances has become more and more common. As a corollary, the advantage of running a closed system of communication has dwindled, and journalists have increasingly been able to produce knowledge of a similar kind at speeds matching or even exceeding that of diplomats. As a result, diplomats lose out on temporality. Indeed, according to his chargé d'affaires, the Norwegian minister to Russia in 1917 kept his reporting home to a minimum, giving as his reason that his colleagues in the ministry could read the international press (Omang 1958: 73). During a private visit to Copenhagen in 2003, I stayed with Gard, an old Norwegian diplomat friend. I was meeting Denmark's leading foreign policy scholar for a working lunch on Nordic strategies regarding European integration. Since reporting on Denmark's EU policy is among the key tasks of Norwegian diplomats in Copenhagen, I asked if Gard would not like to tag along and pick up some extra points for his next report home. Gard politely refused, saying that he would just work up a report on the strength of the weekend papers. One may say of the diplomatization of journalist work, as one may of state bureaucrats' work, that it is a triumph for diplomacy to be copied. One may also say, however, that the very triumph spawns a challenge to the diplomat, who has to deal with others doing similar work in similar ways.

In his work on German journalists, Boyer (2005: 43) argues convincingly that intellectuals are "artisans of epistemic form" and highlights how, historically, the German journalist was held to be an empty holding station for information. The resulting lack of cultural capital placed him at the bottom of the intellectual pecking order. In Norway, another Teutonic power, the situation was similar. These days, however, it is harder to enter journalism school than it is to enter medical school. I bring this up to make the point that the power of epistemic form seems to co-vary with, among other things, what kind of information is handled with what kind of exclusivity by what kind of people. I have given examples of how the Norwegian foreign ministry uses its status as the key node in foreign policy networks to exclude and include others from the sundry political networks of which it is part, and also to take a cut of exclusive information (cf. Strathern 1996). Diplomatization of other spheres makes this harder to do. Although it has always been part of the diplomat's work to be a good networker, it makes perfect sense for diplomats to resist the ongoing tendency to network with different state and nonstate agencies.

It is tempting to lift this *problématique* to a general level. Sovereignty, it has been argued, always had a spiritual dimension (Dumézil [1940] 1988). Often its definition seems secular, as when Thomson (1995: 214) defines it as "an institution which imparts to the state what I call meta-political authority. That is, with the institution of sovereignty states are empowered or authorized to decide what is political in the first place." Even here the spiritual dimension is implied, inasmuch as it is usually a key ingredient of authority claims (Osiander 1994;, Krasner 1984, 1988; chapter 2 above).[6] Diplomacy remains a key marker of sovereignty (Durkheim [1913] 1992: 85; Scott 1998: 315). With globalization weakening state boundaries and with global neoliberalism changing the boundaries between state and nonstate, new practices put the discursive principle of sovereignty under pressure. It stands to reason that diplomats, whose social standing has for the last five hundred years been tied to that of the sovereign they have represented, must feel the pressure. Genealogically, in Western tradition, the diplomat is the angel visiting upon earth. With the weakening of sovereignty, which packs part of its power from indexing the sacred, what is left of the diplomat's halo is fading further.

To follow this perhaps exalted train of thought, the diplomatization of new spheres of social life seems to be matched by the spread of that other main source of present-day diplomacy—bureaucratization. A hundred anthropologists have, redundantly given that the category in point is ideal-typical and so an analytical one, pointed out that the Weberian bureaucrat is the human being that never was (e.g., Handelman and Layton 1978, Lewellen 1992, Gledhill 1994). Since Arendt's (1963) study of Eichmann in Jerusalem, social scientists have increasingly considered indifference, not rationality, to be the hallmark of bureaucracy (Herzfeld 1992). Michael Barnett's (1997, 2002) analyses of how the setup of work at the United Nations first made him an instant Rwanda expert and then, when reports

---

6. Thomson (1995: 214) goes on to argue that "With sovereignty, states do not simply have ultimate authority over things political; they have the authority to relegate activities, issues, and practices to the economic, social, cultural, and scientific realms of authority or to the states' own realm—the political. This is not to say that activities defined as apolitical are not intensely political but only that states will not treat them as political." Compare this to the following forty-year-old broadside from a key figure in political anthropology: "The political philosophers who taught me a generation ago were quite clear that whatever was to be called 'political' must have something to do with the state: if phrases like "University politics" or "Church politics" were used, then they meant that these institutions were playing a part in State politics: otherwise the phrases were simply metaphors. But political structures can be recognized at all levels and in all kinds of activities and can, when appropriate, be compared with one another. The anthropologist must do this. Research has uncovered and made sense of societies which have no authorities and are not states and yet enable their people to live orderly lives" (Bailey 1969: 12). Since Thomson's understanding is now increasingly dominant within political science, clearly political science knowledge production has come closer to that of political anthropology. For key examples where sovereignty is concerned, see Ashley 1984, 1987; Walker 1988, 1993.

about an unfolding genocide began to trickle in, made him give priority to matters organizational and hence indifferent to other aspects of what was going on, demonstrate that this reading is no less apposite now than it was under high modernity. Indeed, something about the particularization of the work process and routinization may make the bureaucratic way of being in the world spread, so that the life of bureaucrats has become and is becoming representative of more general processes of the formation of self under postmodernity.

Catherine Casey's study of life in a U.S.-based transnational hi-tech company presents empirical findings that point in this direction. In industrial societies, she argues, the major principle of the division of labor is that each profession has a more or less fixed domain. Under what she terms "designer capitalism," however, the building blocks are no longer professions, but what she calls "discursive means of production," which may be learned in ways other than educational training for membership in a particular profession. From the employer's point of view, subject positions tied to professions become less central, but no one new set of subject positions emerges to take their place. Thus, "replacing occupation as a primary locus of class and self-identification in the corporate workplace is team and knowledge. . . . Relationship to a product, to team-family members and to the company displaces identification with occupation and its historic repository of skills, knowledges and allegiances" (Casey 1995: 109). This situation, she argues, produces a "colluded self," a narcissistic way of being in the world which is dependent, overagreeable, compulsively dedicated, and passionate about company output (Casey 1995: 191). Designer capitalism produces designer employees. Diplomats, who make a living from mediating among disparate and not necessarily connected worlds and who change their place in the ministry on average every three years, must be considered among the pioneers of this kind of work. "When you've been in the ministry for two years and done two [three-year] tours, you've forgotten your profession," George answered when I noted that he complained about his dull everyday routine and suggested that he go back to his onetime profession as an economics researcher.

Diplomats have always taken pride in their practical knowledge, such as the ability to "keep a bracket" (not give in on a formulation) during a negotiation, what they themselves refer to by a German term as their *Fingerspitzengefühl,* that is, their ability to feel their way, or, in Casey's terms, their dependence on "discursive means of production." The pressure on diplomats to produce instant knowledge leads to a lot of improvisation, ad-libbing, and corner-cutting (cf. Callon 1998). Perhaps with the arrival of designer capitalism, a form of diplomatization is hitting working life. But if it is, then it is exactly because diplomacy's object is indeterminate. A cosmopolitan habitus of the type that has traditionally characterized the diplomat—available, mediating, eager to please—now spreads to ever new spheres in postindustrial societies.

Self-reflection

"Come on, Iver," I hear myself think, does that little snippet of political process in the high north really belong in the conclusion to a work of anthropology? It must be possible to speak about political processes and negotiations of identities more anthropologically, without worrying about what is actually being decided. But I have to face up to it: I cannot let go of my infatuation with outcome. Actually, I do not even really want to. Strathern (2004: 23) was writing about me when she wrote about "knowledge workers" who bring knowledge taken from a community with them when they leave one job for another (see chapter 3).

This is true not only of jobs but of academic disciplines and professions as well. There can be no discipline without discipline. My degrees in political science and my years in a think tank doing applied, outcome-oriented work have disciplined me in more senses than one. The micromechanisms of power that mold me to serve the needs of anthropological knowledge production clash with my embodied practices. I have shown to others my chapter on the emergence of diplomacy. What is the problem, they say; if the outcome of world history was today's diplomatic system, then why worry about the ifs and buts? When I repeat my point that it is of interest to study *how* European practices prevailed, against *what* kind of opposition, they listen politely (we are, after all, friends and colleagues), but I can see that there is no longer anyone at home. I talk about constitution, they talk about outcome. Casey may be right in underlining how professional identities are broken down in many work places, but between academic disciplines, the counterforces are strong. On the other hand, only some seventy years ago, it was the rule in Britain that anthropological doctoral students came from other disciplines. If hybridization and multiple identities are hallmarks of the present era, it would be strange for anthropology to be exempt. Perhaps heavily disciplined academic disciplines turn out to have been a phenomenon of high modernity only.

I believe, in fact, that it is the blossoming of political anthropology that keeps the classical study of politics alive. If we go to the classics of political theory, we find a focus on the preconditions for political order and a focus on how that order is maintained. Present-day political scientists seem to have forgotten about preconditions. With very few exceptions, they take the existence of particular institutions, or the need to create them, as a starting point of analysis. To take an example, they study *how* elections are held and how they should be held, and who wins, but not *why* they are held, and how they interact with other social practices. An anthropologist would find it interesting that donors spent around $1 billion on the Congo's first-ever election in 2006 and would concentrate on how that event reflected and changed social processes. A political scientist would ask if the election adhered to established practices that have emerged elsewhere, which parties ran, and who won.[7] Anthropologists focus on the constitutive, political scientists on the outcome. Anthropologists tend to define politics as a question of who we are, political scientists tend to define it as who gets what, when, how. To use the terms of classical political theory, anthropologists focus on the preconditions for political order, and political scientists on how that order is maintained.

Ian Hacking problematizes modes of knowledge as what he calls styles of reasoning. Styles of reasoning are characterized by the objects that constitute the world to be known, preconditions for making truth claims, and "criteria of proof and demonstration" (Hacking 2002: 4)—that is, an ontology, an epistemology, and a methodology. The difference in object of study (constitution vs. outcome) reflects an ontic difference between seeing the social world as emergent, like most anthropologists, and seeing it as structurally given or in terms of methodological individualism, like most political scientists.[8] This ontic difference is tied in with how the two disciplines

---

7. To dedifferentiate, my source here is actually the work of a political scientist; Autesserre 2010.

8. Despite its name, methodological individualism is clearly an ontic commitment to treating individuals as given resource maximizers. Note that one may dedifferentiate the two givens

lean toward different epistemological commitments (in Weberian terms, understanding vs. explanation) as well as toward different methodologies (some variant on the phenomenological themes of intent and reflexivity vs. defining the object as a "dependent variable" to be studied along with other stuff that is held to be invariant—independent variables). I am moving on the ideal-typical level here, to capture why I had to leave political science to do this study and what the (obviously incomplete) transition from political science to anthropology has involved for me.

In fact, the cross-pressures of academic disciplines have been a greater challenge for me than that classic dilemma which Steven Turner (1994: 19) refers to as "the Mauss problem," that is, how to square the roles of participant and observer. Too much doxa means too little observing distance; too fluent practices spell too little observing. I have noted how, in the crunch, diplomats could brush off my input by activating a discursive resource: "you academics" concentrate on the conceptual, whereas "we diplomats" concentrate on the operative. To them, I was a participant, but one whose competences were lopsided. I myself did not experience the dilemma as pressing. I was helped (as well as handicapped) by the developments that I have sketched: researchers are among the groups that diplomats have drawn on to govern from afar. When the British founded Chatham House in 1920, only two years after the end of the Great War, it was, among other things, to increase the interface between the Foreign Office on the one hand, and what was rapidly becoming an academic discipline—International Relations—specializing in the same subject matter on the other. Chatham House was the explicit inspiration and prime model for the Norwegian Institute of International Affairs, which was founded in 1959 and where I had worked for ten years when I was approached by the MFA. Indeed, one of the reasons that I was approached, and nobody made any bones about it, was that I worked in what the MFA considered the corner of academic life closest to them. The emergence of think tanks such as Chatham House and NUPI is another example of how foreign ministries increase their action capacity by means of governmentality. When, in the United States, the military attempted to enroll anthropologists in its efforts,

---

by arguing that an *ontic* commitment to a world of given individuals may actually be treated as a *structural* commitment; if the social world consists of maximizing individuals, then this would be a structural precondition for any one action.

this provoked immediate debate, probably because the *problématique* was new (at least where the specific employee was concerned; Gusterson 2007). Political science started, back in the seventeenth century, as a state-induced science of governing people. Small wonder that relations to the state are doxic, and small wonder that the discipline's gaze is top-down. This disciplinary closeness to the subject matter and to the state is a problem in its own right, and certainly my own knowledge-producing practices are marked by what some people would call a *pudenda origo* in political science. In terms of the Mauss problem, however, my socialization as a political scientist meant that I was already situated in a way not unlike the diplomat. Estrangements were provoked by differences on the methodological and stylistic levels. Such a situation has its costs and benefits. There was something reassuring when diplomat readers time and again commented to the effect that "Yes, but we have not thought of it in exactly those terms and by the way, who else would be interested?" To avail myself of a cherished political science practice: if we add differing modes of data collection, we arrive at a four-by-three matrix of how the three modes of knowledge production differ, as in Figure 3.

If I were to identify the major challenge in my transition from political science to anthropology, however, it has to do with style, with how to

	Anthropology	Political science	Diplomacy
Ontology	Reality constructed	Structure or agents given	Agents given
Epistemology (understood as)	Constructing	Excavating truth	Instrumental
Methodology	Reflexivity	Identify means and intent	Identify means and intent
Data collection	Reading and field work	Reading and interviews	Reading and meetings

Figure 3. Ideal-typical styles of reasoning in anthropology, political science, and diplomacy.

write up the material. For someone theorizing styles of knowledge production, Hacking actually pays very little attention to style (see, instead,
Derrida [1978] 1985). Writing anthropology is different from writing political science. A decade ago, Finn, one of my political science students,
reported that his first political science professor had written down the
following piece of advice on the blackboard for neophytes to read: "Write
boringly (*skriv kjedelig*)." To him, and arguably to political scientists at
large, writing should reflect the idea that you are writing from nowhere,
about objectively given stuff. Consider what Ardener (1989: 213–14)
has to say about the change of horizon that characterizes the fieldwork
experience

> There was a time when the relativity of cultural categories was raised to a
> philosophical bogey as "relativism." Anthropology then was discovering a
> mismatch between the categories of the observer and those generated by
> the purported object—other people. When the differences are more sub-
> tle, the gap is narrower between these two; the mismatch is virtually simul-
> taneous. Since mismatch is our experience of relativity, then the reduction
> of "transmission time" (between the observer and the purported object)
> and the narrowing of the mismatch (between the categories of the observer
> and the other), demonstrates that the process that we first called relativ-
> ization is not a form of anti-objectivism, but (as its application to "famil-
> iar" experience more clearly shows) is on the contrary our only mode of
> objectivization.

This problem simply does not arise for most political scientists, for whom
the object of study is objective and given. There is no such book title as
"Writing Political Science" (but cf. Shapiro 1988). Moreover, political science finds self-reflection of the sort in which I am engaging to be mean-
ingless. From the perspective of political science, all the contortions that
the situation identified by Ardener brings to anthropological writing are
simply so many misconceptions that keep anthropologists from getting on
with the job. "The job" is, of course, what *they* define as *their* job, namely
objectively to tell the reader what kind of process led to what outcome. I
still identify with that attitude, at least partly. I spent months poring over
my notes on class and gender before finally transforming them into what
is now chapter 5 in this book. The agonizing was due to my poor uptake
of prolonged anthropological training, for I simply could not decide what

to do with stuff that was obviously interesting, in the sense that it constituted the social world in which I had moved, but which at the same time was seemingly without much importance for political outcome. After a decade of formal and informal anthropological training, I was still suffering from outcome blindness.

On the level of stylistics as well, the foregrounding of outcome is key. All five political scientists who read the first draft of this book made the same comment: be more explicit and tie everything better in with the conclusion. If everything should build toward the conclusion, and the conclusion should be reached by means of explanation, then it follows that the writing style itself should be teleological. Anthropological talk about showing it, not saying it; about letting the data decide the form of presentation; about being reticent about passing judgment on statements by interlocutors—all this goes directly against the grain of political science. Marcus (1998: 119) maintains that the ethnographer

> tries to get at a form of local knowledge that is about the kind of difference that is not accessible by working out internal cultural logics. It is about difference that arises from the anxieties of knowing that one is somehow tied into what is happening elsewhere but, as noted, without those connections being clear or precisely articulated through available internal cultural models. In effect, subjects are participating in discourses that are thoroughly localized but that are not their own.

That definitely covers the case of the diplomat and me, but there was, in addition, the anxiety identified by Strathern, of being in the grip of a kind of academic reasoning and knowledge production about which I still feel deeply ambivalent. "Despite their very different values and commitments," Marcus (1998: 125) argues further, "the ethnographer and his subject in this project are nevertheless broadly engaged in a pursuit of knowledge with resemblances in form and context that they can recognize." Again, that holds true for my relationship to diplomats, but it does not necessarily hold true for relations between anthropologists and political scientists. Although the subfield of political anthropology has blossomed over the last half century, cross-fertilization between that subfield and political science has, nonetheless, remained rudimentary. Judging by the kinds of comments that anthropologists and political scientists have offered on chapters in this book, the immediate problem (which may, to repeat myself, be traced back to differing ontic and epistemic commitments) is writing style. I grappled with this problem when it came to what to foreground, how to foreground it, and how to hook the implied reader.

The argument for the pervasive importance of style may be strengthened by applying this book's model of culture not to diplomatic culture but to American academic culture. The two American disciplines of cultural anthropology and political science share some narrative sociabilities. In both cases, socialization takes place in classrooms, the key sites for quotidian life are university institutes, the key sites for display are conferences laid on by institutions that are historically and functionally isomorphic (the American Anthropological Association, the American Political Science Association, the International Studies Association; one could add others such as the American Sociological Association), and hierarchy is tied to publication in journals and book series. Furthermore, the two disciplines share several practices. Examples include elections to AAA, APSA, and ISA, the organization of conferences (in hotels, panel-based, including a plenary address that is subsequently published in the flagship journal, etc.), and peer review procedures for book and journal publication. Some practices, sartorial being one of them, differ between the two disciplines. Still, the practices of presentation emerge as a key site of difference, with writing style the paramount example.

It would be misleading to say that diplomats are hired guns, for their work is most in abeyance during wartime. But they are certainly hired. For the last four hundred years or so, their main employer has been a sovereign, and their arena and object of maintenance has been the states system. That system is still a key part of the world system. One way of understanding the development by which diplomats try to broaden interfaces with other groups, and preferably govern them from afar, is as a response to how the states system's place within the world system is rapidly being relativized. But if so, then diplomats are key to that system. Marcus (1998: 223) argues that "The insularity of nuclear diplomacy discourse is striking." Well, no capable diplomat, nuclear or otherwise, is an island. Marcus also argues, à propos of multi-sited field work, that "some ethnography may not move around literally but may nonetheless embed itself in a multi-sited context. This is different than assuming or constructing a world-system context" (Marcus 1998: 95). It is not different for a study of diplomacy and diplomats, however. Diplomats are constitutive of the world system. Their work, it is true, is highly ritualized—but a discipline that treats ritual specialists as a core subject is hardly in a position to fault them for that. Ours is an alienated world. To the degree that diplomats succeed in mediating that alienation, diplomacy is a scheme to improve the human condition that has succeeded.

References

Abbott, Andrew. 1988. *The System of Professions: An Essay on the Division of Expert Labor.* Chicago: University of Chicago Press.

Acker, Joan. 2006. *Class Questions: Feminist Answers.* Lanham, Md.: Rowman & Littlefield.

———. 1993. *Doing Comparable Worth: Gender, Class, and Pay Equity.* Philadelphia: Temple University Press.

Adcock, Frank, and D. J. Mosely. (1975) 1996. *Diplomacy in Ancient Greece.* London: Thames & Hudson.

Allen, N. J. 2000. *Categories and Classifications: Maussian Reflections on the Social.* Oxford: Berghahn.

Allison, Graham T. 1971. *Essence of Decision: Explaining the Cuban Missile Crisis.* Boston: Little, Brown.

Amadou, Anne-Lise. 1973. "En norsk modell for Marcel Proust" [A Norwegian model for Marcel Proust]. *Edda* (5): 311–16.

Anderson, M. S. 1993. *The Rise of Modern Diplomacy 1450–1919.* London: Longman.

Anderson, Sonia. 1989. *An English Consul in Turkey: Paul Rycaut at Smyrna, 1667–1678.* Oxford: Clarendon Press.

Anon. 1997. "Integrasjon i et nøtteskall, eller i Hanoi (III)" [Integration in a nutshell, or in Hanoi (III)]. *UD-posten* [Norwegian MFA bulletin] (3): 13.

Archer, Margaret. 1995. *Realist Social Theory: The Morphogenic Approach.* Cambridge: Cambridge University Press.

Ardener, Edwin. 1989. "Remote Areas: Some Theoretical Considerations." In *The Voice of Prophecy and Other Essays,* edited by Malcolm Chapman, 211–23. Oxford: Blackwell.

Arendt, Hannah. 1963. *Eichmann in Jerusalem: A Report on the Banality of Evil.* New York: Viking.

Aron, Raymond. (1962) 1966. *Peace and War: A Theory of International Relations.* Garden City, N.Y.: Doubleday.

Ashley, Richard K. 1988. "Untying the Sovereign State: A Double Reading of the Anarchy Problematique" *Millennium* 17 (2): 227–62.

———. 1987. "The Geopolitics of Geopolitical Space: Toward a Critical Social Theory of International Politics" *Alternatives* 12 (4): 403–34.

———. 1981. "Political Realism and Human Interests." *International Studies Quarterly* 25 (2): 204–36.

Autesserre, Séverine. 2010. *The Trouble with the Congo: Local Violence and the Failure of International Peacebuilding.* New York: Cambridge University Press.

Avruch, Kevin. 2000. "Reciprocity, Equality, and Status-Anxiety in the Amarna Letters." In *Amarna Diplomacy: The Beginnings of International Relations,* edited by Raymond Cohen and Richard Westbrook, 154–64. Baltimore: Johns Hopkins University Press.

Bagge, Sverre. 1987. *The Political Thought of the King's Mirror* Odense: Odense University Press.

Bailey, F. G. (1969) *Stratagems and Spoils. A Social Anthropology of Politics.* Oxford: Basil Blackwell.

Bakhtin, Mikhail M. 1981. *The Dialogic Imagination: Four Essays.* Austin: University of Texas Press.

———. (1963) 1984. *Problems of Dostoevsky's Poetics.* Minneapolis: University of Minnesota Press.

Barnes, Barry. 2001. "Practice as Collective Action." In *The Practice Turn in Contemporary Theory,* edited by Theodore R. Schatzky, Karin Knorr Cetina, and Eike von Savigny, 17–28. London: Routledge.

———. 1974. *Scientific Knowledge and Sociological Theory.* London: Routledge & Kegan Paul.

Barnett, Michael N. (2002) *Eyewitness to a Genocide: The United Nations and Rwanda.* Ithaca: Cornell University Press.

———. 1997. "The UN Security Council, Indifference, and Genocide in Rwanda." *Cultural Anthropology* 12 (4): 551–78.

Barrett, Michèle. 1985. Introduction to *The Origin of the Family, Private Property and the State,* by Friedrich Engels, 1–30. Harmondsworth, UK: Penguin.

Bartelson, Jens. 2006. "The Concept of Sovereignty Revisited." *European Journal of International Law* 17 (2): 463–74.

———. 1995. *A Genealogy of Sovereignty.* Cambridge: Cambridge University Press.

Barth, Fredrik. 1993. *Balinese Worlds.* Chicago: University of Chicago Press.

———, ed. 1969. *Ethnic Groups and Boundaries.* Oslo: Norwegian University Press.

Barthes, Roland. (1968) 1977. "The Death of the Author." In *Image Music Text,* edited by Roland Barthes, 142–48. London: Fontana.

Bauman, Zygmunt. 1992. *Postmodern Ethics.* Oxford: Blackwell.

Berridge, Geoffrey R. 1995. *Diplomacy: Theory and Practice.* London: Prentice Hall.

Berridge, G. R., and Alan James. 2001. *A Dictionary of Diplomacy* Houndmills, UK: Palgrave.

Billig, Yvonne Due, and Mats Alvesson. 1994. *Gender, Managers, and Organizations.* Berlin: Walter de Gruyter.

Bjørgo, Narve. 1975. "Udenrigstjeneste: Norge" [Foreign service: Norway]. In *Kulturhistorisk leksikon for nordisk middelalder* [Encyclopedia of the cultural history of the Nordic middle ages], 19:243–47. Oslo: Gyldendal.

Bjørgo, Tore, Øystein Rian, and Alf Kaartvedt. 1995. *Selvstendighet og union: Fra middelalderen til 1905. Norsk utenrikspolitikks historie [Independence and union: From the middle ages to 1905: The history of Norwegian foreign policy].* Vol. 1. Oslo: Universitetsforlaget.

Boas, Franz. (1911) 1983. *The Mind of Primitive Man.* London: Macmillan.

Boudon, Raymond. 1979. *The Logic of Social Action: An Introduction to Sociological Analysis.* London: Routledge & Kegan Paul.

Bourdieu, Pierre. 1991. *Language and Symbolic Power.* Cambridge: Polity Press.

———. (1980) 1990. *The Logic of Practice.* Stanford, Calif.: Stanford University Press.

———. (1979) 1984. *Distinction: A Social Critique of the Judgement of Taste.* London: Routledge.

———. 1977. *Outline of a Theory of Practice.* Cambridge: Cambridge University Press.

Boyd, William. 1981. *A Good Man in Africa.* London: Hamilton.

Boyer, Dominic. 2005. *Spirit and System: Media, Intellectuals, and the Dialectic in Modern German Culture.* Chicago: University of Chicago Press.

———. 2003. "Censorship as a Vocation: The Institutions, Practices, and Cultural Logic of Media Control in the German Democratic Republic." *Comparative Studies in Society and History* 45 (3): 511–45.

Brooke-Rose, Christine. 1975. *Thru.* London: Hamish Hamilton.

Bull, Hedley. 1977. *The Anarchical Society. A Study of Order in World Politics.* London: Macmillan.

Bull, Hedley, and Adam Watson. 1984. *The Expansion of International Society.* Oxford: Clarendon Press.

Butler, Judith. 1993. *Bodies That Matter: The Discursive Limits of "Sex."* New York: Routledge.

Butterfield, Herbert. 1966. "The New Diplomacy and Historical Diplomacy." In *Diplomatic Investigations: Essays in the Theory of International Politics,* edited by Martin Wight and Herbert Butterfield, 181–92. London: Allen & Unwin.

———. 1953. *Christianity, Diplomacy and War.* New York: Abingdon-Cokesbury.

Callan, Hilary. 1975. "The Premiss of Dedication: Notes towards an Ethnography of Diplomats' wives." In *Perceiving Women,* edited by Shirley Ardener, 87–104. London: Dent.

Callon, Michel. 1998. "An Essay on Framing and Overflowing: Economic Externalities Revisited by Sociology." In *The Laws of the Markets,* edited by Michel Callon, 244–69. Oxford: Blackwell.

Campbell, Anne. 1993. *Men, Women, and Aggression*. New York: Basic.

Carter, Alice Clare. 1975. *Neutrality or Commitment: The Evolution of Dutch Foreign Policy, 1667–1795*. London: Arnold.

Casey, Catherine. 1995. *Work, Self and Society: After Industrialism*. London: Routledge.

Certeau, Michel de. 1984. *The Practice of Everyday Life*. Berkeley: University of California Press.

Chowdhry, Geeta, and Sheila Nair, eds. 2002. *Power, Postcolonialism and International Relations: Reading Race, Gender and Class*. London: Routledge.

Christiansen, Carl. 1908. *Bidrag til dansk statshusholdnings historie under de to første Enevoldskonger* [Contribution to the history of the Danish state household under the two first absolute kings]. Vol. 1. Copenhagen: Nordiske forfatteres forlag.

Clark, Eric. 1973. *Corps Diplomatique*. London: Allan Lane.

Clark, Isobel. 1984. "The Negation of Structure: A Note on British Council Wives." In *The Incorporated Wife*, edited by Hilary Callan and Shirley Ardener, 135–42. London: Croom Helm.

Clifford, James, and George E. Marcus. 1986. *Writing Culture: The Poetics and Politics of Ethnography*. Berkeley: University of California Press.

Cohen, Abner. 1981. *The Politics of Elite Culture: Explorations in the Dramaturgy of Power in a Modern African Society*. Berkeley: University of California Press.

Cohen, Raymond, and Richard Westbrook. 2000. "Conclusion: The Beginnings of International Relations." In *Amarna Diplomacy: The Beginnings of International Relations*, edited by Raymond Cohen and Richard Westbrook, 225–36. Baltimore: Johns Hopkins University Press.

Colban, Erik. 1952. *Femti år* [Fifty years]. Oslo: Aschehoug.

Collins, H. M. 2001. "What Is Tacit Knowledge?" In *The Practice Turn in Contemporary Theory*, edited by Theodore R. Schatzky, Karin Knorr-Cetina, and Eike von Savigny, 107–19. London: Routledge.

Comaroff, Jean, and John Comaroff. 1992. *Ethnography and the Historical Imagination*. Boulder, Colo.: Westview Press.

———. 1991. *Of Revelation and Revolution: Christianity, Colonialism, and Consciousness in South Africa*. Chicago: University of Chicago Press.

Connell, Robert W. 1995. *Masculinities*. Berkeley: University of California Press.

———. 1987. *Gender and Power: Society, the Person, and Sexual Politics*. Stanford, Calif.: Stanford University Press.

Constantine Porphyrogenitus. 1967. *De Administrando Imperio*. Washington, D.C.: Dumbarton Oaks Center for Byzantine Studies.

Constantinou, Costas. 1996. *On the Way to Diplomacy*. Minneapolis: University of Minnesota Press.

Coronil, Fernando. 1997. *The Magical State: Nature, Money, and Modernity in Venezuela*. Chicago: University of Chicago Press.

Crompton, Rosemary. 1998. *Class and Stratification: An Introduction to Current Debates*. 2nd. ed. Cambridge: Polity.

Crystal, David. 1987. *The Cambridge Encyclopedia of Language*. Cambridge: Cambridge University Press.

Csordas, Thomas J., ed. 1994. *Embodiment and Experience: The Existential Ground of Culture and Self.* Cambridge: Cambridge University Press.

Cuttino, G. P. 1985. *English Medieval Diplomacy* Bloomington: Indiana University Press.

———. 1971. *English Diplomatic Administration, 1259–1339* Oxford: Clarendon Press.

Dawson, Christopher, ed. 1955. *The Mongol Mission.* New York: Sheed & Ward.

Deacon, Terrence W. 1997. *The Symbolic Species: The Co-Evolution of Language and the Human Brain.* Harmondsworth, UK: Penguin.

Dennis, Matthew. 1993. *Cultivating a Landscape of Peace: Iroquois-European Encounters in Seventeenth-Century America* Ithaca, N.Y.: Cornell University Press.

Der Derian, James. 1996. "Hedley Bull and the Idea of Diplomatic Culture." In *International Society after the Cold War: Anarchy and Order Reconsidered,* edited by Rick Fawn and Jeremy Larkins. 84–100. Houndmills, UK: Macmillan.

———. 1993. "Diplomacy." In *The Oxford Companion to Politics of the World,* edited by Joel Krieger and William A. Joseph, 244–66. New York: Oxford University Press.

———. 1987. *On Diplomacy: A Genealogy of Western Estrangement.* Oxford: Blackwell.

Derrida, Jacques. (1978) 1985. "The Question of Style." In *The New Nietzsche: Contemporary Styles of Interpretation,* 2nd ed., edited by David B. Allison, 176–89. Cambridge, Mass.: MIT Press.

Dery, David. 1998. "'Papereality' and Learning in Bureaucratic Organizations." *Administration and Society* 29 (6): 677–89.

Dickie, John. 2004. *New Mandarins: How British Foreign Policy Works* London: I. B. Tauris.

Dickinson, Joycelyne Gledhill. 1955. *The Congress of Arras 1435* Oxford: Clarendon Press.

Doran, Susan, and Glenn Richardson. 2005. "Introduction—Tudor Monarchs and Their Neighbours." In *Tudor England and Its Neighbours,* edited by Susan Doran and Glenn Richardson, 1–13. London: Palgrave.

Dosse, François. 1998. *History of Structuralism.* 2 vols. Minneapolis: University of Minnesota Press.

Doty, Roxanne Lynn. 1997. "Aporia: A Critical Exploration of the Agent-Structure Problematique in International Relations Theory." *European Journal of International Relations* 3 (3): 365–92.

Douglas, Mary. (1966) 1996. *Purity and Danger: An Analysis of Concepts of Pollution and Taboo.* London: Routledge.

———. 1986. *How Institutions Think.* Syracuse, N.Y.: Syracuse University Press.

Døving, Runar. 2003. *Rype med lettøl: En antropologi fra Norge* [Grouse with nonalcoholic beer: An anthropology from Norway]. Oslo: Pax.

Dumézil, Georges. (1940) 1988. *Mitra-Varuna: An Essay on Two Indo-European Representations of Sovereignty* New York: Zone.

Durkheim, Émile. (1913) 1992. *Professional Ethics and Civic Morals.* London: Routledge.

———. (1912) 1995. *The Elementary Forms of Religious Life.* New York: Free Press.

Durkheim, Émile, and Marcel Mauss. (1913) 1971. "Note on the Notion of Civilization." *Social Research* 38 (4): 808–13.

———. (1903) 1963. *Primitive Classification*. Chicago: University of Chicago Press.

Eisenstein, Zillah. 1994. *The Color of Gender: Reimagining Democracy,* Berkeley: University of California Press.

Enloe, Cynthia. 1989. *Bananas, Beaches and Bases: Making Feminist Sense of International Politics.* London: Pandora.

Eribon, Didier. (1989) 1991. *Michel Foucault.* London: Faber & Faber.

Eriksen, Thomas Hylland. 1993. *Ethnicity and Nationalism: Anthropological Perspectives.* London: Pluto.

Eriksen, Thomas Hylland, and Iver B. Neumann. 1993. "International Relations as a Cultural System: An Agenda for Research." *Cooperation and Conflict* 28 (3): 233–64.

Evans-Pritchard, E. E. 1940. *The Nuer: A Description of the Modes of Livelihood and Political Institutions of a Nilotic People.* Oxford: Clarendon Press.

Fabian, Joseph. 1983. *Time and the Other.* New York: Columbia University Press.

Fair, John D. 1992. *Harold Temperley: A Scholar and Romantic in the Public Realm.* Cranbury, N.J.: Associated University Presses.

Fairclough, Norman. 1995. *Critical Discourse Analysis: The Critical Study of Language.* London: Longman.

Fallows, James. 2001. "Councils of War." *Atlantic Monthly* (December): 42–45.

Farnell, Brenda. 2000. "Getting Out of Habitus: An Alternative Model of Dynamically Embodied Social Action." *Journal of the Royal Anthropological Society* 6 (3): 397–418.

Fay, Hans. 1959. *På post i fem verdensdeler* [On post in five continents]. Oslo: Dreyer.

Feldbæk, Ole. 2000. "Vækst og reformer—dansk forvaltning 1720–1814" [Growth and reforms—Danish administration 1720–1814]. In *Dansk forvaltningshistorie I. Stat, forvaltning og samfund: Fra middelalderen til 1901* [Danish administrative history I. State, administration, and society: From the middle ages to 1901], edited by Leon E. Jespersen, E. Ladewig Petersen, and Ditlev Tamm, 227–340. Copenhagen: Jurist-og økonomforbundets forlag.

Ferguson, James C., and Akhil Gupta. 2002. "Spatializing States: Toward an Ethnography of Neoliberal Governmentality." *American Ethnologist* 29 (4): 981–1002.

Finch, Janet. 1983. *Married to the Job: Wives' Incorporation in Men's Work.* London: Allen & Unwin.

Fischer, Paul, and Nils Svenningsen. 1970. *Den danske udenrigstjeneste* [The Danish foreign service], vol. 2: *1919–1970,* edited by Klaus Kjølsen and Viggo Sjøqvist. Copenhagen: J. H. Schultz.

Flood, Christopher G. 2002. *Political Myth.* London: Routledge.

Fournier, Marcel. 1994. *Marcel Mauss.* Paris: Fayard.

Foucault, Michel. 2000. "Governmentality." In *Power: Essential Works of Michel Foucault 1954–1984,* edited by James D. Faubion, 3:201–22. Harmondsworth, UK: Penguin.

———. 1994. "L'éthique du souci de soi comme pratique de la liberté." In *Dits et écrits 1954–1988,* vol. 4: *1980–1988,* 708–29. Paris: Gallimard.

———. 1985. *The History of Sexuality,* Vol. 2: *The Uses of Pleasure.* Harmondsworth, UK: Penguin.

———. 1984. *The History of Sexuality,* vol. 1: *An Introduction.* Harmondsworth, UK: Penguin.

———. 1980. "Two Lectures." In *Power/Knowledge: Selected Interviews and Other Writings 1972–1977,* edited by Colin Gordon, 78–108. Brighton: Harvester.

———. 1979. *Michel Foucault: Power/Truth/Strategy,* edited by Meaghan Morris and Paul Patton. Sydney: Feral.

———. (1970) 1972. *The Archaeology of Knowledge.* London: Tavistock.

———. (1968) 1991. "Answer to a Question." In *The Foucault Effect: Studies in Governmentality,* edited by Graham Burchell, Colin Gordon, and Peter Miller, 53–72. London: Harvester Whitsheaf.

Frey, Linda S., and Marsha L. Frey. 1999. *The History of Diplomatic Immunity.* Columbus: Ohio State University Press.

Fure, Odd-Bjørn. 1996. Mellomkrigstid 1920–1940: *Norsk utenrikspolitikks historie, vol. 3* [The inter-war period 1920–1940: History of Norwegian Foreign Policy, vol 3]. Oslo: Universitetsforlaget.

Galtung, Ingegerd. 1983. "Fellesdiplomatiet og konsulatsaken 1814–1905" [Union diplomacy and the consular quarrel]. In *Fra diplomatiets verden* [From the world of diplomacy], edited by Ingegerd Galtung and Alf R. Bjerke, 16–24. Oslo: Atheneum.

Galtung, Johan, and Kari Holmboe Ruge. 1965. "Patterns of Diplomacy—a Study of Recruitment and Career Patterns in Norwegian Diplomacy." *Journal of Peace Research* 2 (2): 101–35.

Garfinkel, Harold. 1967. *Studies in Ethnomethodology.* Englewood Cliffs, N.J.: Prentice-Hall.

Geanakoplos, Deno John. 1976. *Interaction of the "Sibling" Byzantine and Western Cultures in the Middle Ages and Italian Renaissance.* New Haven, Conn.: Yale University Press.

Geertz, Clifford. 1983. "From the Native's Point of View: On the Nature of Anthropological Understanding." In *Local Knowledge: Further Essays in Interpretive Anthropology,* edited by Clifford Geertz, 55–70. London: Fontana.

———. 1980. *Negara: The Theatre State in Nineteenth-Century Bali.* Princeton, N.J.: Princeton University Press.

———. 1973. "Thick Description: Toward an Interpretive Theory of Culture." In *The Interpretation of Cultures,* 3–30. New York: Basic.

Gelting, Michael H., and Peter Korsgaard. 1983. "Forholdet til udlandet" [Relations abroad]. In *Rigsarkivet og hjælpemidlerne til dets benyttelse* [The National Archive and aids for its use], vol. 1, edited by Wilhelm von Rosen, 301–15. Copenhagen: Rigsarkivet, Gad.

Giddens, Anthony. 1984. *The Constitution of Society: Outline of the Theory of Structuration.* Cambridge: Polity.

Gilbert, G. Nigel, and Michael Mulkay. 1984. *Opening Pandora's Box: A Sociological Analysis of Scientists' Discourse.* Cambridge: Cambridge University Press.

Gledhill, John. 1994. *Power and Its Disguises: Perspectives on Political Anthropology.* London: Pluto.

Goffmann, Erving. 1961. *Asylums.* Harmondsworth, UK: Penguin.

———. 1959. *The Presentation of Self in Everyday Life.* Garden City, N.Y.: Doubleday.

Gong, Garrit W. 1984. *The Standard of "Civilization" in International Society.* Oxford: Clarendon Press.

Goody, Jack. 1986. *The Logic of Writing and the Organization of Society.* Cambridge: Cambridge University Pres.

Gordon, Colin. 1991. "Governmental Rationality: An Introduction." In *The Foucault Effect: Studies in Governmentality,* edited by Graham Burchell, Colin Gordon, and Peter Miller, 1–51. London: Harvester Wheatsheaf.

Grant, J. R. 1965. "Greek Diplomacy." *Classical Quarterly,* n.s. 15 (2): 261–66.

Gudmundson, Ulla. 2004. "Comments." In *Cultural Barriers, Cultural Bridges: Experience and Evidence from Diplomacy and Politics,* edited by Olav F. Knudsen, 21–23, 97–102. Stockholm: Swedish Institute of International Affairs.

Gullestad, Marianne. 1996a. *Everyday Life Philosophers: Modernity, Morality and Autobiography in Norway.* Oslo: Scandinavian University Press.

———. 1996b. *Imagined Childhoods: Self and Society in Autobiographical Accounts.* Oslo: Scandinavian University Press.

———. 1984. *Kitchen-Table Society: A Case Study of Family Life and Friendship of Young Working-Class Mothers in Urban Norway.* Oslo: Norwegian University Press.

Gupta, Akhil, and James Ferguson. 1997. "Culture, Power, Place: Ethnography at the End of an Era." In *Culture, Power, Place: Explorations in Critical Anthropology,* edited by Akhil Gupta and James Ferguson, 1–29. Durham, N.C.: Duke University Press.

Gustafsson, Harald. 2000. *Gamla riken, nya stater: Statsbildning, politisk kultur och identitet under Kalmarunionens upplösningsskede 1512–1541* [Old reichs, new states: State formation, political culture, and identity during the dissolution of the Kalmar Union 1512–1541]. Stockholm: Atlantis.

Gusterson, Hugh. 2007. "Anthropology and Militarism." *Annual Review of Anthropology* 36: 155–75.

———. 1996. *Nuclear Rites. A Weapons Laboratory at the End of the Cold War.* Berkeley: University of California Press.

Hacking, Ian (2002) *Historical Ontology.* Cambridge: Harvard University Press.

Halford, Susan, Mike Savage, and Anne Witz. 1996. *Gender, Careers and Organizations: Current Developments in Banking, Nursing and Local Government.* Houndmills, UK: Macmillan.

Halliday, M. A. K. 1998. "Situasjonskonteksten" [The situation context]. In *Å skape mening med språk. En samling artikler av M. A. K. Halliday, R. Hasan og J. R. Martin* [Creating meaning with language: A collection of essays], edited by Kjell Lars Berge, Patrick Coppock, and Eva Maagerø. Oslo: Landslaget for norskundervisning, Cappelen Akademiske.

Hamilton, Keith, and Richard Langhorne. 1995. *The Practice of Diplomacy: Its Evolution, Theory and Administration.* London: Routledge.

Handelman, Don, and Elliot Leyton. 1978. "Introduction: A Recognition of Bureaucracy." In *Bureaucracy and World View. Studies in the Logic of Official Interpretation,* 1–14. St John's: Institute of Social and Economic Research, Memorial University of Newfoundland.

Hannay, David. 2008. *New World Disorder: The UN after the Cold War—An Insider's View*. London: I. B. Tauris.

Hannerz, Ulf. 2003. *Foreign News: Exploring the World of Foreign Correspondents*. Chicago: University of Chicago Press.

———. 1996. *Transnational Connections: Culture, People, Places*. London: Routledge.

Hansen, Lene, and Ole Wæver, eds. 2002. *European Integration and National Identity: The Challenge of the Nordic States*. London: Routledge.

Hatton, Ragnhild, and M. S. Anderson, eds. 1970. *Studies in Diplomatic History: Essays in Memory of David Bayne Horn*. London: Longman.

Heiberg, Inger. 1983. "Fra fine franske teer, via 'spinnesiden' til Utef [From fancy French teas via the fair sex to UTEF]. In *Fra Diplomatiets Verden* [From the world of diplomacy], edited by Ingegerd Galtung and Alf R. Bjerke, 141–43. Oslo: Atheneum.

Helle, Knut. 1972. *Konge og gode menn i norsk riksstyring ca. 1150–1319* [The King and good men in the rule of the Norwegian reich ca. 1150–1319]. Bergen: Universitetsforlaget.

Hellesund, Tone. 2003. *Kapitler fra singellivets historie* [Chapters from the history of the life of singles]. Oslo: Universitetsforlaget.

Hernes, Helga Maria. 1982. *Staten—Kvinner ingen adgang?* [The state: Women no entry?] Oslo: Universitetsforlaget.

Herzfeld, Michael. 1992. *The Social Production of Indifference: Exploring the Symbolic Roots of Western Bureaucracy*. New York: Berg.

Hinsley, F. H. 1963. *Sovereignty*. Cambridge, UK: Cambridge.

Hochschild, Arlie Russell. 1983. *The Managed Heart: The Commercialization of Human Feeling*. Berkeley: University of California Press.

Hocking, Brian, ed. 1999. *Foreign Ministries in a Time of Change*. London: Macmillan

Hodge, Robert, and Gunther Kress. 1988. *Social Semiotics*. Cambridge: Polity.

Holbraad, Carsten. 1970. *The Concert of Europe: A Study in German and British International Theory 1815–1914*. London: Longman.

Hollis, Martin. 1985. "Of Masks and Men." In *The Category of the Person: Anthropology, Philosophy, History*, edited by Michael Carrithers, Steven Collins and Steven Lukes, 217–33. Cambridge: Cambridge University Press.

Holmes, Douglas R., and George E. Marcus. 2004. "Cultures of Expertise and the Management of Globalization: Towards the Re-Functioning of Ethnography." In *Global Assemblages: Technology, Politics, and Ethics as Anthropological Problems*, edited by Aihwa Ong and Stephen J. Collier, 235–52. Oxford: Blackwell.

Horn, David Bayne. 1961. *The British Diplomatic Service 1689–1789*. Oxford: Clarendon Press.

Ingold, Tim. 2000. *The Perception of the Environment: Essays in Livelihood, Dwelling, and Skill*. London: Routledge.

Irving, David. 1978. *The War Path: Hitler's Germany, 1933–1939*. London: Michael Joseph.

Isocrates. 2000. "Encomium of Helen." In *Isocrates I*, translated by David C. Mirhady and Yun Lee Too, 32–48. Austin: University of Texas Press.

Jackson, Patrick T. 2004. "Symposium: Is the State a Person? Why Should We Care?" *Review of International Studies* 30 (2): 255–316.

Jackson, Patrick Thaddeus, and Daniel H. Nexon. 1999. "Relations before States: Substance, Process and the Study of World Politics." *European Journal of International Relations* 5 (3): 291–332.

Jacobsen, Karen. 1994. Om ansettelse i UD i 1947 og tjeneste ved legasjonen/GK Montreal [On employ in the MFA in 1947 and service at the legation/CG Montreal]. Uncatalogued material collected for the Norwegian MFA's ninetieth anniversary, 1995.

Jespersen, Leon E. 2000. "Tiden 1596–1660: Mellem personlig kongemagt og bureaukrati" [The period 1596–1660: Between personal royal power and bureaucracy]. In *Dansk forvaltningshistorie,* vol. 1: *Stat, forvaltning og samfund: Fra middelalderen til 1901* [Danish Administrative History I. State, Administration, and Society: From the Middle Ages to 1901], edited by Leon E. Jespersen, Ladewig Petersen, and Ditlev Tamm, 95–158. Copenhagen: Jurist-og økonomforbundets forlag.

Johansen, Arve. 1983. "De utenrikspolitiske sendemenn i Norge på 1200-tallet" [The thirteenth-century foreign policy envoys in Norway]. Master's thesis, University of Tromsø.

Jones, C. P. 1999. *Kinship Diplomacy in the Ancient World.* Cambridge, Mass.: Harvard University Press.

Jones, Ray. 1971. *The Nineteenth-Century Foreign Office: An Administrative History.* London: Weidenfeld & Nicolson.

Jones, Raymond A. 1983. *The British Diplomatic Service, 1815–1914.* Waterloo, Ont.: Wilfred Laurier University Press.

Jones, Susan Stedman. (1996) 2001. "What Does Durkheim Mean by 'Thing'?" In *Durkheim: Critical Assessments of Leading Sociologists,* 1:300–312. London: Routledge.

Jönsson, Christer, and Martin Hall. 2005. *Essence of Diplomacy.* London: Palgrave.

Kant, Immanuel. (1781) 1993. *Critique of Pure Reason.* London: Dent.

Kanter, Rosabeth Moss. 1977. *Men and Women of the Corporation.* New York: Basic.

Keens-Soper, Maurice. 1972. "The French Political Academy, 1712: A School for Ambassadors." European Studies Review 11 (4): 329–55.

Kertzer, David I. 1988. *Ritual, Politics, and Power.* New Haven, Conn.: Yale University Press.

Kessler-Harris, Alice. 1982. *Out to Work: A History of Wage-Earning Women in the United States.* New York: Oxford University Press.

Kissinger, Henry. 2004. *Diplomacy.* New York: Simon & Schuster.

———. 1957. *A World Restored: Metternich, Castlereagh, and the Problem of Peace, 1815–22.* Boston: Houghton Mifflin.

Kittler, Friedrich A. (1986) 1999. *Gramophone, Film, Typewriter.* Stanford, Calif.: Stanford University Press.

Kjølsen, Klaus. 1991. *Det diplomatiske fag: Den danske udenrigstjenestes forvaltning 1700–1770* [The diplomatic métier: The Administration of the Danish foreign service 1700–1770]. Odense: Odense universitetsforlag.

Kjølsen, Klaus, and Viggo Sjøqvist, eds. 1970. *Den Danske udenrigstjeneste* [The Danish foreign service], vol. 1: *1770–1919.* Copenhagen: J. H. Schultz.

Klausen, Arne Martin, ed. 1986. Den norske væremåten: Antropologisk søkelys på norsk kultur [The Norwegian way of being: Anthropological focus on Norwegian culture]. Oslo: Cappelen.

Knudsen, Sten. 1998. *For Sjåfør og ambassadør: NTL i Utenrikstjenesten 1948–1998* [For driver and ambassador: NTL in the Foreign Service 1948–1998]. Oslo: Norsk Tjenestemannslag, Utenriksdepartementet.

Koht, Halvdan. 1956. "Nordmenn i Utanriksteneste före 1814" [Norwegians in diplomatic service before 1814]. In *Afhandlinger tilegnede Arkivmanden og Historikeren, Rigsarkivar, dr. phil. Axel Linvald af nordiske Fagfæller på halvfjerdsårsdagen 28. januar 1956* [Dissertations dedicated to archivist, historian, national archivist, Dr. Axel Linvald by Nordic colleagues], edited by Johan Hvidtfeldt and Harald Jørgensen, 41–63. Copenhagen: Rosenkilde & Bagger.

Koselleck, Reinhart. (1979) 1985. *Futures Past: on the Semantics of Historical Time*. Cambridge, Mass.: MIT Press.

Kratochwil, Friedrich V. 1989. *Rules, Norms, and Decisions: On the Conditions of Practical and Legal Reasoning in International Relations and Domestic Affairs*. Cambridge: Cambridge University Press.

Krasner, Steven. 1988. "Sovereignty: An Institutional Perspective." *Comparative Political Studies* 21 (1): 66–94.

———. 1984. "Approaches to the State: Alternative Conceptions and Historical Dynamics." *Comparative Politics* 16 (2): 223–46.

Kuhn, Thomas. 1970. *The Structure of Scientific Revolutions*. Chicago: University of Chicago Press.

Kuper, Adam. 1999. *Culture: The Anthropologists' Account*. Cambridge, Mass.: Harvard University Press.

Kvistad, John Mikal. 1995. *The Barents Spirit: A Bridge-Building Project in the Wake of the Cold War* Oslo: Institute of Defence Studies, report no. 95/2.

Laclau, Ernesto, and Chantal Mouffe. 1985: *Hegemony and Socialist Strategy. Towards a Radical Democratic Politics*. London: Verso.

Laffey, Mark, and Jutta Weldes. 1997. "Beyond Belief: Ideas and Symbolic Technologies in the Study of International Relations." *European Journal of International Relations* 3 (2): 193–237.

Lamont, Michele. 1992. *Money, Morals and Manners: The Culture of the French and the American Upper-Middle Class*. Chicago: University of Chicago Press.

Laqueur, Thomas. 1990. *Making Sex: Body and Gender from the Greeks to Freud*. Cambridge, Mass.: Harvard University Press.

Leira, Halvard. 2011. "Making Politics Foreign: A Tale of Two Countries." PhD diss. submitted to the Department of Political Science, University of Oslo.

———. 2008. "Justus Lipsius, Political Humanism and the Disciplining of 17th Century Statecraft." *Review of International Studies* 34 (3): 669–92.

———. 2002. "Internasjonal idealisme og Norge: Utenrikspolitisk tenkning fra Justus Lipsius til Halvdan Koht" [International idealism and Norway: Foreing policy thinking from Justus Lipsius to Halvdan Koht]. Master's thesis, University of Oslo.

Leira, Halvard, and Iver B. Neumann. Forthcoming. "Merchants, Pirates and Spies: The Emergence of the Consul."

———. 2008. "Consular Representation in an Emerging State: The Case of Norway." *The Hague Journal of Diplomacy* 3 (1): 1–19.

———. 2007. "The Emergence and Practices of the Oslo Diplomatic Corps." In *The Diplomatic Corps as an Institution of International Society,* edited by Paul Sharp and Geoffrey Wiseman, 83–102. Harmondsworth, UK: Palgrave.

Lewellen, Ted C. 1992. *Political Anthropology: An Introduction.* 2nd ed. Westport, Conn.: Bergin & Garvey.

Lewis, Bernard. 1988. *The Political Language of Islam.* Chicago: University of Chicago Press.

Li, Tania Murray. 2007. *The Will to Improve: Governmentality, Development, and the Practice of Politics.* Durham, N.C.: Duke University Press.

———. 2005. "Beyond 'the State' and Failed Schemes." *American Anthropologist* 107 (3): 383–94.

Lien, Marianne E., Hilde Lidén, and Halvard Vike, eds. 2001. *Likhetens paradokser: Antropologiske undersøkelser i det moderne Norge* [Paradoxes of equality: Anthropological explorations in modern Norway]. Oslo: Universitetsforlaget.

Lincoln, Bruce. 1989. *Discourse and the Constitution of Society: Comparative Studies of Myth, Ritual, and Classification.* New York: Oxford University Press.

Lind, Gunnar. 2000. "Den heroiske tid? Administrationen under den tidlige enevælde 1660–1720" [The heroic era? Administration during the early absolutist state 1660–1720]. In *Dansk forvaltningshistorie,* vol. 1: *Stat, forvaltning og samfund: Fra middelalderen til 1901* [Danish Administrative History I: State, Administration, and Society: From the Middle Ages to 1901], edited by Leon E. Jespersen, E. Ladewig Petersen, and Ditlev Tamm, 159–225. Copenhagen: Jurist-og økonomforbundets forlag.

Lipman-Blumen, Jean. 1984. *Gender Roles and Power.* Englewood Cliffs, N.J.: Prentice Hall.

Liverani, Mario. 2000. "The Great Powers' Club." In *Amarna Diplomacy: The Beginnings of International Relations,* edited by Raymond Cohen and Richard Westbrook, 15–27. Baltimore: Johns Hopkins University Press.

———. 1990. *Prestige and Interest: International Relations in the Near East ca. 1600–1100 BC.* Padua: Sargon.

Luce, T. J., and A. J. Woodman, eds. 1993. *Tacitus and the Tacitean Tradition.* Princeton, N.J.: Princeton University Press.

Lukes, Steven. 1975. *Émile Durkheim: His Life and Work. A Historical and Critical Study.* London: Penguin.

Lyotard, Jean-François. 1988. *The Differend: Phrases in Dispute.* Minneapolis: University of Minnesota Press.

Macdonell, Diane. 1986. *Theories of Discourse: An Introduction.* Oxford: Basil Blackwell.

Marcus, George E. 1998. *Ethnography Through Thick and Thin.* Princeton, N.J.: Princeton University Press.

Martin, Patricia Yancey. 2003. "'Said and Done' Versus 'Saying and Doing': Gendering Practices, Practicing Gender at Work." *Gender and Society* 17 (3): 342–66.

Martin, Patricia Yancey, and David Collinson. 2002. "'Over the Pond and Across the Water': Developing the Field of 'Gendered Organizations.'" *Gender, Work and Organization* 9 (3): 244–65.

Mattingly, Garrett. 1955. *Renaissance Diplomacy.* New York: Dover.

Mauss, Marcel. 1990. *The Gift: The Form and Reason for Exchange in Archaic Society.* London: Routledge.

——. (1936) 1979. "The Notion of Body Techniques." In *Sociology and Psychology: Essays,* 95–123. London: Routledge & Kegan Paul.

Mazrui, Ali. 1977. *Africa's International Relations: The Diplomacy of Dependency and Change.* London: Heinemann.

Melissen, Jan. 1999. *Innovation in Diplomatic Practice.* Houndmills, UK: Macmillan.

Merchant, Livingston. 1964. "New Techniques in Diplomacy." In *The Dimensions of Diplomacy,* edited by E. A. J. Johnson, 117–35. Baltimore: Johns Hopkins University Press.

Minson, Jeffrey. 1998. "Ethics in the Service of the State." In *Governing Australia: Studies in Contemporary Rationalities of Government,* edited by Mitchell Dean and Barry Hindess, 47–69. Melbourne: Cambridge University Press.

Moore, Henrietta L. 1994. *A Passion for Difference: Essays in Anthropology and Gender.* Bloomington: Indiana University Press.

Munn-Rankin, J. M. 1956. "Diplomacy in Western Asia in the Early Second Millennium BC." *Iraq* 18: 68–110.

Murray, Craig. 2007. *Dirty Diplomacy: The Rough-and-Tumble Adventures of a Scotch-Drinking, Skirt-Chasing, Dictator-Busting and Thoroughly Unrepentant Ambassador Stuck on the Frontline of the War against Terror* New York: Scribner.

Neumann, Iver B. Forthcoming. "Peace and Reconciliation Efforts as Systems-Maintaining Diplomacy: The Case of Norway."

——. Forthcoming, 2012. "Euro-Centric Diplomacy: Challenging but Manageable." *European Journal of International Relations.*

——. 2008a. "Discourse Analysis." In *Quantitative Methods in International Relations: A Pluralist Guide,* edited by Audie Klotz and Deepa Prakash, 61–77. Houndmills, UK: Palgrave.

——. 2008b. "Globalisation and Diplomacy." In *Global Governance and Diplomacy,* edited by Andrew F. Cooper, Brian Hocking and William Maley, 15–28. London: Palgrave.

——. 2007. "When Did Norway and Denmark Get Distinctively Foreign Policies?" *Cooperation and Conflict* 42 (1): 53–72.

——. 2006a. "Naturalizing Geography: Harry Potter and the Realms of Muggles, Magic Folks, and Monsters." In *Harry Potter in International Relations,* edited by Daniel H. Nexon and Iver B. Neumann, 157–75. Lanham, Md.: Rowman & Littlefield.

——. 2006b. "Sublime Diplomacy: Byzantine, Early Modern, Contemporary." *Millennium* 34 (3): 865–88.

——. 2004a. "The English School on Diplomacy." In *Diplomacy,* edited by Christer Jönsson and Richard Langhorne, 92–116. London: Sage.

——. 2004b. "Introduksjon: Mauss i fransk tradisjon" [Introduction: Mauss in the French tradition]. In *Marcel Mauss: Kropp og person, to essays* [Marcel Mauss: Two essays], translated, annotated, and introduced by Iver B. Neumann, 7–64. Oslo: Cappelen.

——. 2002a. Introduction to *Michel Foucault: Forelesninger om regjering og styringsmakt* [Lectures on governmentality and indirect power], translated, annotated, and introduced by Iver B. Neumann, 9–40. Oslo: Cappelen.

———. 2002b. "Returning Practice to the Linguistic Turn: The Case of Diplomacy." *Millennium* 32 (3): 627–52.

———. 2002c. "This Little Piggy Stayed at Home: Why Norway Is Not a Member of the EU." In *European Integration and National Identity: The Challenge of the Nordic States,* edited by Lene Hansen and Ole Wæver, 88–129. London: Routledge.

———. 2001. "Grab a Phaser, Ambassador: Diplomacy in Star Trek." *Millennium* 30 (3): 603–24.

———. 1999. *Uses of the Other: The "East" in European Identity Formation.* Minneapolis: University of Minnesota Press.

Neumann, Iver B., and Halvard Leira. 2007. "The Emergence and Practices of the Oslo Diplomatic Corps." In *The Diplomatic Corps as an Institution of International Society,* edited by Paul Sharp and Geoffrey Wiseman, 83–102. Harmondsworth, UK: Palgrave.

———. 2005. *Aktiv og avventende: Utenrikstjenestens liv 1905–2005* [Active and waiting: Life of the foreign service 1905–2005]. Oslo: Pax.

Neumann, Iver B., and Ole Jacob Sending. 2010. *Governing the Global Polity: Governmentality and Agency in World Politics* Ann Arbor: University of Michigan Press.

Nickles, David Paull. 2008. "U.S. Diplomatic Etiquette during the Nineteenth Century." In *The Diplomats' World: A Cultural History of Diplomacy, 1815–1914,* edited by Markus Mösslang and Torsten Riotte, 287–316. Oxford: Oxford University Press.

———. 2003. *Under the Wire: How the Telegraph Changed Diplomacy.* Cambridge, Mass.: Harvard University Press.

Nicol, Donald M. 1988. *Byzantium and Venice: A Study in Diplomatic and Cultural Relations.* Cambridge: Cambridge University Press.

Nicolson, Harold. (1939) 1963. *Diplomacy.* 3rd ed. London: Oxford University Press.

———. (1954) 1988. *The Evolution of The Diplomatic Method* London: Cassell.

Nien, Nguyen Dy. 2004. *Ho Chi Minh Thought on Diplomacy.* Hanoi: Gioi.

Numelin, Ragnar. 1954. *Diplomati.* Helsingfors: Söderstrøm.

———. 1950. *The Beginnings of Diplomacy.* London: Oxford University Press.

Nustad, Knut G. 1999. "Perspectives on Development: Politics and Strategies in a Durban Squatter Settlement." Paper presented at the Nordic Africa Days, The Nordic Africa Institute, Uppsala, Sweden.

Nustad, Knut, and Christian Krohn-Hansen, eds. 2005. *State Formation: Anthropological Perspectives.* London: Pluto.

Oikonomides, Nicolas. 1992. "Byzantine Diplomacy, AD 1204–1453: Means and Ends." In *Byzantine Diplomacy. Papers from the Twenty-fourth Spring Symposium of Byzantine Studies, Cambridge, March 1990,* edited by Jonathan Shepard and Simon Franklin, 73–88. Aldershot, UK: Variorum.

Olesen, Jens E. 2000. "Middelalderen til 1536: Fra rejsekongedømme til administrationscentrum" [The middle ages to 1536: From itinerant kingdom to administrative center]. In *Dansk forvaltningshistorie,* vol. 1: *Stat, forvaltning og samfund: Fra middelalderen til 1901* [Danish Administrative History, vol. 1: State, Administration, and Society: From the Middle Ages to 1901], edited by Leon E. Jespersen, E. Ladewig Petersen, and Ditlev Tamm, 3–48. Copenhagen: Jurist-og økonomforbundets forlag.

Olick, Jeffrey K., and Joyce Robbins. 1998. "Social Memory Studies: From 'Collective Memory' to the Historical Sociology of Mnemonic Practices." *Annual Review of Sociology* (24): 105–40.

Olsen, Johan P., and B. Guy Peters, eds. 1996. *Lessons from Experience: Experiential Learning in Administrative Reforms in Eight Democracies.* Oslo: Scandinavian University Press.

Omang, Reidar. 1955, 1958. *Norsk utenrikstjeneste* [The Norwegian foreign service]. 2 vols. Oslo: Gyldendal.

Ortner, Sherry B. 1989. *High Religion: A Cultural and Political History of Sherpa Buddhism.* Princeton, N.J.: Princeton University Press.

———. 1982. "Theory in Anthropology since the Sixties." *Comparative Studies in Society and History* 26 (1): 126–66.

Ortner, Sherry B., and Harriet Whitehead. 1984. *Sexual Meanings: The Cultural Construction of Gender and Sexuality.* Cambridge: Cambridge University Press.

Ørvik, Nils, et al. 1977. *Departmental Decision-Making. A Research Report.* Oslo: Universitetsforlaget.

Osiander, Andreas. 1994. *The States System of Europe, 1640–1990: Peacemaking and the Conditions of International Stability.* Oxford: Clarendon Press.

Otte, T. G. 2008. "'Outdoor Relief for the Aristocracy'? European Nobility and Diplomacy, 1850–1914." In *The Diplomats' World: A Cultural History of Diplomacy, 1815–1914,* edited by Markus Mösslang and Torsten Riotte, 23–58. Oxford: Oxford University Press.

———. 2001. "Satow." In *Diplomatic Theory from Machiavelli to Kissinger,* edited by G. B. Berridge, Maurice Keens-Soper, and T. G. Otte, 125–50. Houndmills, UK: Palgrave.

Pateman, Carole. 1989. *The Disorder of Women: Democracy, Feminism and Political Theory.* Stanford, Calif.: Stanford University Press.

———. 1986. "Introduction: The Theoretical Subversiveness of Feminism." In *Feminist Challenges,* edited by Carole Pateman and Elizabeth Grozs, 4–20. Winchester, Mass.: Allen & Unwin.

Petersen, E. Ladewig. 2000. "Reformationstiden 1536–96: Modernisering—justering." In *Dansk forvaltningshistorie, vol. 1: Stat, forvaltning og samfund: Fra middelalderen til 1901,* edited by Leon E. Jespersen, E. Ladewig Petersen and Ditlev Tamm, 49–93. Copenhagen: Jurist-og økonomforbundets forlag.

Peterson, V. Spike. 1992. Introduction to *Gendered States: Feminist (Re)Visions of International Relations Theory,* edited by V. Spike Peterson, 1–29. Boulder, Colo.: Lynne Rienner.

Pleck, Joseph H. 1981. *The Myth of Masculinity.* Cambridge, Mass.: MIT Press.

Potter, Jonathan, and Margaret Wetherell. 1987. *Discourse and Social Psychology.* London: Sage.

Queller, Donald E. (1973) 1980. "The Development of Ambassadorial Relazioni." In *Medieval Diplomacy and the Fourth Crusade,* 174–96. London: Variorum.

Radcliffe-Brown, A. R. 1958. *Method in Social Anthropology,* edited by M. N. Srinivas. Chicago: University of Chicago Press.

Ræder, Gudrun. 1975. *De uunnværlige flinke* [The indispensable clever ones]. Oslo: Gyldendal.

Rana, Krishan S. 2007. "Representing India in the Diplomatic Corps." In *The Diplomatic Corps as an Institution of International Society*, edited by Paul Sharp and Geoffrey Wiseman, 125–41. Houndmills, UK: Palgrave.

Ransom, John S. 1997. *Foucault's Discipline. The Politics of Subjectivity*. Durham, N.C.: Duke University Press.

Reed, Adam. 2005. "'My Blog is Me': Text and Person in UK Online Journal Culture (and Anthropology)." *Ethnos* 70 (2): 220–42.

Renfrew, Colin, and John Cherry, eds. 1986. *Peer Polity Interaction and Socio-Political Change*. Cambridge: Cambridge University Press.

Reus-Smit, Christian. 1999. *The Moral Purpose of the State: Culture, Social Identity, and Institutional Rationality in International Relations*. Princeton, N.J.: Princeton University Press.

Riksarkivets beståndöversikt, pt. 1, vol. 2. 1996. Stockholm: Svenska Riksarkivet.

Riles, Annelise. 2006. "[Deadlines]: Removing the Brackets on Politics in Bureaucratic and Anthropological Analysis." In *Documents: Artifacts of Modern Knowledge*, edited by Annelise Riles, 71–92. Ann Arbor: University of Michigan Press.

Ringmar, Erik. 1996. *Identity, Interest and Action: A Cultural Explanation of Sweden's Intervention in the Thirty Years War*. Cambridge: Cambridge University Press.

Riste, Olav. 2005. *Norway's Foreign Relations: A History*. Oslo: Universitetsforlaget.

Ross, Carne. 2007. *Independent Diplomat: Dispatches from an Unaccountable Elite* Ithaca, N.Y.: Cornell University Press.

Rostow, Walt W. 1964. "The Planning of Foreign Policy." In *The Dimensions of Diplomacy*, edited by E. A. J. Johnson, 41–55. Baltimore: Johns Hopkins University Press.

Sahlins, Marshall. 1987. *Islands of History*. London: Tavistock.

———. 1981. *Historical Metaphors and Mythical Realities: Structure in the Early History of the Sandwich Islands Kingdom*. Ann Arbor: University of Michigan Press.

Said, Edward. 1978. *Orientalism*. Harmondsworth, UK: Penguin.

Satow, Sir Ernest. (1917) 1922. A *Guide to Diplomatic Practice*. 2nd ed. London: Longmans.

———. (1917) 1979. *Satow's Guide to Diplomatic Practice*, edited by Lord Gore-Booth. 5th ed. London: Longman.

Saussure, Ferdinand de. (1916) 1986. *Course in General Linguistics*. La Salle, Ill.: Open Court Press.

Schatzky, Theodore R. 2001a. "Introduction: Practice Theory." In *The Practice Turn in Contemporary Theory*, edited by Theodore R. Schatzky, Karin Knorr Cetina, and Eike von Savigny, 1–14. London: Routledge.

———. 2001b. "Practice Minded Orders." In *The Practice Turn in Contemporary Theory*, edited by Theodore R. Schatzky, Karin Knorr Cetina, and Eike von Savigny, 42–55. London: Routledge.

Schatzky, Theodore R., Karin Knorr Cetina, and Eike Von Savigny. 2001. *The Practice Turn in Contemporary Theory*. London: Routledge.

Schlesinger, Arthur M. 1967. A *Thousand Days: John F. Kennedy at the White House*. London: Mayflower-Dell.

Schytte, Andreas. 1773–76. *Staternes indvortes Regiering* [The internal governing of states]. 5 vols. Copenhagen: Gyldendal.

———. 1774–75. *Staternes udvortes Regiering* [The external government of states]. 2 vols. Copenhagen: Gyldendal.

Scott, James C. 1998. *Seeing Like a State: How Certain Schemes to Improve the Human Condition Have Failed.* New Haven, Conn.: Yale University Press.

Seidler, Victor J. 1994. *Unreasonable Men: Masculinity and Social Theory.* London: Routledge.

Seip, Jens Arup. (1974) 1997. *Utsikt over Norges historie [Overview of Norwegain history].* Oslo: Gyldendal.

Shapiro, Michael J. 1988. *The Politics of Representation: Writing Practices in Biography, Photography, and Policy Analysis.* Madison: University of Wisconsin Press.

Sharp, Paul. 2009. *Diplomatic Theory of International Relations.* Cambridge: Cambridge University Press.

———. 2002. "The English School, Herbert Butterfield, and Diplomacy." Paper presented to the Annual International Studies Association Conference, New Orleans.

Shore, Cris. 2000. *Building Europe: The Cultural Policies of European Integration.* London: Routledge.

Shore, Cris, and Susan Wright. 1997. "Policy: A New Field of Research." In *Anthropology of Policy: Critical Perspectives on Governance and Power,* edited by Susan Wright and Cris Shore, 3–39. London: Routledge.

Shore, Cris, and Stephen Nugent, eds. 2002. *Elite Cultures: Anthropological Perspectives.* London: Routledge.

Skeggs, Beverly. 1997. *Formations of Class and Gender.* London: Sage.

Slagstad, Rune. 1998. *De nasjonale strateger [Natioanl strategists].* Oslo: Pax.

Smith, Adam T. 2003. *The Political Landscape: Constellations of Authority in Early Complex Polities.* Berkeley: University of California Press.

Sofer, Sasson. 2000. "Being a 'Pathetic Hero' in International Politics: The Diplomat as a Historical Actor." Paper presented to the annual International Studies Association Conference. Los Angeles.

Sogner, Sølvi, and Kari Telste. 2005. *Ut og søkje teneste—historia om tenestejentene* [Out seeking employ: The history of maids]. Oslo: Samlaget.

Somers, Margaret R. 1994. "The Narrative Constitution of Identity: A Relational and Network Approach." *Theory and Society* 23 (5): 605–49.

Steensgaard, Niels. 1967. "Consuls and Nations in the Levant from 1570 to 1650." *Scandinavian Economic History Review* 15: 1–27.

Stein, Gil. 1999. *Rethinking World Systems: Diasporas, Colonies, and Interaction in Uruk Mesopotamia* Tucson: University of Arizona Press.

Stendal, Synnøve Hinnaland. 2003. *. . . Under en forvandlingens lov: En analyse av stortingsdebatten om kvinnelige prester i 1930-årene* [. . . Under the law of change: An analysis of the 1930s parliamentary debate concerning female ministers of the church]. Lund: Arcus.

Stocking, George W. 1995. *After Tylor: British Social Anthropology 1888–1951.* Madison: University of Wisconsin Press.

Stokke, Olav. 1979. *Norge og Den tredje verden* [Norway and the Third World]. Oslo: Universitetsforlaget.

Stoltenberg, Thorvald. 1983. "Statssekretær i Utenriksdepartementet [Undersecretary in the Norwegian MFA]." In *Fra Diplomatiets Verden* [From the world of diplomacy], edited by Ingegerd Galtung and Alf R. Bjerke, 63–65. Oslo: Atheneum.

Strathern, Marilyn. 2004. *Commons and Borderlands: Working Papers on Interdisciplinarity. Accountability and the Flow of Knowledge.* Wantage, UK: Sean Kingston.

———. 1996. "Cutting the Network." *Journal of the Royal Anthropological Institute,* n.s., 2 (3): 517–35.

———. 1987. "The Limits of Auto-Anthropology." In *Anthropology at Home,* edited by Allison Jackson, 16–37. London: Tavistock.

Suganami, Hidemi. 1989. *The Domestic Analogy and World Order Proposals.* Cambridge: Cambridge University Press.

———. 1984. "Japan's Entry into International Society." In *The Expansion of International Society,* edited by Hedley Bull and Adam Watson, 185–99. Oxford: Clarendon Press.

Svennevig, Tormod Petter. 1996. *I Østerled: Kapitler fra et liv i utenrikstjenesten* [Going east: Chapters from a life in the foreign service]. Oslo: Gyldendal.

Swidler, Ann. 2001. "What Anchors Cultural Practices?" In *The Practice Turn in Contemporary Theory,* edited by Theodore R. Schatzky, Karin Knorr Cetina, and Eike von Savigny, 74–92. London: Routledge.

Szakolczai, Árpád. 1998. *Max Weber and Michel Foucault: Parallel Life-Works.* London: Routledge.

Taftø, Synnøve Fjellbakk. 1997. *Skjolødmøysagaen* [Saga of the female warrior]. Elverum: Samfunnstrykk.

Taylor, Charles. 1989. *Sources of the Self: The Making of the Modern Identity.* Cambridge: Cambridge University Press.

Thayer, Charles W. 1960. *Diplomat.* New York: Harper.

Thomson, Janice E. 1995. "State Sovereignty in International Relations: Bridging the Gap between Theory and Empirical Research." *International Studies Quarterly* 39 (2): 213–33.

———. 1994. *Mercenaries, Pirates, and Sovereigns: State-Building and Extraterritorial Violence in Early Modern Europe* Princeton, N.J.: Princeton University Press.

———. 1990. "State Practices, International Norms, and the Decline of Mercenarism." *International Studies Quarterly* 34 (1): 23–47.

Todorov, Tzvetan. 1984. *Mikhail Bakhtin: The Dialogical Principle.* Manchester: Manchester University Press.

Torfing, Jacob. 1999. *New Theories of Discourse: Laclau, Mouffe and Žižek.* Oxford: Blackwell.

Towns, Ann E. 2010. *Women and States: Norms and Hierarchies in International Society.* Cambridge: Cambridge University Press.

———. 2004. "Norms and Inequality in International Society: Global Politics of Women and the State." PhD diss., University of Minnesota.

Trouillot, Michel-Rolph. 2001. "The Anthropology of the State in the Age of Globalization: Close Encounters of the Deceptive Kind." *Current Anthropology* 42 (1): 125–39.

Try, Hans. 1979. *To kulturer en stat 1851–1884: Norges historie* [Two cultures, one state 1851–1884: History of Norway], vol. 11. Oslo: Cappelen.

Tully, James. (1983) 1988. "The Pen Is a Mighty Sword: Quentin Skinner's Analysis of Politics." In *Meaning and Context. Quentin Skinner and His Critics,* edited by James Tully, 7–25. Cambridge: Polity.

Tunander, Ola. 1994. "Inventing the Barents Region: Overcoming the East-West Divide." In *The Barents Region: Cooperation in Arctic Europe,* edited by Olav Schram Stokke and Ola Tunander, 31–45. London: Sage.

Tunberg, Sven, Carl-Fredrik Palmstierna, et al. 1935. *Den svenska utrikesförvaltningens historia* [History of Swedish Foreign Administration]. Uppsala: Almquist and Wiksell.

Turner, Bryan S. 2004, *Regulating Bodies: Essays in Medical Sociology.* Harmondsworth: Routledge.

Turner, Victor W. 1967. *The Forest of Symbols: Aspects of Ndembu Ritual.* Ithaca, N.Y.: Cornell University Press.

———. 1964. "Symbols in Ndembu Ritual." In *Closed Systems and Open Minds: The Limits of Naivety in Social Anthropology,* edited by Max Gluckman, 20–51. London: Oliver & Boyd.

Utenriksdepartementet. 2002. *Utenriksdepartementets kontoplan* [Chart of accounts for the MFA]. Oslo: Utenriksdepartementet.

Van der Roos, Janneke. 1996. "Femokrat, hva slags fugl er nå det?" [Femocrat, what kind of bird is that?]. In *Hun og han: Kjønnsforskning og politikk* [Gender research and politics], edited by Harriet Holter, 195–219. Oslo: Pax.

Vernadsky, George. 1948. *Kievan Russia.* New Haven: Yale University Press.

Vike, Hallvard. 1996. "Conquering the Unreal: Politics and Bureaucracy in a Norwegian Town." Department of Social Anthropology, University of Oslo.

Vollebæk, Knut. 1998. "Norsk sikkerhetspolitikk i et Europa i endring" [Norwegian security policy in a changing Europe]. *Internasjonal Politikk* 56 (2): 313–29.

Wæver, Ole. 2001. "Identity, Communities and Foreign Policy: Discourse Analysis as Foreign Policy Theory." In *European Integration and National Identity: The Challenge of the Nordic States,* edited by Lene Hansen and Ole Wæver, 20–49. London: Routledge.

Walker, R. B. J. 1993. *Inside/Outside.* Cambridge: Cambridge University Press.

———. 1988. *One World, Many Worlds: Struggles for a Just World Peace.* Boulder: Lynne Rienner.

Warner, W. Lloyd, et al., eds. 1963. *Yankee City.* New Haven, Conn.: Yale University Press.

Watson, Adam. (1982) 1984. *Diplomacy: The Dialogue between States.* London: Methuen.

Weber, Eugen. 1977. *Peasants into Frenchmen: The Modernization of Rural France, 1870–1914.* London: Chatto and Windus.

Weber, Max. 1968. *Economy and Society.* Berkeley: University of California Press.

Webster, C. K. 1919. *The Congress of Vienna, 1814–1815.* London: Oxford University Press.

Weeden, Lisa. 2002. "Conceptualizing Culture: Possibilities for Political Science." *American Political Science Review* 96 (4): 713–28.

Wendt, Alexander. 1999. *Social Theory of International Politics.* Cambridge: Cambridge University Press.

West, Candace, and D. H. Zimmermann. 1987. "Doing Gender." *Gender and Society* 1 (2): 125–51.

Whitehead, Stephen M. 2002. *Men and Masculinities: Key Themes and New Directions.* Cambridge: Polity.

Wight, Martin. 1966. "Western Values in International Relations." In *Diplomatic Investigations: Essays in the Theory of International Politics,* edited by Martin Wight and Herbert Butterfield, 89–131. London: Unwin.

Wight, Martin. 1977. *Systems of States,* edited by Hedley Bull. Leicester: Leicester University Press.

Williams, Patrick, and Laura Chrisman, eds. 1993. *Colonial Desire: Hybridity, Theory, Culture and Race.* London: Routledge.

Wolfe, Robert. 1998. "*Still* Lying Abroad? On the Institution of the Resident Ambassador." Diplomacy and Statecraft 9 (2): 23–54.

Ye'or, Bat. 1985. *The Dhimmi: A Historical Survey of Jews and Christians under Islam.* London: Associated University Presses.

Yilmaz, Suhnaz. 2011. *Turkish-American Relations (1800–1952): Between the Stars, Stripes and the Crescent.* New York: Routledge.

Yurchak, Alexei. 2006. *Everything Was Forever, Until It Was No More: The Last Soviet Generation.* Princeton, N.J.: Princeton University Press.

Zabusky, Stacia E. 1995. *Launching Europe: An Ethnography of European Cooperation in Space Science* Princeton, N.J.: Princeton University Press.

Zhang, Yongjin. Forthcoming. "A Curious and Exotic Encounter—Europeans as Supplicants in the Chinese Imperium, 1514–1792." In *Before the Arrival of the Anarchical Society: A Study of International Order, 1492–1792,* edited by Yongjin Zhang, Shogo Suzuki, and Joel Quirk.

Zorin, V. A., et al., eds. 1959. *Istoriya diplomatii* [The history of diplomacy], vol. 1. 2nd ed. Moscow: Gospolitizdat.

INDEX

Note: Page numbers in *italics* indicate figures.